REMEMBER THE TIME

REMEMBER

the

TIME

Protecting Michael Jackson in His Final Days

BILL WHITFIELD
AND JAVON BEARD

with **Tanner Colby**

WEINSTEIN
BOOKS

Printed in the United States of America.

Cataloging-in-Publication Data for this book is available from
the Library of Congress.

ISBN 978-1-60286-250-0 (print)
ISBN 978-1-60286-251-7 (e-book)

Published by Weinstein Books
A member of the Perseus Books Group
www.weinsteinbooks.com

Weinstein Books are available at special discounts for bulk purchases
in the U.S. by corporations, institutions and other organizations.
For more information, please contact the Special Markets Department
at the Perseus Books Group, 2300 Chestnut Street, Suite 200,
Philadelphia, PA 19103, call (800) 810-4145, ext. 5000,
or e-mail special.markets@perseusbooks.com.

FIRST EDITION

2 4 6 8 9 7 5 3

I dedicate this book to Prince, Paris, and Blanket.
Their father guided and prepared them for a world
that he knew would be challenging for them.
Through his spirit he will continue to guide them and,
when called upon, I will be there for them as well.

—Bill

I dedicate this book to my twin, Jovon.
I wish you were here to share this moment with me.
Rest in peace. Gone but never forgotten. Love you always!
I also dedicate this book to Michael Jackson. Thank you
for believing in me and giving me the opportunity of a life time.
And to Prince, Paris, and Blanket. It was a pleasure serving you.
You guys were one of the highlights of coming to work every day.
I'm always here if you need me.

—Javon

INTRODUCTION

You would not be reading this if Michael Jackson was still alive.

For over two and a half years, from December 2006 until his death in June 2009, we were employed as the personal security team for Michael Jackson, the most famous and most successful entertainer in history. For a significant part of that time, we were the only gatekeepers between his family and the outside world, and we have a story to tell.

The world of personal security is not something that most people are familiar with. People see us on TV, and they probably think we're just a bunch of thick-necked bruisers in black suits standing by the door. That's not who we are. We're not bouncers. Many of us are former law-enforcement, sometimes ex-military, people who have studied and trained in the art of private security. In today's celebrity-obsessed culture, the lives of movie stars and professional athletes are valuable currency. Their privacy is under constant assault. Executive protection is a serious business. We're entrusted with the welfare of spouses, children, and classified documents. We run countersurveillance in hotels, restaurants, and hospital rooms. We set up false identities to move people around the globe in secret. And when we leave, if we've done our jobs right, it's like we were never there. But we're always there—standing in the background, listening, and observing. We know the things the tabloids pretend to know. We know the things you *wish* you knew.

In private security, getting hired is not just based on experience and skill. Someone has to vouch for you. You don't bring someone into this business unless you know they can be trusted. People who tell stories out of school, they don't stick around. That's how it works. You see everything. You hear everything. You know nothing. If you're asked, you don't recall. If you're subpoenaed, you make yourself scarce. That's how it works in this profession, and that is how we handle the affairs of our clients today.

Michael Jackson was not a typical client. We were the sworn keepers of his secrets in life, but his death has forced us into a position we've never been entirely comfortable with. The questions surrounding his death—who had access to him at what times and for what purpose—put a glaring spotlight on our role as his first line of defense. We've tried to keep our profile as low as possible. We've turned down repeated cash offers from tabloids trying to get us to spill secrets about the more controversial aspects of Mr. Jackson's life. Compelled to testify in the murder trial of Dr. Conrad Murray and deposed in the civil litigation between the Jackson estate and AEG Live, the promoters for Mr. Jackson's never-performed comeback show, *This Is It*, we answered the questions put to us, truthfully and to the best of our knowledge, but provided no more information beyond what was legally required of us. We had no desire to be dragged into that circus.

We have spoken publicly only twice before, in brief televised interviews with *Nightline* and *Good Morning America*, which aired in March 2010. Our purpose in doing so was simple: to tell the truth about the Michael Jackson we knew. We wanted the world to see a glimpse of the good man and wonderful father that we had the privilege of serving. Mr. Jackson's fans, whom he deeply appreciated and loved, deserve to see that part of him. Our purpose has not changed. We decided that a book written by us—a direct account unfiltered by reporters and commentators—would be the most effective means to set the record straight.

We have tried our best to strike a balance between the need for honesty and our obligation to secrecy. The individuals that you will see named in this book—Mr. Jackson's famous siblings; Raymone Bain, his manager; Grace Rwaramba, his children's nanny—are all public figures well known to anyone who has followed Michael Jackson's story in the past. Therefore we feel there is little breach of confidentiality in identifying them here. They have been included because it would be impossible to tell the story without doing so. Otherwise, we have done our best to leave the names of private individuals out of our account. Besides, more than enough has been written about the hordes of lawyers, managers, and hangers-on who populated the fringes of Mr. Jackson's life. Our focus is on the only person in this story that readers really care about.

In many ways, this is a story that only we can tell. While hundreds of people came in and out of Michael Jackson's life at various points, in his final years, before *This Is It*, there was almost no one else around. Days and weeks went by when it was just us, Mr. Jackson, and his three children, Prince, Paris, and Blanket. Mr. Jackson has been robbed of the chance to tell the story himself. His children were too young to remember or fully grasp everything that transpired, and they deserve to have these events recorded and remembered as they actually happened. So that leaves us.

Just as there are those who seek to drag Mr. Jackson's name through the mud, there are those who insist that he was a saint, an angelic figure to be put on a pedestal. He was neither. Michael Jackson was, like all of us, a complicated human being. A deeply religious man who gave millions to charity and brightened our lives with his talent, he also struggled with personal pain in a way that few can really understand. This book celebrates the good times and great achievements of his life, but it does not shy away from the more difficult and troubling moments that he endured. Our aim is simply to present the whole story in an honest, sympathetic light in order to give a well-rounded view of the events that we witnessed.

Lastly, given the unseemly behavior that has surrounded the handling of Michael Jackson's tremendous fortune, we would like to make one thing clear: we are not writing this book for financial reward. As we mentioned, we have already turned down substantial cash offers to tell our story. When Mr. Jackson died, we had two years left on our contract with his management company. Though we were legally within our rights to pursue what was owed to us, we had no desire to join the stampede of creditors rushing in to get their pound of flesh. When Mr. Jackson passed away, we considered any outstanding debts to be wiped clean. Unlike many others, we have pursued no claims against his estate.

So far, we haven't even been paid for this book. While some close to Mr. Jackson raced to get six-figure paydays for tell-all memoirs in the wake of his death, we have chosen a different route. When we signed the contract for *Remember the Time*, we personally received no money at all. The modest, up-front advance that our publisher paid did not go to us. It was used to cover the expenses of producing the book: traveling to meet with editors, hiring a professional writer to help us craft our story, etc. Beyond that, the time and energy required to see this project to completion came out of our own pocket. It has not been an easy journey. In preparing this book for publication, we have endured and overcome many obstacles that were put in front of us. As with everything involving Mr. Jackson, we encountered the ugliness of his world in trying to do right by him.

We want our reward to come from you, the fans, and only if you decide that we have earned it. Michael Jackson still has a vast legion of dedicated followers worldwide. You deserve an honest and thoughtful testimony of his life. You deserve to know who he really was. We believe that this book will finally give that to you. If you agree, if you put your hard-earned cash on the counter to buy it, that will let us know our efforts were worthwhile. Either way, we will still sleep easy knowing that we have been true to Mr. Jackson's legacy while remaining true to our own principles. Protecting Michael Jackson was an experience like no other. It brought us a deeper and more profound understanding of the man and his music, and it changed the way we look at the world forever. We are sharing our story with you now in the hope that you will be changed by it as well.

PROLOGUE

December 22, 2006
McCarran International Airport
Las Vegas, NV

Bill: It was three days before Christmas, around ten o'clock at night, and I was sitting in a motorcade of four black Cadillac Escalades out on the tarmac. I'd been hired for a security detail. A client was flying into Las Vegas on a private jet from outside the country; I was there to escort him from the airport to a gated house in the Summerlin neighborhood, over on the northwest side of town. I was in the passenger seat of the lead SUV. The vehicle designated as the mother car—meaning the one that would transport the client— was just behind me. I was scanning the air above us, looking for the plane.

People think of Las Vegas as nothing but neon lights, hot pavement, and desert. But in the winter? At night? Once the sun sets, the temperature drops quick. Out at the airport, it was well below freezing. I had the heater turned up full blast to keep out the cold while we waited. The fact that we'd been given vehicle access to the tarmac, that was unusual. It wasn't something I was used to, even for big-name clients. But in this town, in this line of work, unusual is the norm. It's Vegas. An armed motorcade like this one might be hired for a movie star or a CEO, an athlete or a politician.

Hell, I might've been hired to help a deposed dictator fleeing a revolution in some third-world country somewhere. I didn't actually know who I was there to pick up.

A couple days earlier, I'd come home from a three-month assignment that spanned two countries and five states. All I wanted was to rest and spend time with my daughter. Then I got a call from an associate of mine, Jeff Adams. Jeff and I were tight, almost like family. We'd worked together many times. He asked me if I was available to lead a security detail for a high-profile dignitary arriving in Las Vegas in two weeks. I would pick him up and escort him from point A to point B. Jeff said, "I've been in touch with the client's assistant, a man named John Feldman. I told him about your background. He wants you to fax him your résumé and a copy of your driver's license so they can do a background check on you." He gave me an overseas fax number, and I jotted it down.

"Who's the client?" I asked.

Jeff paused. He said, "I can't give you that information just yet. But trust me, you'll be glad you took this one—and you'll need to be armed."

I was a little apprehensive about committing, not knowing who it was for. But I'd been in the business long enough to know that sometimes this was just how things worked. Until trust is established, information is on a need-to-know basis. You're contracted for two hours, you show up, execute the assignment, and that's that. I'd done plenty of details just like it. I told him to count me in.

Over the next two weeks, these people did a background check on me, brought me on board, and I began making the arrangements. Two days before the client was to arrive, Jeff and I did what's known as a pre-advance detail, mapping out the best route from the airport to this person's new home, driving the route together, making note of every stop sign, timing the traffic lights, mapping out any congested areas we might encounter along the way. We decided that I would handle transportation from the airport to the house, and Jeff would be waiting for us when we got there.

On the day of the detail, I arrived at the airport at seven-thirty. I'd told the car service to have its vehicles there by eight. When they arrived, I conducted a thorough inspection of each one. As I was doing that, I noticed that the rearview mirrors were equipped with video cameras aimed at the vehicle passenger seats. I called Jeff. "No cameras," he said. "Period." So I went vehicle to vehicle and disconnected each one.

At ten o'clock, we proceeded onto the tarmac. At 10:35, a Gulfstream V landed and taxied in our direction. I instructed the drivers to pull alongside the plane as the stairway was dropped. I exited my vehicle and walked back to the mother car, which had stopped right at the foot of the steps. I stood there and waited, ready to open the rear door for the passengers. The flight crew and the other drivers started loading the luggage into the SUVs.

First to deplane was a man in his late forties, black guy, neatly groomed but not particularly noteworthy. Then a woman came out. She had a sleeping child in her arms, and she carried him carefully down the steps. They were followed by two other children, both about elementary school age. They all climbed in the car. I thought, Okay, that must be it. I went to close the door and one of the kids spoke up and said, "Where's Daddy?"

Daddy?

I looked back up at the plane. This man was coming down. He was dressed in all black, his face covered with a black scarf. As he got closer, I noticed his feet: slip-on loafers, slender ankles and white socks sticking out of these high-water pants. He came down, passed me, and climbed into the SUV with the children. I closed the door, got back in the lead vehicle, and we left the airport.

With the holiday traffic, it took us forty-five minutes to get to the house. Jeff was waiting. We pulled into the driveway; the gate closed behind us. My car stopped in front, and the mother car drove around the side to let the family out in private. I helped unload the luggage—there were at least thirty bags—and we brought it all inside. Then I went back out to the driveway.

Jeff came out of the house. Over the two-way radio, he said, "We good?"

"Code 4," I said.

At that point, I figured I was done. I got my subject from point A to point B. It's a wrap. But the curiosity was killing me. I walked over to Jeff and said, "So tell me. Who is that guy?"

Jeff got this big grin on his face. "Didn't you see him?" he said.

I shrugged. "Sure. I saw a skinny dude, a chick, and three kids."

Jeff leaned in and whispered, "That's Michael Jackson."

I just stared at him. "Get the fuck outta here!"

He put his right hand in the air. "Death before dishonor," he said. "Real talk."

I didn't believe it. He laughed at me a bit. Then the assistant, Feldman, the first guy who'd come off the jet, called for us to come inside. As we went in, I was like, Yo, *really*? Am I really gettin' ready to meet Michael Jackson?

We went inside and this same guy was coming over to me with no scarf covering his face, and I was like, *Oh shit*. There I was, standing in front of Michael Jackson, shaking his hand. It was surreal. Jeff introduced us. In this soft, quiet voice, Mr. Jackson said, "Hello, it's nice to meet you."

I said, "It's an honor to meet you, sir. I've been a huge fan for a long time."

Huge fan? I *never* said that kind of thing to clients. Doing what I do, I've gotten used to being around famous people. But my heart was pounding in my chest; the hairs on my neck were standing up. I was trying to maintain my professionalism, but inside I was like a little kid. I *was* a huge fan. I still had my old Jackson 5 albums, the 45s and 33s, all of them. I still remembered watching him and his brothers on *Soul Train*, watching him do the robot to "Dancing Machine."

We talked a bit about Motown Records, because I'd done some work for them and he'd seen that on my résumé. His children were behind him. Paris and Prince both said hello. Blanket was very reserved and quiet, hiding behind his father and giving a little wave.

Mr. Jackson said, "Kids, this is Bill. He's our new security."

I was like, Huh? New security? What's he talking about? I'd been told this was point A to point B. Pick up a check and go home. An alarm started going off in the back of my head. And then Mr. Jackson said—more like a statement than a question—"You'll be staying the night, right?"

"Um . . . yes. Yessir."

"Great," he said. "We'll see you in the morning."

They all said good night and went upstairs. I looked at both Jeff and Feldman. I said, "We need to talk." We went out and stood in the driveway, and I said, "What's going on here? Where's this dude's security?"

"Nation of Islam was holding his security down for a while," Jeff explained. "He got some flak about that, so he's making some changes."

Feldman apologized for any confusion and asked me if I'd be comfortable staying the night, and perhaps longer.

I said to Jeff, "Is that the real Michael Jackson? Don't play with me, man. It's too cold, and I'm in no mood to be running around Las Vegas with some Michael Jackson impersonator."

"Trust me," he said. "This is the real dude. He looked at your résumé, saw you were with Motown, and straight up said he wanted you for this."

"Okay. So when does the rest of the team get here?"

Feldman looked at Jeff and then back at me and he said, "I thought you knew. There is no team. You're it."

What? Uh-uh. No, no, no. Now I was pissed off. I was being put in a position that I was not prepared for. There are people out there who love this guy with a passion, and there are crazy people who hate him, and they'll do anything to get at him. Any time I'd seen Michael Jackson on TV, he had a whole crew of people with him. I was all by myself. I didn't know the property or the interior layout of the house. I didn't have any of the gear I'd need for a detail like this.

I started to get a bad feeling. Something's not right, I thought. I'd been doing this too long to believe that Michael Jackson, the King of Pop, was traveling with *no* security. Just an assistant and a nanny? Where was the staff? The manager? The entourage?

What I didn't know then, but what I would quickly learn, was that the Michael Jackson who flew into Las Vegas that night was not the same Michael Jackson who'd left the country the year before. There was no entourage that night because there was no*body*, period. He was all alone. The most famous man on the planet, and we were the only ones who even knew he was back in the United States.

I agreed to stay, because what else do you do? The man told his children I was there to protect them. After a while, the assistant and the nanny left. They were staying at a hotel nearby. Then Jeff left too. He had another job he was already contracted for. Now it was just me. I did a sweep of the property, checked all the doors and windows, then set up on a folding chair in the garage. It was freezing. Garage wasn't insulated. Twenty-eight degrees and I had on nothing but a two-piece suit, dress shirt, and tie.

It still hadn't set in. None of it. I was trippin'. I wanted to call everybody I knew, but of course I couldn't. And who would believe me anyway?

"Hey, guess what? I'm in a house with Michael Jackson and his family."

"Who you with?"

"It's just me. In the garage."

"Man, somebody's playin' a joke on your ass."

I stayed up all night, alert and cold. Every sound, every car that went by, I was up, looking around, checking it out. But mostly I just sat there, shivering my ass off and wondering, Where are all his people? Is some lunatic about to come climbing over the gate? What the hell am I even doing here?

About a quarter past seven, the sun finally came up. I heard the interior door to the house unlocking. It opened, and this tiny voice said, "Excuse me."

I glanced up. It was the little girl, Paris. She stepped into the garage, holding out this cup. It was hot chocolate, with some of those little melted marshmallows in it. She just stood there quietly and looked at me and held out this cup and said, "Daddy said to give you this."

PART ONE

CAN WE GO BACK
TO NEVERLAND?

1

On June 19, 2005, Michael Jackson boarded a private jet with his three children and disappeared. Ten days later, following a brief stop-over in Europe, he landed in the remote island kingdom of Bahrain in the Persian Gulf, which would be his home for the next year. Jackson, the universally recognized King of Pop, had gone into exile.

Michael Joseph Jackson was born on August 29, 1958, in the Midwestern steel town of Gary, Indiana, the seventh of nine children of Joe and Katherine Jackson. A musical prodigy almost from the time he could walk, Jackson soon joined his older brothers Jackie, Tito, Jermaine, and Marlon in the singing group managed by their father. They named themselves The Jackson 5. From the age of six, Michael was on the road with his brothers nearly every week, playing regional talent shows, nightclubs, and music festivals. By the time he turned twelve, he was one of the most popular entertainers in the country. Before he was twenty-five, thanks to the success of his now-iconic album, *Thriller*, he'd become the most recognizable human being on the planet.

Jackson's spectacular career began to unravel in August 1993 when he was publicly accused of child molestation. While maintaining his innocence, to avoid a lengthy trial and further invasion of his private life, he agreed to settle the case out of court for a reported $22 million. That decision would haunt him for the rest of his days, casting a shadow of public suspicion over his every move. In the years that followed, Jackson's life stumbled and faltered and finally imploded when a second accusation of abuse surfaced in 2003, prompting a full criminal investigation by Santa Barbara district attorney Tom Sneddon, who had been on a mission to convict the singer ever since the first allegations had been made a decade earlier.

In April 2004, Sneddon convened a grand jury, which voted to indict the singer on charges of endangering the welfare of a minor. Jackson, determined to prove his innocence once and for all, agreed to stand trial. In January 2005, the case of *The People of California v. Michael Joseph Jackson* began, capturing the attention of the entire world. But after a two-year investigation and a six-month trial, Santa Barbara's overzealous prosecutor had failed to produce a single piece of evidence proving any criminal misconduct on Jackson's part. The jury voted unanimously to acquit, and on June 13, 2005, Michael Jackson walked out of the courtroom an exonerated man.

Exonerated but broken. Still reeling from the trial, and facing a crush of legal and financial problems that had built up during the years it had consumed his life, Jackson left America for Bahrain. There he lived as a guest of Sheikh Abdullah bin Hamad bin Isa Al Khalifa, a friend of Jermaine Jackson, who had introduced them. Sheikh Abdullah, the second son of the king of Bahrain and governor of the kingdom's southern province, had aspirations of becoming a music mogul and saw in Jackson the perfect vehicle for building his entertainment enterprise. The two men formed a record label and announced big plans. But their relationship quickly soured, and in the summer of 2006, the singer left Bahrain and spent the next six months living in Ireland. Jackson was in love with the peaceful remoteness of the Emerald Isle, but his legal and financial problems could not be resolved by hiding out overseas. He needed to go back to work, and so the decision was made to move his family to Las Vegas, with the aim of securing a headlining slot at one of the hotels on the famous Las Vegas Strip.

Jackson, who once toured the world with two cargo planes'

worth of equipment and personnel, returned from his eighteen months abroad with only a skeleton crew: his children, their nanny, Grace Rwaramba, and his personal assistant, John Feldman. Since his days as a child star, the core part of Michael Jackson's entourage had always been his personal security team, who shadowed nearly all of his public movements. In the run-up to the 2005 trial, the singer's protection had been handled by the Nation of Islam. The Nation's presence in Jackson's life had stirred up controversy in the media, so when Jackson returned to the United States, his management decided not to continue using the Nation for the singer's personal security. Through private security consultant Jeff Adams, who had ties to Jackson's team, word went out that new people were needed to work the singer's protective detail. Of the résumés that came back, one candidate caught Jackson's eye.

Born in 1965, Bill Whitfield grew up in the New York suburb of New Rochelle and went on to pursue a career in law enforcement. By the early 1990s, he'd become a father to his only daughter and was moonlighting in the world of private protection, which would soon become his primary career. At the time, New York's hip-hop scene was exploding, moving up from the streets of the Bronx to become a billion-dollar industry. Through his cousin, Maxwell Dixon—also known as Grand Puba, MC of the group Brand Nubian—Bill was introduced to various players in the business and began working private security details for rappers, musicians, and professional athletes. In 1995, he left law enforcement permanently to head up the security team of Andre Harrell, the founder of Uptown Records, who had just been appointed CEO of Motown Records. Working with Harrell for the next four years, Bill put together the connections that would soon yield him a star-studded list of clients, including Harrell's protégé from Uptown, Sean "P. Diddy" Combs.

In 2001, Bill was contracted for a security detail in Las Vegas and found that he liked the city. As a hub of the entertainment business and a playground for the rich and famous, it offered no shortage of work for someone in his profession. Taking full custody of his daughter, he moved west and built a successful career as an independent private security consultant, working with top NBA athletes, touring musicians, corporate VIPs, and even presidential candidates.

By the time he received a call from Jeff Adams to transport a mystery client from McCarran International's executive terminal to a gated mansion across town, Bill Whitfield had been working at the top of his chosen profession for over a decade. But nothing he'd done in all that time had fully prepared him for the direction his life would take when the sun came up on an empty Las Vegas garage and a young Paris Jackson poked her head in to offer him a cup of hot chocolate, with some of those little melted marshmallows in it.

Bill: That whole first morning I mostly just sat in the garage, trying to fathom what was going on. I stayed until about six that evening. Then Jeff came and relieved me. I took a few hours and went home and saw my daughter. I had to tell her what was going on. She knew I'd worked for a lot of celebrities, but Michael Jackson? I told her and she looked straight at me and said, "You lyin', Daddy."

I had no way to prove it to her, either. It's not like I was taking pictures with Michael Jackson and his kids. But I had to convince her. Not only was it the holidays, but her birthday was coming up, too. New Year's Eve is her birthday, and I had to tell her that I was going to be working through Christmas Eve, Christmas Day, *and* her birthday. As a single dad, believe me, she didn't let me live that down. She broke down crying in front of me.

That was the one moment I stopped to think about whether I should take this job or not. I was conflicted. On the one hand, I had my family. But on the other—it's hard to explain. I just felt this pull, this obligation to see this thing through. Here was this man and his family in this odd situation, and there was nobody looking out for them. I had to see where this was going to go. I talked things out with my daughter, showered up, got something to eat, and went back that night.

There was a family Mr. Jackson was friendly with, the Cascios, an Italian family from New Jersey. He'd been friends with them going way back to the *Thriller* days. One of their sons, Angel, was in Vegas for the holidays, and he showed up to visit the day before Christmas. Once Angel was there, Mr. Jackson decided he wanted to go to FAO Schwarz at the Forum Shops inside Caesars Palace. He wanted to do some last-minute Christmas shopping.

That was the first time we tried to take him out of the house. We took every precaution we knew to take. It was still chaos. Jeff and I spent the morning driving the route from the house to the mall, surveying the parking lots for the safest access in and out of the store. We called and made arrangements with mall security to let them know which way we were going to come in. Didn't tell them it was Michael Jackson. We'd never tell them that; we'd always say "high-profile dignitary," so they'd know to be prepared but wouldn't have any information to leak to the press.

We hired three SUVs from the same car service we used at the airport. We loaded up Mr. Jackson, Feldman, Angel, and the kids, and then we drove over to the shops, going in through the parking garage and then through the back door of Galerie Lassen, this store that sells lots of expensive paintings. We met up with mall security and from there we decided to separate the kids from their dad. Jeff and Angel took Paris, Prince, and Blanket so they could shop on their own. Feldman and I stayed with Mr. Jackson. We gave them about five minutes to get ahead of us, then we headed out into the mall.

We hadn't set foot inside but maybe a minute when someone spotted him and screamed, *"Michael Jackson! It's Michael Jackson!"* People were stopping and staring. Mr. Jackson was saying hello, shaking people's hands. They were yelling, *"We love you, Michael!"* and Mr. Jackson kept saying, "I love you more! Thank you so much.

God bless you." He was almost in tears, genuinely touched by all this love they were showering on him.

It was a little rough but not totally overwhelming, at first. Then it started to build. At that point, nobody even knew he was back in the country, so the shock of seeing him was that much bigger. People started swarming around him, wanting to touch him. People were *screaming*, their faces all contorted with all this freaked-out, passionate emotion. Within seconds it turned into complete and total madness.

I've been in some messed-up situations with celebrities before, but this was like nothing I'd ever experienced in my life. Being in the middle of that kind of onslaught, people coming at you from all sides, it's frightening. There's very little you can do to control the situation; the only rational response is to get out of there as fast as possible. Almost as soon as it started, Mr. Jackson turned to me and said, "We need to leave before someone gets hurt." We radioed the other team to take the kids out a different way and rendezvous with us in the parking garage. Mall security and the Las Vegas police helped us clear a path back to the vehicles. Then we drove everybody home.

Once we got back to the house, we called FAO Schwarz and made arrangements for Mr. Jackson to go again after store hours, when all the customers and tourists were gone. That night, we went shopping, all alone in the mall. He dropped about ten thousand dollars on toys. He picked out a whole bunch of stuff: train sets, action figures, lots of girly-girly stuff for Paris. Then he wanted all of it gift-wrapped. For everything he picked out, we had to write down the name of who was getting what and make sure the store clerks had everything straight. We took Mr. Jackson home, I drove back to the mall, got the presents, and brought them into the house, arranging everything under the Christmas tree.

The tree was there when they first arrived in Las Vegas. The whole house was already decorated inside with ornaments. The property management company knew he was coming, and I'm pretty sure it was Mr. Jackson's directive, the house being decked out like that. He was raised a Jehovah's Witness. Jehovah's Witnesses don't celebrate Christmas, but he celebrated it because of his kids. He wanted them to have that experience. He wanted everything to be a perfect surprise for them when they woke up the next morning—including the puppy. He'd planned a special gift for Prince: a seven-week-old chocolate Labrador puppy. But the people that Feldman arranged to get the dog from had arrived too early on Christmas Eve. Mr. Jackson didn't want Prince to see the dog, and there was nobody else to step up, so I said, "I'll take him for the night."

I took the dog home, kept him at my house. Cute dog. Did not shut up. Whined and whimpered all damn night. I'd barely slept a couple hours when my phone started ringing off the hook. It was only six a.m., but somehow Prince had gotten wind of the surprise and wanted the puppy as soon as possible. So I dragged my ass out of bed, put the puppy in the car, and drove it over. Little guy was whimpering and whining the whole way. But the second I brought him inside Mr. Jackson's house? He shut right up. He was suddenly as sweet and lovable as he could be, like he knew he was finally home. Prince went crazy. He loved that dog. Named it Kenya.

For those first few days the family didn't do anything, didn't go anywhere. It was mostly just me running a lot of errands. Pick up this, go get that. Feldman would order prepared meals for them from Whole Foods—always Whole Foods—then either he or I would go and pick them up. Occasionally, when I was patrolling the property, I'd see the family at the kitchen table, having breakfast or something. But I didn't have any real interaction with them. They stayed in the house. Any communication I had went through Feldman.

Mr. Jackson's mother came to visit during that week before New Year's. No other family members, just her and her driver. She came to the house and brought gifts for the kids. When she pulled up to the house, Mr. Jackson and the little ones were all right there to open the front door for her. There was a lot of excitement. A lot of "Hi, Grandma! Hi, Grandma!" That sort of thing. It was pretty clear they hadn't seen each other in a while.

I was keeping an eye on most of this from the garage, where I'd set myself up with a makeshift command post. Every couple hours I'd patrol the perimeter. The whole neighborhood was quiet. Dead of winter. Streets empty. Word hadn't leaked out yet that Mr. Jackson was living here, so there were no fans, no paparazzi lined up outside the gate. It was eerie, sort of like the calm before the storm, you know? It was only a matter of time before people found out that this was Michael Jackson's house. When they did, who knew what kind of madness was going to come crashing through the front gate. And we weren't prepared.

"What are we doing about security?" was a major discussion, every day, between Feldman, Jeff, and myself. We needed more bodies, people we could trust. New Year's Eve was coming up fast, and Mr. Jackson had passed down word that he wanted to take the kids to see the David Copperfield show at the MGM Grand. We couldn't take the family back down to the Strip, on New Year's Eve, without the right people to handle it. Jeff said he'd reach out to his cousin, Javon, who lives here in Vegas. I'd never met him before, but if Jeff vouched for him I was ready to accept him.

And to be honest, at that point, Jeff's word was all I had to go on. The whole situation still felt very strange. Something wasn't right, the way this was being handled. I just couldn't put my finger on it yet. I had a lot of questions. I didn't ask them. In this line of work, you don't ask questions. When I hire someone to do personal security, if they have too many questions, to me that means they're not focused on the job. They're too worried about the who, the what, the why—things that aren't really their business. It's a sign that person can't be trusted.

Besides, if you really want to know something? When you're on a detail long enough, you'll find out. It will come. You start overhearing conversations. You start getting emails, taking phone calls. You see who's visiting, so on. You keep your thoughts to yourself. You just watch and listen, and pretty soon all your questions will be answered without you having to ask them.

2

Growing up, Michael Jackson idolized James Brown, the Godfather of Soul, the Hardest-Working Man in Show Business. Watching Brown on television and from the wings at Harlem's Apollo Theater, the young performer studied and absorbed the master's every move. Though he would go on to learn at the feet of Motown greats like Marvin Gaye, Diana Ross, and Smokey Robinson, Michael Jackson would insist throughout his life that James Brown had been his deepest and most lasting influence.

On Christmas Eve, as Jackson and his family were preparing to celebrate the holidays, his childhood idol was checking into a hospital in Atlanta, Georgia, complaining of exhaustion and a debilitating cough. Just hours later, in the early morning of Christmas Day, the seventy-three-year-old Brown died of congestive heart failure brought on by complications from pneumonia. On December 30, leaving his children in the care of their nanny, Jackson flew to Augusta, Georgia, and attended Brown's memorial service, joining several other luminaries onstage to eulogize the departed singer. It was Jackson's first public appearance in the United States since leaving the country a year and a half before.

While waiting for Jackson to return, Bill Whitfield and Jeff Adams began making arrangements to beef up the family's security detail for New Year's Eve. Adams, already contracted to another client, would not be on hand much longer, so he reached out to his cousin Javon

Beard. Twenty-six years old and a father of three, Javon Beard grew up in the heart of South Central Los Angeles, his father a postal worker and his mother a clerk for FedEx. One of six children, Beard had an older sister, a twin brother, younger twin sisters, and a younger baby brother. His own twin, Jovon, was born with cerebral palsy and died at the age of seven.

The Beards lived with their grandmother near the corner of 46th and Western, an area notorious for drug activity and gang violence at the height of the crack-cocaine era. Javon escaped the streets by throwing himself into the basketball team at Inglewood High School, one of the most competitive squads in the country, with the hope that his athletic talents would open the door to a college degree. But one night, filling up at a gas station a few blocks from home, Javon was shot in the arm during an attempted carjacking. His dream of an athletic career and a college scholarship over, he graduated from Inglewood and took a full-time job as a security guard at the Hyperion Treatment Plant, where he was promoted to head of security.

After years of dealing with the harsh Los Angeles streets, Javon decided to leave South Central for a safer, more stable environment. While visiting family in Las Vegas in 2004, he interviewed for a position at the Summer Bay time-share resort, got the job, and moved out the very next week. He worked his way up from a front-desk security post to be an executive housekeeper/security manager, overseeing a staff of two hundred security and maintenance personnel.

Unlike Bill Whitfield, Javon Beard had never done high-profile celebrity protection in his life, but he did possess the one qualification that mattered: he was family, and he could be trusted. So on New Year's Eve, just hours before the Jackson family planned to head out for the night, Jeff Adams reached out to his cousin to offer him a once-in-a-lifetime opportunity.

Javon: I had "Smooth Criminal" set up as the ringtone on my cell phone, so that's what I heard when I got Jeff's call. It was around one-thirty in the afternoon. At first I thought he was calling to coordinate for that night, because all our family members were coming in for this big New Year's party I'd put together. I'd rented a suite at the Bellagio, been planning on it for months. But as soon as I picked up the call, I could tell his tone was real strange. He was being short with me. He said, "What are you doing right now?"

I said, "I'm getting ready for tonight."

I was really pressed for time. The city closes the Strip to vehicle traffic on New Year's so people can come down to see the fireworks. I told Jeff, "I'm trying to get down to the Strip because they close it at five, and it's almost two now."

"You at the house?"

"Yeah, I'm at the house."

"I'm on my way."

"What for?"

"I need to talk to you, and it can't be on the phone. I'll be there in fifteen minutes. Don't go nowhere."

Then he hung up, real abrupt. Didn't even say good-bye.

When he got to the house, I was out front, loading the car. I had a friend there helping me pack. Jeff looked at this guy and said he needed to talk to me in private. So we went inside, he sat me down and said, "Okay, I know you're not going to want to do this. I know you've got plans, but I've got a serious favor to ask and I need someone I can trust. Can you work tonight?"

I said, "*Hell*, no."

First off, it was New Year's. Second, I already had this suite at the Bellagio. You're talking seven hundred dollars a night with a two-night minimum, and my credit card had already been charged. I was out fourteen hundred dollars, and that was the discount rate; I'd had to book months in advance to get it.

I didn't need the work, either. I'd made my way up at the

time-share, was making $65,000 a year. I was doing good, and now I was ready to kick back and celebrate. I said to Jeff, "Man, I'm straight. I've got my bread coming in right now. I'm not looking to ruin my New Year's plans for a one-night detail." He kept on me. Finally I said, "Who's the client?"

He said, "I can't tell you. All I can say is it's a high-profile dignitary."

I laughed. I said, "Jeff, you know you my cousin, but I'm not even listenin' to that. I'm not about to cancel my plans unless you tell me facts."

He thought about it for a second and said, "Okay, I'm breaking confidentiality here, but since you're family I'll tell you." Then he leaned in close and said, "It's Michael Jackson."

"Get the fuck outta here!"

"I'm *serious*. It's Michael Jackson."

I could tell by the look on his face that he wasn't messing with me. He explained the whole situation. "More than likely it's going to be a permanent job if you want," he said. "Just go on this detail tonight, and it could turn into a whole lot more."

I said, "No way, Jeff. I know how the personal security business works from watching you. It's touch and go, and I've already got a steady thing."

He told me it was pretty definite but the one thing he couldn't vouch for was whether Mr. Jackson was going to like me or not. He said, "The guy's picky sometimes. He can be very choosy about who represents him." Finally he said, "Look, I know Mr. Jackson's going to end up liking you, so I'm going to make it worth your while. I'll help you tell the family that you're not going to make the party. I'll take the heat for that, and I'll pay for the room."

I said, "You're gonna give me fourteen hundred dollars?"

He reached in his pocket and pulled out a thousand in cash. "It's all I've got on me," he said, "but come with me to an ATM and I'll get you the rest."

Once he did that? I knew it was good. I told him I was on board.

He said, "Do you have a black suit?" I did, but it was at the cleaners, and they were closed. The suits I had at the house were all bright colors—people who know me know I'm kind of a colorful guy—and with security it's strictly black or navy blue. Can't wear nothing else. So Jeff said, "Okay, we need to go and get you a new suit."

It was already after two o'clock on New Year's Eve, and since I'm six foot five, we had to hurry up and find a 48 Long that didn't need to be tailored—there's no tailors working on New Year's. We went to the Boulevard Mall, then the Meadows Mall. Finally we hit the Burlington Coat Factory and found a suit that fit me perfectly. We bought it, rushed back to my place, I put an iron on it, and headed to Mr. Jackson's house.

We pulled up to the house a little before five. I was getting nervous. Bill came out and opened the gate for us. That was my first time meeting Bill. He looked at me and said, "You ready to be a part of this?"

I said, "I hope so." But I was still really nervous about the whole thing. I didn't really know if it was something I could handle.

Bill said, "Well, you are tall. Might be good for something."

We drove up to the door. Jeff got out and went inside, left me in the car for about thirty minutes. I kept checking my watch, checking my suit, making sure my tie was fixed. Finally, Jeff came out and said, "Okay, let's go in. I spoke highly of you and he respects my opinion, so I think it's going to be a done deal."

Then he took me inside. Mr. Jackson came down the stairs. He had a surgical mask on, was wearing one of those white, Hanes V-neck T-shirts and pajama pants with his little white socks sticking out. First thing I noticed was just how frail and thin he was. When I went to shake his hand, I was careful just to lightly touch him. I was scared I was going to break him, because he seemed so fragile.

He started to say something, but I couldn't understand him because his voice was all muffled with that surgical mask on. I was trying to be all humble and respectful, but he was talking and I kept going, "Huh? Excuse me?" Then he lifted the mask up a bit and said, "Hello, Javon. I've heard a lot about you. Are you ready to be a part of my security team?"

I said, "Absolutely, sir. I'm very excited to be a part of the team. I hope it'll become something permanent."

He said, "I don't see why not. Can I trust you?"

"Yes, sir. You definitely can."

"Okay, welcome then."

He called the kids down. Prince and Paris walked right up and shook my hand. Mr. Jackson had to push Blanket to say hi. Then they ran right back to doing whatever they were doing before. Mr. Jackson said, "Don't pay them no mind. This is routine for them. They're used to meeting so many new people. But they mean well."

We talked a bit more and then he went back upstairs. Me, Bill, and Jeff spent the next few hours planning the detail. They took me on a walk through the property, showed me what was what. About ten o'clock that night, Mr. Jackson and the kids came down all dressed up and we drove over to the MGM Grand. The hotel management arranged for us to come in through the stage door.

The show had already started when we got there. We slipped in; Mr. Jackson and the kids took their seats in the front row. I sat right behind them. Bill posted up by the exit door, stage left. We watched the show, then slipped out before the lights came back up. Mr. Jackson took his kids to meet David Copperfield backstage. They chatted for a few minutes. Then we got in the vehicles and took them home to bed.

The next morning I called my office, gave them my notice, and I went to work for Michael Jackson.

3

In 1990, Michael Jackson opened the gates of his Neverland Valley Ranch to the public for the first time. Named after the fantastical island in J. M. Barrie's classic *Peter Pan*—the place where children never grow up—the sprawling, 2,700-acre estate was nestled deep in the Santa Ynez Mountains, about a hundred miles north of Los Angeles.

The new home was a significant upgrade for the then thirty-one-year-old singer, who had spent his earliest years in a tiny, two-bedroom cottage in Gary, Indiana. Even at the pinnacle of his success in the 1980s, Jackson had continued to live with his parents at Hayvenhurst, the Jackson family compound in Encino, California. Finally ready to move out on his own, Jackson bought Neverland, then called the Sycamore Valley Ranch, for $17 million in March 1988. He went on to spend two years and an additional $55 million converting it into a spectacular playground and showplace for his imagination.

Neverland's visitors entered the ranch at its train station, boarding a steam engine that took them up to the main house. The house itself, a massive Tudor-style mansion, was situated on a five-acre lake with a man-made waterfall. Hidden speakers, disguised as rocks, were strategically placed throughout the gardens to play music all through the day. Bronze statues of children at play and life-sized mannequins of Peter Pan and Tinker Bell and other classic children's characters populated the grounds. Neverland had its own amusement park, complete with a Ferris wheel, bumper cars, and roller coasters; its own movie theater, filled with rows of plush velvet seats and a fully stocked concession stand; and even its own zoo, showcasing giraffes, lions, and zebras. With a staff of over sixty employees, the estate reportedly cost over $4 million a year to operate.

Neverland, Jackson often said, was his sanctuary, a place to recapture the childhood he'd lost when he was pushed into stardom at such an early age. Given the life he'd lived, Jackson wanted to share Neverland with children of all ages, particularly those for whom childhood had brought more hardship than joy. Among his many charitable activities, he opened his amusement park to children's hospitals and inner-city church groups year round, for free, entertaining thousands of sick and disadvantaged kids over the years.

But on November 18, 2003, Jackson's sanctuary was destroyed. That morning, armed with a search warrant, a team of seventy Santa Barbara sheriffs raided the estate, looking for evidence to corroborate the accusations of child abuse that had been leveled against him. For the next fourteen hours, officers went room to room, ransacking the mansion and rifling through the singer's personal effects; Jackson, in Las Vegas to promote his 9/11 charity single, "What More Can I Give," was powerless to stop it. The entire search was documented by video camera and later shown in court, exposing Jackson's private world for everyone to see. After the raid, Jackson declared that Neverland was no longer his home. When he had to live there during his trial, he refused to go back in the main residence; he stayed in one of his own guesthouses. When the trial was over, he vowed he would never return.

With Jackson living abroad, Neverland fell into steep decline. He could no longer cover the estate's considerable operating costs. The roller coasters sat idle. The grounds were no longer maintained. The animals in the zoo could not be properly cared for. By the end of 2005, Neverland's workers' compensation insurance had lapsed, and Jackson owed his staff over $300,000 in back wages. On March 9,

2006, the state of California served notice that the property had to be closed until the outstanding labor issues were resolved. The estate was officially shuttered. Its few remaining staffers were let go, leaving one security guard posted at the front gate. The animals were donated to zoos and wildlife preserves in California, Arizona, and elsewhere. The train station and the amusement park were mothballed and left to collect dust.

When Jackson moved to Las Vegas at the end of 2006, his management rented him a house at 2785 South Monte Cristo Way. As with a lot of Las Vegas architecture, the fifteen-thousand-square-foot, seven-bedroom, ten-bath mansion was a bit over the top. Just inside the house's gated entrance was a circular drive that surrounded a small fountain and led to a covered portico outside the main entrance. Inside, a grand, two-story foyer opened on to an absurdly oversized living room with a vaulted ceiling gilded with massive chandeliers. To the foyer's left was a private movie theater; to the right, a sweeping marble staircase that led upstairs to the children's bedrooms and Jackson's two-thousand-square-foot master suite, which ran the entire length of the north face of the house. At the rear of the ground floor, the kitchen and dining area overlooked the pool house and private tennis court in the backyard.

Outside, tucked out of view from the street, sat the garage, reached via a driveway that split off from the courtyard in the front. It was here that Bill and Javon set up their base of operations—and they had their work cut out for them. While the opulent home may have seemed fit for a celebrity of Michael Jackson's stature, his new security team quickly realized that it was anything but.

Bill: Mr. Jackson didn't choose the house; someone else made the arrangements on his behalf while he was overseas. From a security point of view, it was a nightmare, located on the wide-open corner of an intersection, exposed on two sides. The neighbors could see directly into the backyard where the children played. And once word got out that Michael Jackson was living there? We had paparazzi climbing the trees, trying to get shots of him and the kids. The front doors were visible from the street, and they were glass-paned, which meant you could see straight into the house from outside the gate. We had to suggest that Mr. Jackson not use the front door unless he was receiving guests. For routine comings and goings, he went through the garage.

The house came with a security system. There were digital cameras covering the property, all wired to a room upstairs with a bank of monitors. I spent a day up there messing with all that gear, only to find that a lot of the equipment wasn't even working. Out of fifteen cameras on the property, maybe four or five of them worked. That was horrible.

It was a horrible house. It was the kind of house where the garage had been designed with a space for a limousine, but the way the driveway was angled, you couldn't actually drive a limousine into the garage. If you wanted to put a limousine in that spot you'd have to drop it in from the roof.

Javon: It was a nice place to look at, eye-candy wise. Marble floors. Marble staircase. Big chandeliers. But the plumbing and everything? Terrible. There was this beautiful water fountain in front of the house. Mr. Jackson loved the fountain, but for some reason we could never figure out, all the water completely drained out of it every two days. Every time it emptied out, we'd have to go and fill it with the garden hose. Every time it rained, the whole side yard flooded, leaving this deep, mud-filled trench running the whole length of the house.

The plumbing inside wasn't much better. Mr. Jackson's bedroom flooded a number of times. We were only there a couple weeks when the water heater blew. Dead of winter and for several days there was no hot water. We had to pack Mr. Jackson and his family up and make arrangements for them to stay at the Marriott until a new water heater was installed. Central heating didn't work properly, either; we had to go out and get space heaters for the children's bedrooms. If too many appliances were turned on at once, the breakers would flip and all the lights would go out.

This place was trying to be so fancy that it had an elevator. Mr. Jackson got stuck in the elevator. The kids came running outside one day, yelling, "Daddy's stuck! Daddy's stuck!" We went in, and he was trapped between floors. We had to go upstairs and lift him out. He thought it was his fault. He kept saying, "Did I push the wrong button? What did I do?" But it wasn't his fault. That elevator broke down all the time.

Bill: All kinds of stuff went wrong. Service technicians were always on the property. Mr. Jackson complained about it all the time. And it's not that the house was chosen to save money. It had been on the market for about seven years. No one had ever lived in it, and Mr. Jackson rented it for six months for $1 million. One million for six months. What kind of bullshit is that?

We tried to make all the improvements we could. For the amount of work the security system required, I would've had to call a company to come in and install a whole new system. But if I did that, I'd be taking a risk of someone finding out personal details about Mr. Jackson living here. Plus, I really didn't like an outside company knowing exactly what kind of security measures we had in place. So I decided it was best that we get it done inside the team.

The main piece of equipment we installed was what's called an inground intrusion detection system. It's these small sensors linked together on a fiber-optic network that runs underground. That gave us detection around every inch of the property. If so much as an empty tin can was tossed over the outside wall, we'd be alerted immediately.

Javon: We had to lay wires all through the grounds and run every single one of them back to the garage. We installed lights with motion sensors, new cameras that covered the yard and the perimeter outside the fence. We quickly learned that money was no object for Mr. Jackson when it came to security. He would front any bill when it came to that. Cameras, weapons, whatever. We'd say, "We need to get this and it's going to cost such and such amount." He'd just pay it. He'd say, "Make that happen."

Bill: We bought a CPM-700 countersurveillance sweeper. Costs about five thousand dollars. It picks up electronic recording devices. We took that everywhere. Hotel rooms, conference rooms, restaurants. He was adamant about it. During his trial in '05, someone had made a secret recording of a conversation between him and his lawyer and then tried to sell it. So he was concerned about that, being taped. If we went anywhere, before he'd even get out of the car, he'd say, "Did we scan everything?"

We never found any bugs. Not that we expected to, because people rarely knew we were coming. There were times when we detected something, some strange frequency, but we couldn't find the source of it. He'd insist on having the room changed anyway.

Javon: He was furious when we caught one of the drivers from the car service with a camera in their car. Most limousine services out here, even taxis, use cameras to record their passengers. It's standard practice. The car service we were using, we told them to disconnect any recording devices in the vehicles. But we were in the car one day, and there was a red light on the visor. We saw it and said, "What's that light?"

The driver said, "Oh, that's the camera."

"What camera? We told you no cameras. All this is being recorded?"

"Well, it's—"

"No, no. We're gonna need that tape. Give us the tape."

So arrangements were made to get the tape back. And when Mr. Jackson got wind of it? If you even said the word "camera" to him, he was done. He started calling his manager. "I need my vehicles," he told her. "Get my cars out here."

About a week later, the vehicles showed up; they were shipped out from Neverland. He had three identical black SUVs, GMC Yukons, the same cars he used during his trial in Santa Barbara. They were all fitted with triple-tinted windows. We installed a privacy curtain between the front and backseat of the primary vehicle that Mr. Jackson rode in.

When the trucks arrived, a Bentley and a Rolls-Royce were delivered too. They were both black. The interior of one of them was 14-karat gold. It had been a gift for Mr. Jackson from some Middle Eastern prince or something. There was a minibar in the back of this thing. Even the ice bucket was 14-karat gold. Those two cars, the Bentley and the Rolls, they sat in the garage.

Bill: He hated those cars. That's when we really started to see that there was some friction between Mr. Jackson and his people, that they didn't always understand his needs and wants. One night we were going on some detail, and Feldman said, "We're gonna drive the Rolls-Royce tonight. Just you wait. He's gonna love this."

So we got the Rolls detailed. Mr. Jackson came out to the garage, we had this car all shiny and beautiful, and he just stared at it. He said, "What is this?"

Feldman said, "We brought it from Neverland, sir."

"I know where it's *from*," Mr. Jackson said. "Why is it here?"

"I thought you wanted to keep driving them—"

"No, no, I don't like these cars. These cars always break down. I was with Liz one night in the Rolls and it broke down and we were stuck."

He didn't like those cars. We drove the trucks.

Javon: I was the primary driver. I took him everywhere he needed to go, kept the cars washed and cleaned. One thing I learned real quick was whenever we were driving him, he only listened to classical music. He'd send us to the store to buy it by the armload. He'd say, "I need some CDs. Classical. Get all the classical CDs you can find." So one of us would go to the store, go to the classical section, grab a bunch, bring them home. If he got in the backseat and either me or Bill had the radio on an R & B station, one of us would quickly turn it to classical. Every now and then, he'd want to listen to the R & B, but otherwise it was classical pretty much all of the time.

Bill: Typically, I was there until midnight or so. I'd wait and go home once the kids were in bed and everything was set for the night. Couple times a week, Javon or I would stay overnight, work through until morning, but we also hired three guys to come in to work the graveyard shift. Whole place would be locked down, alarms set. I gave them direct orders: if anyone breaches the wall, shoot first then call me.

Javon: We were still working out of the garage, and there was very little space for us to maneuver or get comfortable. And you know, if it's winter, the garage is the coldest part of the house. We were in there all night, on a twenty-four-hour shift, freezing our asses off. Thank God, a couple weeks later we got the security trailer.

Mr. Jackson's manager was a woman named Raymone Bain. She'd been his publicist during the trial and now she was managing him. The first time Ms. Raymone came to the house, she saw us set up in this cold, cramped garage and she couldn't believe it. She said, "Why don't you get the trailer from Neverland?"

"Trailer? What trailer?"

"There's a security trailer at Neverland."

So we got the trailer out here. That was a blessing. Trailer had a sink, a shower, a bathroom, a full-size bed. It served as our command center. We rerouted all the surveillance cables that had been running into the garage. We posted up a full blueprint of the interior layout of the house as well as a map of the entire city of Las Vegas. We surveyed every block of the surrounding residential area, mapped all the possible routes for ingress and egress. Given how exposed the house was, we did everything we could to compensate.

Bill: We installed panic buttons in different rooms in the house—in his bedroom, in the family room. In the event of an emergency, Mr. Jackson or the kids could alert us right away. The alarm didn't sound inside the house, just in the trailer, to alert us. And it was a loud-ass alarm, tell you that much. I remember the first time it went off. It was early one morning. I heard it and ran out of the trailer and around the back of the house. I got to the kitchen door, drew my weapon, and burst inside, like I was ready for some real shit to be going down.

They were all just sitting at the breakfast table, eating their cereal. They saw me and they froze: Mr. Jackson on the left, Paris at the head of the table, Prince sitting on my right, across from Mr. Jackson. I didn't see Blanket. He was across the room by the TV, which was where the panic button was mounted on the wall. He was just walking around, hitting buttons. They all sat there at the table, staring at me, and then Blanket blurted out, "Bill, is that a real gun?!"

Little dude thought it was cool. Mr. Jackson did not. Pulling an automatic weapon in the family room with his kids eating breakfast? Oh, he got on me about that.

Javon: He didn't like the kids seeing weapons, but he did appreciate that we were well armed. We both carried semiautomatic Glock pistols with extended magazines. We had Tasers. Each of them delivered a charge of 1.2 million volts, powerful enough to take down a three-hundred-pound man. We had a cache of backup weapons: MP5 fully automatic submachine guns, military-style AR-15s, 12-gauge automatic shotguns, and concealable MAC-10s. We had three cases of ammunition, close to three thousand rounds for everything we had. We wore lightweight body armor under our suits at all times. Some may say it was overkill, but those people don't know the kind of threats that Mr. Jackson received on a regular basis. We planned and prepared for the worst, but we hoped and prayed for the best.

Bill: Anyone who came to the house—repairmen, service technicians, whoever—they all had to sign confidentiality agreements before they were allowed on the property. It was a contract that carried a $10 million penalty for disclosing any details about Mr. Jackson, his home, his children, any of it. If they didn't sign, they didn't come in. We also searched them and confiscated their cell phones. If they didn't comply, they didn't come in. Those that were allowed on the property had a member from the security team accompany them throughout the house until they were finished.

That was standard procedure for everybody, even the clowns we'd hire for the kids' birthday parties. The clowns didn't know whose party they were coming to perform at until they got there. They'd show up, we'd hit them with this industrial-strength non-disclosure form, and they'd go, "Huh?" Then we'd search 'em, wand 'em, and take their phones.

"We need to hold on to this phone until you leave."

"But what if someone calls?"

"Do you want to be our clown or not?"

And they'd hand over the phone.

Mr. Jackson trusted no one. The man was paranoid, very paranoid. Didn't sleep much. He was always going around the house at three, four in the morning, checking the locks on all the doors. The nights I stayed over in the trailer I saw him do it a number of times.

We had thousands of dollars in surveillance gear covering every inch of this property, armed security guards patrolling the grounds, and still he was going door to door, checking the deadbolts. I'd show up in the morning, and the overnight guys would give me a report. "Dude was checkin' doors again," they'd say. It just became normal to us.

Javon: He'd frequently come outside in the dead of night to make sure we were in the trailer. He'd poke his head in and say, "Just checking that you guys are here."

We'd say, "Sir, we're not going anywhere."

Bill: There was a direct phone line to the trailer, and only Mr. Jackson had the number. We'd get calls in the middle of the night. He heard something. He was worried about something. Didn't take much to set him off.

One night, we were on duty and, around two-thirty in the morning, we heard the door to the house slam and then all of a sudden there was this loud banging on the trailer door. We opened it and Mr. Jackson was standing there, holding the kids close to him. The kids were all half asleep and discombobulated, wearing pajamas, shivering in the freezing cold.

Mr. Jackson had this look of panic on his face, his eyes wide open. "Somebody's *inside* the house," he said. "They're trying to break into my bedroom through the terrace door."

My first thought was that we should leave, just take the cars and bounce. But Javon was saying, "Check the room! Let's check the room!" So we stayed to investigate. We brought Mr. Jackson and the kids inside the trailer. Javon stayed with them. I drew my weapon, went into the house, and made my way upstairs to Mr. Jackson's bedroom.

The thought in the back of my mind was that someone must have climbed up the back balcony. Once I was inside his room, I could hear what he was talking about. There was this rustling sound coming from outside the door to the balcony, like someone trying to get in. I crept up and threw the door open and looked out. Nobody there. But now I could hear the sound better. Sounded more like flapping. I looked up and there was a wing sticking out of this vent, frantically flapping around. A pigeon. All this over a pigeon.

I reached up and grabbed it. I pulled it out of the vent and threw it over the balcony. I couldn't tell if it took off or what. I may have broken its wing. All I saw was the thing going straight down. I went back downstairs and told Mr. Jackson it was just a bird. Of course now he was all concerned about the bird. He was like, "You didn't kill it, did you?"

"No, sir," I said. "Of course not. I just let it go."

"Oh, good."

Javon: By that point, it was well past three in the morning. Prince was like, "*Da-ad*, can we go back to bed now, *please*? We've got school in the morning, and I'm tired."

So they all shuffled back into the house to go to bed. As they walked in, Mr. Jackson said, "See, kids? Better safe than sorry."

Bill: A couple weeks later, maybe mid-February, about one-thirty in the morning, I got this frantic call from his manager, Raymone. She was all worked up, saying, "You gotta get Mr. Jackson out of the house!"

"What's the problem?"

She wouldn't tell me. She just kept saying, "Get him outta the house! I booked you a room at a hotel. Get him outta the house!"

I figured it had to be something serious. I told Javon to get the cars ready, and I ran into the house. When I got upstairs, Mr. Jackson was running around in the dark. It was pitch black inside; he didn't want the lights turned on, like he was scared somebody was going to see him. He had the kids going room to room with flashlights, getting their stuff together, packing to leave. He was whispering to them, "Let's go! Let's go! C'mon! No, we don't need that! Just grab a few things!"

I didn't know what was happening. I said, "Sir, what's wrong? What's going on?"

He wouldn't say. He just said, "Raymone called. There's a threat. We have to leave. We have to leave. *Right now.*"

Javon: I had the cars ready, and I was outside in the security trailer. There was nothing on any of the monitors; none of the sensors had been tripped. Before we left, me and Bill checked the whole house. Nothing. We went to Mr. Jackson and said, "Sir, everything's fine. The house is secure. Trust us, no one's getting in here."

But he was in a full panic. He was almost incoherent, like he wasn't even hearing a word we told him. He just kept saying, "We gotta go! We gotta go!"

Bill: We had no idea what was going on, but we loaded the suitcases and the kids into the trucks and took everyone to the Green Valley Ranch, a resort nearby in Henderson. The manager was waiting for us at the loading dock when we pulled in. We crept up in there in the middle of the night, with no advance security check, nothing.

We got him settled in his room, and we took the room across the hall. The next morning, I went over and talked to him. He was fuming. He said, "I shouldn't have to leave my house for nobody. I shouldn't have to run from nobody. Isn't that what I have you guys for?"

I said, "Sir, who are you running *from?*"

Finally he told me what was up. Raymone had received a phone call from this former security guard at Neverland, an employee that Mr. Jackson supposedly owed money to. This guy had called her up and he got real vocal and real threatening about what he was going to do to get his money. He said he was coming to Vegas and was going to climb the wall to Mr. Jackson's house. So Raymone called Mr. Jackson and sent him into a panic.

I said, "And *that's* why we left? Mr. Jackson, you are safe in your house. We're more than capable of protecting your family. If Raymone had told me what was going on, I would have taken care of it."

That caught him off guard. He seemed a little pissed off.

We stayed at the Green Valley Ranch one more night, then packed everybody up and went back to the house. The kids were pretty worn out. Usually, they seemed to take this kind of stuff in stride; they were accustomed to the rhythm of their father's life. Secret back doors, security alarms, panic buttons—that was their everyday. They were little troopers. But every now and then, you'd see the craziness take its toll. This was one of those times. Here they were, in a new city, living in a strange house. Then suddenly they're leaving that house, running out in the middle of the night, popping into this hotel, then turning around and leaving the hotel. And no real explanation for any of it.

As we drove back to the house, everyone was being real quiet in the backseat. Then Blanket looked up at his daddy and said, "Daddy, can we go back to the other house? Can we go back to Neverland?"

Mr. Jackson shook his head and said, "No. We can't ever go back there. That place has been contaminated by evil."

4

In May 1970, the Jackson 5 flew into Philadelphia to kick off their first national tour as an official Motown act. They had signed with the famous Detroit label just two years before, and their debut single, "I Want You Back," had been released the previous fall, shooting straight to No. 1 on the *Billboard* charts. That feat would be matched by each of their next three singles, making the Jackson 5 the first recording act in history to have four consecutive debut songs reach the top of the charts. Through record sales and radio play, the group's popularity had been building, and when their plane landed at Philadelphia International Airport, over three thousand fans mobbed the terminal. The following night, during their performance, a cordon of one hundred police officers was required to keep the crowd of sixteen thousand from rushing the stage.

Michael Jackson was only eleven years old, but the script of his life had already been written. For the next four decades, massive crowds would shadow his every public move, laying siege to his hotel rooms and camping outside the gates of his homes. When *Thriller* was released on November 30, 1982, the adulation he'd experienced as part of the Jackson 5 was eclipsed by a level of fame unprecedented in the history of entertainment. *Thriller* stayed in the *Billboard* Top 10 for eighty weeks. Thirty-seven of those weeks were spent at No. 1. Seven of its nine tracks became Top 10 singles. The album won eight Grammys out of a record-setting twelve nominations. In its first year alone, *Thriller* sold over 22 million copies. As one Jackson observer noted, *Thriller* transcended its status as a mere musical album and became something more like a household appliance—it was something that everybody just had.

Pop superstars had existed before Michael Jackson, of course. Frank Sinatra, Elvis, and the Beatles all dominated the music scene in their respective eras. But Michael Jackson appeared at a propitious—and, in hindsight, fleeting—moment in the evolution of both music and technology. Broadcast and satellite television were just cementing their hold on the international media landscape, and the rapid digital distribution of the Internet age had not yet fragmented that landscape into a million little niches. It was a brief window in which the world was uniquely primed for a global commercial phenomenon, and that phenomenon was Michael Jackson, the newly crowned King of Pop.

When *Thriller*'s follow-up, *Bad*, was released in August 1987, it became the No. 1 album not just in America but in a record-setting twenty-five countries. It generated five No. 1 singles and sold 17 million copies in its first year, two-thirds of those sales coming from outside the United States. *Bad* would also launch Jackson's first-ever solo tour. He put on 123 concerts in fifteen countries on four continents, playing to a total audience of 4.5 million and grossing a total $125 million, making *Bad*, up to that point, the most highly-attended and highest-earning tour of all time. In every city Jackson played, he moved through the streets with an armed motorcade fit for a head of state.

By the turn of the century, Jackson's popularity had dimmed somewhat. When his last studio album *Invincible* was released in 2001, many considered it a commercial disappointment compared to his earlier work. Still, it sold 11 million copies worldwide, more than most artists could dream of. Even if casual listeners had moved on, Jackson still had a passionate fan base. This was particularly true outside the United States, where the allegations made against him were given far less credence in the popular media.

Indeed, the more Jackson was attacked in the tabloids, the more devoted his community of fans became; loyalty to the singer in the face of adversity became its own badge of honor. Millions of listeners in dozens of countries formed an elaborate network of clubs and groups, publishing newsletters, trading memorabilia. The most die-hard among them followed Jackson from country to country, wherever he went. And during his months-long trial in 2005, hundreds of them converged to stand vigil outside the courthouse, cheering his every coming and going and praying for his acquittal.

What made the phenomenon of Jackson's fan base unique was not just their devotion to him, but his reciprocal embrace of them. As much as the singer would come to despise the prison that fame had put him in, he never lost his love for the people who had made him famous. The fans, Jackson believed, not the record execs and the concert promoters, were the ones responsible for his success. He felt personally indebted to each and every one. Their steadfast loyalty was something the singer had rarely experienced in his private life. And because his fans never lost faith in him, Michael Jackson never forgot about them.

Bill: For the first couple weeks, everything was quiet. Then we started to see cars. People would drive by the house. Some would linger, stop and look, and then drive off. There was this one car, a red car that would park across the street from the house and just sit there. I'd watch it through the security cameras. This was at least a couple times a week. Sometimes daily.

Eventually I got a glimpse of the driver. It was a woman, petite, with light-brown hair. She would get out of the car and she would just pace. I'd heard about the kind of fans who were attracted to Michael Jackson. They were in love with him. From a security standpoint, I perceived them as a threat at first. When you see a car parked outside the gate, you don't know if it's just a fan or someone worse, a stalker, someone who's completely unhinged. I'd never seen this person before, so one afternoon I went out to the car and talked to her. She was from California. She said she didn't live far from Neverland. She said she knew Michael and that she was a friend of his. I said, "So you're just gonna sit out here?"

She said, "It's okay. He knows."

Whenever we went on a detail, this girl would get out of her car and stand up to be seen, hoping he'd notice her. It was usually just me or Javon in the car and we wouldn't stop. The first time we were leaving the house with Mr. Jackson in the back, she stood up out of her car and I said, "There's that girl again."

Mr. Jackson looked up and said, "Who?"

I said, "That girl right there."

He said, "Oh, yes. I know her. Slow down."

We stopped and he put the window down and they had a conversation like they were old pals. "How are the kids doing?" "How do you like Vegas?" "Are you going to stay here long?" Hearing them speak, I didn't get the feeling that she was a stalker. She was just a real, dedicated fan. The conversation sounded innocent, friendly, trusting. A little flirtatious, to be honest. They just talked. It came to the point I had to remind him, "Sir, we have to go."

He told her what time we'd be back and that he hoped he'd see her then, just like you'd say, "See you later," to a good friend. As we drove away, he said, "Yeah, she goes everywhere I go."

Near the end of January, Mr. Jackson did an interview with the Associated Press, confirming that he was back in the country. After that, the fans really started coming. They were parked outside all day. Usually about four or five cars. Sometimes more. They'd come to the house each morning, park in front of the house, sit out there in lawn chairs, go home at night. Whenever our vehicles left the property, Mr. Jackson would roll down the window and say, "Hi. We'll be back in about twenty minutes." We'd take off, and they'd just sit and wait. We'd come back, he'd wave at them, go back in the house, and then they'd sit and wait some more. It was his presence, his aura. They just wanted to be near him.

Javon: The neighbors hated it. The fans were usually well behaved, but this was a high-end residential neighborhood. The CEO of Sprint lived next door. Gary Payton, the NBA player, was two doors down. You had these million-dollar homes and all these people setting up camp on the street. As far as the neighbors were concerned, the fans were a nuisance. Folks were always calling the cops. They would show up and hassle the fans until they left. Then the next day, the fans would be right back at it.

Bill: One day, there were three cop cars out there, and Mr. Jackson saw them from his window. He came out to the security trailer and told me, "I don't want my fans being harassed. I need you to let the police know that it's okay for them to be here as long as they're on my side of the property."

I went out and told the officers that. Cop asked me if I was a resident. I said, "No, but I'm doing a personal security detail for the owner of this house."

He said, "Who is that?"

I didn't answer. I just gave him a shrug. Then one of the fans said, "Michael Jackson lives there."

I didn't confirm or deny it. I just said. "The owner of the house does not have a problem with these people being out here."

The fans started clapping and saying, "You see? You see?"

The officer warned them that if they made any noise and he had to come back, arrests would be made. I didn't feel like that was the end of it, and it wasn't. Neighbors kept complaining, and the police kept coming back. Finally, Mr. Jackson said he was going to talk to his attorney. I don't know who they spoke to or what strings were pulled, but after that the police never came back and the fans stayed.

Javon: They were there through the winter months. They were there through the summer months. It'd be hot as hell out there, and they'd just be camped out on the pavement, waiting. On really hot days, Mr. Jackson would send us out with soft drinks and plates of snacks. The ones who stayed long enough, he sent us out there to give them folding chairs. We even rolled out the lawn furniture from the pool house.

There was this one girl who was adamant about seeing Mr. Jackson. She was there every single day. Every. Single. Day. She claimed a permanent place for herself on the pavement right next to the driveway, and she was always trying to pass Mr. Jackson things through the window of the car. One time, she ran up and handed Mr. Jackson a stack of nude photos of herself. Somehow he always found time to stop and chat with her on the way out.

Bill: Every time we left the house, the fans would run up to try and get a glimpse of him. If the kids were in the car, we'd keep the windows up and drive on; Mr. Jackson didn't want anybody getting too close to his kids. But if it was just us, he insisted on stopping and saying hello and signing as many autographs as possible. We were always nervous with that, but he'd insist. Most of them were respectful, courteous, but there were times it would get out of control and I'd have to jump out of the car to back everyone up. Whenever I got into it like that, Mr. Jackson would always talk me down. "Bill, be nice to my fans," he'd say. "They're not going to let anything happen to me. They're harmless."

Part of our apprehension was that at first we didn't understand what his relationship with his fans was. We were surprised to learn that he stayed in touch with some of them, would correspond with them. They would call his manager and send messages through her. When he talked to them, there were a lot of exchanges of "I love you" and "I love you more." They were always bringing him presents, personal things. They'd say, "I made this for you"; "Here's a stuffed animal"; "Here's a Peter Pan trinket."

His relationship with his fans—I'd never seen anything like it with other celebrities. Never. No matter how famous. With other celebrities, you see the groupies hanging around, but these were not groupies. Mr. Jackson actually knew a lot of them individually. He remembered what show he first met them at, how many years they'd known each other. He'd point out fans that he'd seen in other countries. Here we were in Las Vegas, and he was going, "That one there, I remember him from Germany."

It was an interesting relationship, him and the fans. He loved them as much as they loved him. From his bedroom window upstairs, he could look directly out to the street where they were camped out. Sometimes we'd glance up and see him, looking out from behind the curtains, just watching them, observing them. They'd sit and wait; he'd sit and watch.

Javon: The only real problem with the fans was that they drew the paparazzi. Usually it would just be three or four fans, the regulars. But when it became ten or eleven or a couple dozen? That's when we had a paparazzi problem. It was a bigger scene to get a picture of.

The photographers never got much of a glimpse of him, though. We would always load him into the vehicles through the garage. We used decoy vehicles too. I would go out in Mr. Jackson's primary vehicle and start heading one way, and Bill would take the other vehicle with Mr. Jackson to a different location while they were following me.

For the really desperate ones, down the street there was a tree they would climb up in and try and take pictures. I caught a guy up there one time and told him to come down. After he climbed down, I demanded to see his camera. But he wouldn't give it over. He said that everything he was doing was legal and he wasn't trespassing. Basically, he was like, "I'm gonna get my pictures, so get over it." Wasn't much I could do, so I just let him go.

A picture of Mr. Jackson and his kids would have probably been worth tens of thousands, if not hundreds of thousands of dollars. One night, we took Mr. Jackson and his kids to have dinner at the Wynn hotel. I was on post outside the dining room when this guy came up to me, came right up to my side and leaned in and said, "How'd you like to earn an easy fifty thousand?"

"What do you mean?" I said.

"I know who you work for. You give me the exact whereabouts of Michael Jackson and his kids at a specific time next week, and the money's yours. Call me tomorrow if you want to know more."

Then he shoved a business card in my hand and walked off. I didn't say anything to Mr. Jackson. I took the card to Bill and he ran a check on the guy, found out he was a paparazzi. We figured if we just did nothing and ignored it, the problem would pass. So that's what we did. Then about a week later, we were driving in the car, the classical music was on real loud, and Mr. Jackson said, "Javon, can you turn down the radio for a moment? I have a question for you."

I turned the music down. "Yes, Mr. Jackson?"

"Did you get an unusual offer from someone last week?"

I froze. *Oh, shit.* At that moment I knew exactly what had happened: *he'd* sent the photographer, to test me.

"Yes, sir," I said. I turned around to look him in the eye, and I explained how the whole thing had gone down.

He said, "I'm proud of you, Javon." It was like he was real happy that I'd passed the test, that he'd found somebody he could trust. "If you had even called that man's number, I would have fired you. But you did the right thing. The only mistake you made was you didn't tell me that it happened."

"Yes, sir, I know, and I am sorry about that, but I didn't want to worry you."

Bill spoke up and said, "It's my fault, sir. Javon told me about this, and once I found out it was just about a photograph and not a real threat, I was the one that made the decision not to worry you with it."

Mr. Jackson said, "Thank you, but you always have to tell me everything."

"Yes, sir."

Before that, I think he had sort of been on the fence about me. Everything went through Feldman to Bill to me, so I didn't interact with him that much. Once he put me through that test, that's really when he started to feel that he could trust me more.

Bill: Him testing Javon like that showed us just how little trust he had in people in general. Prior to working for Mr. Jackson, my main job had always been handling external threats—stalkers, the paparazzi. That type of stuff I knew how to deal with. But what Mr. Jackson was really paranoid about, the thing he felt he needed most from us, was protection from the people who were already in his life. He wanted us there so he could hide his movements from his own lawyers and managers. He wanted us there to be a buffer between him and his own family.

We knew he and the family were distant. You could tell that much just from reading about them. But we were also given instructions by his managers and the lawyers that made us feel the problems in the family were much worse than your typical, run-of-the-mill dysfunction. Pretty early on, we learned that if Mr. Jackson's family tried to reach out to him and come to the house, we were not supposed to let him know. Raymone said, "Any time his family comes around, call me. Call the management company." Both Feldman and Raymone gave us those directions.

No one in his family was allowed past the front gate without advance notice, with the exception of Mrs. Jackson, his mother. If she showed up, we'd open up the gate and she'd go right on into the house. She could come unannounced. Everyone else needed an appointment, and that was a very delicate situation to handle.

5

In the shifting racial landscape of the 1960s, the success of Motown Records was driven not just by the talent of its artists, but also by the marketing genius of its owner and founder, Berry Gordy. Gordy took black singers and performers and polished their public images to perfection, making them "safe" and appealing to white audiences, who flocked to record stores and bought the label's records by the millions. The Jacksons, a tight-knit, church-going, blue-collar family, were prime candidates for one of Gordy's signature makeovers—living proof of the success that awaited hard-working black families in a newly desegregated America.

This neatly packaged story had the benefit of being at least partially true. Joe Jackson, a crane operator at Inland Steel in East Chicago, channeled his love of music into his children, and his relentless ambition bootstrapped his family from seemingly impossible circumstances into Southern California's land of opportunity. His sons—handsome, wholesome, and well mannered—had shared a triple bunk bed in a single bedroom and rehearsed hours every day after school, staying out of trouble. The Jackson daughters, Rebbie, La Toya, and baby Janet, were cute and precocious and promised to be stars one day in their own right. Katherine, the family's steadfast matriarch, was a devout member of the Jehovah's Witness faith who had raised all her children to be good and decent and God-fearing.

Behind that image, as with all families, lay a more complicated reality. Years later, it would be revealed that Joe didn't just push his children but was physically abusive to them, beating them with belts and electrical cords for the slightest infraction. Joe was also a serial philanderer who used his newfound success to bed a steady stream of willing admirers. In 1974, he fathered a daughter outside of marriage and kept his second family a secret for years.

On more than one occasion, encouraged by her children, Katherine Jackson filed for divorce but later rescinded the petitions at the urging of her church, which frowned on the practice. Katherine and Joe remained legally married but led de facto separated lives. Most of the Jackson children embarked on ill-fated early marriages, some before the age of eighteen, in large part to get out of the house and away from their father. Despite the success that the family had achieved under Joe's direction, one by one, each of the Jackson siblings severed their professional relationship with him as well.

Inevitably, this personal strife tore the Jackson 5 apart. In 1975, the family split from Motown to pursue a more lucrative record deal with CBS/Epic Records. Jermaine, who had married Berry Gordy's daughter Hazel, stayed behind to pursue a solo career. The other brothers, with Randy now added to the lineup, re-formed as The Jacksons (Motown owned the Jackson 5 name). In making the move, Michael insisted that CBS back his solo efforts as well. Starting with 1979's *Off the Wall*—which sold 7 million copies and was the best-selling album ever by a black artist until topped by *Thriller* three years later—he minted a whole new generation of fans for whom his identity as a solo artist eclipsed any association he'd ever had with his brothers.

When Motown's twenty-fifth anniversary special aired on television in May 1983, Michael topped off a medley of classic hits with a show-stopping performance of "Billie Jean," introducing his iconic moonwalk to audiences for the first time. In that moment, the Jackson 5 became a nostalgia act. Michael Jackson was his own man. A year later, he was pressured by the family to stick with his brothers for the

Jacksons' *Victory* tour. On the last night of the tour, playing to a sold-out crowd in Los Angeles, Michael announced to the audience that this performance would be the group's "last and final show." Five years later, in June 1989, CBS decided not to renew the Jacksons' contract. Without Michael involved, the label no longer had any interest.

For the debut single on his 1995 *HIStory* album, "Scream," Michael performed a duet with his younger sister Janet, by then a major superstar in her own right. In September 2001, he rejoined his brothers for a brief reunion during two concerts at New York's Madison Square Garden. Beyond that, in the public eye at least, Michael had very little to do with his famous brothers and sisters. That changed in 2005. When the case against Michael went to trial, his family sat behind him in the courtroom, loudly and publicly supporting him throughout the entire ordeal. Randy Jackson, especially, stepped back into Michael's life in a big way, serving as Michael's manager and helping assemble the legal team, led by attorney Tom Mesereau, that would ultimately win Michael's acquittal.

But after the trial, that re-forged familial bond seemed to break as quickly as it had taken hold. Michael learned that Jermaine had used the trial to try to sell a Jackson family book. Michael and Randy had a massive falling out over business deals Randy had entered into on his brother's behalf during the trial. By the time Michael arrived in Las Vegas in December 2006, he had severed ties with everyone in his family, save his mother. Hearing that their famous brother was back in the country, however, the Jacksons undertook a series of attempts to see him. For the men charged with guarding the gate at 2785 South Monte Cristo Way, keeping the family out became the most difficult, and most confusing, part of the job.

Bill: We had fans that did drive-bys all the time. They'd come, circle the block, stop, look around, drive off. On this one particular day, would have been in early February, we saw a burgundy PT Cruiser going back and forth in front of the house. It had tinted windows, so we couldn't see who it was. This car circled the block maybe four times and drove off. That raised a red flag. The next day, the same PT Cruiser came and pulled right up to the gate. Javon stayed in the trailer to watch the monitors. I went down to the gate to see what was what.

I got down there, and Mr. Jackson's father, Joe Jackson, was getting out of the car. That was the first time I'd ever seen the guy in person; I'd only just seen him on TV before. He's a mean-lookin' dude. Got a unibrow. Looks like Blacula and shit. Whole time I was standing there thinking, Damn, this is *Joe Jackson*. This is the guy used to beat on all them Jackson 5 kids. That's what was going through my mind, looking at him. I stuck my hand through the gate to shake his and said, "How you doing, Mr. Jackson?"

He wouldn't shake my hand. He just eyed me with this nasty look and said, "You're probably one of those putting needles in my son's arm." I didn't respond. He said, "I'm here to see Michael."

I said, "Okay," left him there, and went back to the house to get Mr. Jackson. He was in his room, listening to music very loud. I knocked on the door and he came out, and I said, "Sir, your father's outside."

He said, "Does he have an appointment? Is he on the calendar?"

"I don't believe so, sir."

"No, no, no. I'm working. I cannot be disturbed when I'm being creative. Tell him he has to come back and make an appointment."

When that appointment talk came out of his mouth? That messed me up. I walked back out to the gate, thinking, Damn, I've got to go tell this man that he needs an appointment? To see his son? Uh-uh. I wasn't doing that. I was gonna have to ad lib this one.

I went down to the gate and told him that Mr. Jackson was busy, but if he came back tomorrow, I'd make sure to let his son know he wanted to visit. Then I held out my business card for him. He wouldn't take it. He just went off on me. "I don't need your damn number! If it wasn't for me, none of you bastards would have a job! I'm the one started this shit!"

Once he started rapping all that? Our conversation was over. I walked off. He just stood there on the sidewalk, yelling at nobody in particular. I didn't want to be part of that episode, so I just turned around and went back to the trailer. Eventually he got in his little car and left.

At that point, I started to wonder what kind of situation we'd walked into. I hadn't signed up for this part, getting involved with family.

Javon: A few days after Joe came by, we'd made plans to take the boss and the kids to the movies. The backup team was watching the house, and me and Bill were on our way to the theater a few miles out, to do the pre-detail. Suddenly we got a call over the radio. "They've breached the gate! They've breached the gate!"

Bill grabbed the radio. "Who? Who breached the gate?"

"His family. They're here."

The second we heard that we broke every traffic law on the books getting back. We were driving down the wrong side of the street, going over center lanes and barriers. We *flew* back to the house.

Bill: We pulled up, and I saw a black Hummer inside the gate. I was heated. I was pissed. I was yelling in the car, "How did they get past the gate?!"

The gate to the driveway closed real slow. You always had to watch it closely, because if you opened it for one car, there was usually time for another to come in behind it. We found out later that's what had happened. The chef had come in to make a delivery, and Mr. Jackson's family had been sitting in the street, idling in their car, and waiting for the chance to slip in.

I got out of the truck and saw it was three of his siblings: Randy, Rebbie, and Jackie. They were standing in the circular drive in front of the house. They walked down the driveway to me. I was expecting a confrontation, like with Joe, but they were very cordial, very calm. They introduced themselves. Jackie shook my hand and said, "Hey, how you doin'? Are you Bill?"

"Yes, sir."

"Okay, yeah. We heard about you."

Then Randy jumped in. "Are you Fruit?" he asked.

"Excuse me?"

"You from the Fruit of Islam?"

I said, "No, I'm not."

Randy said, "Oh, okay. Well, we need to talk to our brother."

I said, "I'm sorry, but you need to make an appointment."

Jackie and Rebbie kept their cool, but Randy started copping a little attitude, saying, "No, we need to talk to him *now*."

I quietly stood my ground and laid it out for them. "Mr. Jackson will only see you if you come back and make an appointment."

And that was all we said. After that, I escorted them off the property.

The whole situation was very uneasy. As I walked back in the house, I looked up and could see Mr. Jackson watching all this from behind the curtains of his bedroom window. I went inside and found him. He seemed very agitated. I said, "Sir, is everything okay?"

He said, "How did they just walk right up to my front door?"

I said, "I'm sorry, sir. I'm going to check with the team and find out what happened."

He said, "Bill, that can never happen again."

"Yes, sir."

"Never. Do you understand that?"

"I understand."

Javon: We could tell the family was upset with us. They thought we were the ones cutting them off. A lot of people accused Mr. Jackson's security of trying to limit access to him as a way of controlling him.

But we weren't any part of that. We didn't care one way or another if the family talked to him. It was Mr. Jackson's orders 100 percent.

I don't know what the deal with his family was before we showed up, but on our watch it was obvious that their relationship was null and void. We didn't understand it. You'd think they were the enemy. I was like, What's going on? Why does he not want to see his own family?

Bill: Mr. Jackson and Elizabeth Taylor were old friends, and she was having a seventy-fifth birthday party at a resort out at Lake Las Vegas, this big, red-carpet affair. Her people had heard that Mr. Jackson was living here now, and they reached out to his manager to ask if he would attend. They wanted it to be a surprise for Ms. Taylor; she wouldn't know anything about it until he showed up. Of course Mr. Jackson wanted to go. So about two weeks out from the event, word came down to us, and things started to gear up.

Javon: First thing Mr. Jackson did was call Roberto Cavalli, the designer, to create a custom outfit for him for the party. Cavalli took an emergency flight out here. We picked him up from the MGM Grand, brought him to the house, and he and Mr. Jackson started designing this whole new thing for him just for the party.

Mr. Jackson was obsessing over every detail. He flew his hairstylist and his makeup artist in too. Once we saw that? We knew he was really taking this seriously. We'd been working for him for over a month, and this was the first detail where he said, "Make sure you have on new suits." Not just suits, *new* suits. "Clean the cars. Wax the cars. Make sure your shoes are shined like mirrors." He never did that kind of thing before. Typically, he'd just tell us where he wanted to go, and we'd handle it. This was the first time we'd be stepping out in public, where we knew that the paparazzi and the press were going to be there. So every day, Mr. Jackson was like, "You guys have to look great. I want everybody to look great."

Bill: We hit the mall a few times, slipping in and out in disguises. Went to Tiffany's, to Hallmark. He picked out some gifts, a birthday card. We'd hear him talking in the car, talking to Feldman about how amped he was. We were getting excited just being around him. It was the first time we'd really seen him like this.

Day of the party, he was in good spirits all day long. It was infectious. It spread to everybody in the house. "Hey, Mr. Jackson's in a good mood!" Everybody was pumped. The whole atmosphere of the place changed. The security team, we were checking each other out, making sure we were all set. Suits pressed. Shoes shined. Even our weapons were polished. Shit, we looked *good*.

Javon: We were getting ready to walk out on the red carpet with Michael Jackson. It was surreal to us. We're security, but we're fans too. How could you not be? We were escorting the King of Pop to Elizabeth Taylor's birthday party. This was top of the line. A-list.

Bill: We were ready to roll out, the cars were in the driveway, all set to go, and Mr. Jackson was taking forever to get ready. While we waited, I left to go and gas up one of the vehicles. I came back and they opened the gate for me and I pulled in on the right-hand side of the circular driveway. The gate was closing behind me. I was getting out of the car and the gate was just a couple feet from closing when all of a sudden—*BAM!*—there was this loud crash. I turned around to see this gray Mercedes SUV come smashing full speed into the gate. It started to wobble back open, like a garage door does when it can't close. The Mercedes punched forward, scraping through the opening, and then it raced up the left side of the driveway. I was thinking this was some deranged person about to crash his car into the house. I pulled out my weapon and ran toward the car.

Javon: I was in the garage, waiting to lock up behind Mr. Jackson, who was on his way down. I heard the crash and looked up and saw Bill pull out his joint. The boss was coming through the garage door at that same moment. I screamed, "Mr. Jackson! No!" And I grabbed him and pushed him back into the house and locked him inside. He was all freaked out, going, "What's happening? Is everything okay?"

Bill: Everything felt like it was moving at super speed and in slow motion at the same time. The Mercedes came screeching to a halt right in front of the main door. I came between it and the house, drew my pistol and took aim at the driver. I had the laser sight right on his chest and the only thing running through my mind was, Whoever this is, they're about to get shot. The driver ducked down and out the corner of my eye I saw this woman in the passenger seat. That threw me. I wasn't expecting to see a woman. Then the driver lifted his head up and I saw who it was and I froze. *Holy shit,* I thought. *That's his brother. That's Randy Jackson.*

I eased back a bit. Now I was confused. What was the deal with this family? Here I was, about to shoot his own brother and I was only a split second away from pulling the trigger. All I could think about was the madness that would have broken loose if I'd taken that shot. I could see the headlines: Michael Jackson's Brother Shot by King of Pop's Bodyguards.

Javon: I still couldn't see who it was, just that Bill had the guy pinned down. I ran out the garage to back him up. I was coming down the driveway when Bill put his hand up for me to stop. I was ready to open up a can of whoop-ass, no question, but he waved me off like, "I got this, I got this."

Bill: Randy cracked his window open and yelled, "Get that gun out my face before I call the press."

The press? That was the last thing the boss needed. I went up to the window and said, "Mr. Jackson, you can't be doin' this."

"I'm here to see my brother," he said.

"Not like this, you're not. I'd appreciate it if you'd go back outside the gate. Go back outside, and I'll inform Mr. Jackson that you're here."

"I ain't moving until I see my brother!"

Javon: He started screaming, cussing his brains out, rapping all this stuff about money he's owed and how he's not leaving without it. *"Michael owe me money! I want my fuckin' money! I ain't fuckin' moving till I get my fuckin' money!"*

Bill: I didn't care what he wanted. I just wanted him outside the gate. I put my pistol away, trying to cool things down. I asked him to exit his vehicle so we could talk in a civilized manner. He refused. He just sat there in the car, threatening to call the press if he didn't get to see his brother. I didn't want him to call the press, and I couldn't call the cops because that would just bring the press too. I was stuck. I had this angry little asshole cussing in my face, and I couldn't do anything about it.

I left Javon and the others to watch Randy and went in the house to talk to Mr. Jackson. "Your brother Randy's crashed the gate," I told him. "He says he's here to see you about some financial matters, and he won't leave until he talks to you."

Mr. Jackson raised his eyebrows for a moment. Then he winced and looked away. "Get rid of him," he said.

I went back down to try to talk to Randy again. He wouldn't move. He just sat there in his car, screaming and cussing about his money.

Javon: I had the idea to block Randy in with one of the trucks, bring the boss out through the side entrance, hop into a different car, and then slip away. But Mr. Jackson shot it down. He said, "He'll just find out how to follow us to Liz's party and cause a huge scene; she doesn't deserve that."

Bill: After about thirty more minutes, I went in the house and told Mr. Jackson again that Randy wasn't leaving. Mr. Jackson sat there for a moment, then he let out a sigh and said, "Okay. I'm just going to go to bed."

He went upstairs, closed the door, and didn't come back out.

Javon: That killed us. We were devastated, for Mr. Jackson and for ourselves. I was proud to work for him, and I wanted the chance to do that in public, to show people I worked for Michael Jackson. We had brand-new suits; we were very excited. Elizabeth Taylor's birthday party? Are you kiddin' me?! I'm just a normal guy. It was just human nature for us to be excited.

And Mr. Jackson? He'd been making plans for two weeks. This was so important to him. It would have been one of the last times he and Ms. Taylor ever saw each other, and they were old friends. So for him to write it off and go to bed? That was a moment that let us know, okay, this family has some real power over him. If it had just been some ordinary person that busted through the gate, Mr. Jackson would have been like, "What are you guys waiting for? Escort him off the property and let's go." But this? This threw off his whole night.

Bill: I was pissed. I didn't even want Randy to take the car off the property anymore. I *wanted* him to get out of the car, because I wanted to whip his ass for ruining Mr. Jackson's night.

He sat in the driveway for another two hours. We had to call his father. That was the only option we could think of. Randy's a grown-ass man, and here we were calling his daddy to come and clean up his mess. Joe Jackson showed up, and at first Randy wouldn't even listen to him. He just kept saying how he was going to call the press, saying, "I'm here to get my money."

Joe said, "This is not the place. What the hell are you doing?"

Joe finally convinced Randy to leave, and they drove off. Mr. Jackson's bedroom was right above the driveway. He had to have heard a lot of it. By that point, it was too late to make the party. We tried to make arrangements for him to see Ms. Taylor while she was in town, but she was already leaving that next morning. So they talked on the phone and that was it.

Javon: After that, he didn't leave the house for three days. We didn't hear from him. No phone calls, no communication, nothing. He just shut down.

Bill: A week or so after that, the whole family showed up—all of them. We'd had a long day taking Mr. Jackson to the studio at the Palms, where he was in a recording session with will.i.am from the Black Eyed Peas; they were working on the *Thriller 25* album together. Around midnight, I'd wrapped up my shift and was just getting back to my house when the team called me on the radio. "Bill, his family's here!"

Again? I called Javon. He'd already left the house too. I told him to turn around immediately.

I raced back. Took about fifteen minutes from my place. I went in through the side entrance, met up with Javon. We walked out to the front and saw a bunch of people standing outside the gate. There were a whole lot of familiar faces. Looked like everybody except Randy and Marlon. For a minute it was like I was looking at some kind of Jackson reunion special.

Javon: They all had on hats and sunglasses. It was very incognito. It was so late and so cold that there was only one fan camped out on the street, and there were no paparazzi or anything to make a scene. Which made it even more strange. This big family of famous people standing out on the sidewalk in the middle of the night, and quiet all around.

Bill: I walked up to the gate, asked them what their business was this time of night. They said, "We heard our brother's sick. We came to make sure he's okay."

I told them I hadn't seen any signs that Mr. Jackson wasn't okay. They told me they wanted to see for themselves and weren't leaving until they did. So now I was in a jam. We had strict instructions from Mr. Jackson not to bother him, but at the same time we couldn't just leave the entire Jackson family standing in the street at one in the morning without it turning into a scene, which Mr. Jackson also wouldn't want.

I told them to hold on. I went back to the house, rang the doorbell, waited for Mr. Jackson to come down. The whole time I was thinking, This is not going to go well. When Mr. Jackson came to the door, I said, "Sir, your family is out front, and they insist on seeing you."

He was not happy. He was pissed, and I could tell he was pissed at me for not handling the situation myself. I said, "They heard you were sick and they want to know if you're okay."

"I'm fine, I'm fine," he said. "Tell them I'm fine."

"Sir, they're not leaving until they see you."

He went quiet for a moment, then said, "Okay, I'll meet with them. But I don't want them in the house."

"I can bring them over to the security trailer. You can talk to them in there."

"Fine. But I'll only speak to my brothers."

Then he asked if Randy was there. I said I didn't see him. "Good," he said. "I don't want to see Randy."

I went back to the gate and said, "Mr. Jackson just wants to see his brothers."

This voice from the back said, "What about me?"

At first I couldn't see who it was. Then I realized it was Janet. Part of me wanted to yell, *Wow!* That's Janet Jackson! But I just said, "Sorry, ma'am. He said only his brothers." She was not happy about that.

The brothers came in. I escorted them over to the trailer, and they stepped inside. Then I called Mr. Jackson and he came down and joined them. They closed the door and talked for about twenty minutes. Mr. Jackson came out first. Walked straight into the house. Didn't say anything. The brothers came out, walked to the gate, and that was it. What they talked about, I don't know.

Javon: Later on, we found out that they'd come because of a rumor they'd heard. There were always rumors going around about Mr. Jackson. Sometimes it was completely made up and sometimes it was sort of half true.

This particular time, they'd heard that their brother was sick, but Mr. Jackson wasn't sick. The kids were. Back in January, they'd all come down with colds. Arrangements were made to see a private doctor at his office one evening, after regular hours. The receptionist in that office leaked the story that Michael Jackson had come in, and the family had heard about it. It seemed suspicious to them. They heard he was seen going to a doctor's office in the middle of the night, and they wanted to make sure he was okay.

Bill: That was the difficulty of being Michael Jackson and trying to move around in the world. Just to take his kids to the doctor required days of planning and advance work. You'd use every precaution, and all it took was fifteen seconds walking past the wrong person, some nosy receptionist, and all of a sudden you've got this rumor circulating.

Paris didn't get better. Her cold wouldn't go away, and Mr. Jackson was worried she was coming down with the flu. We couldn't go to the emergency room, and Mr. Jackson didn't trust going back to some strange office. He wanted a doctor who would come to the house. So the word was put out there to find a private physician who made house calls. Jeff Adams, my associate and Javon's cousin, who'd first brought us onto the detail, said his

66

family doctor would stop by as a favor. I was given a name and told when to expect him. On the scheduled night, this silver BMW 745i pulled up to the driveway and a tall, slender gentleman stepped out. He was wearing light blue medical scrubs. He walked up to the gate and introduced himself. "I'm Dr. Conrad Murray," he said. "I'm here for a visit."

I told him he was expected, opened the gate, and directed him as to where he could pull his vehicle in. He drove in, parked, and got out.

I had a confidentiality form waiting. Before I pulled it out, I asked him if he knew who he was here to see. He said no. I told him he'd need to sign the agreement before I could allow him to go inside. He said sure. I pulled it out, and he glanced at the heading on the document and saw the name Michael Jackson. His eyebrows raised up and he gave me this look, like, Are you serious?

I gave him a nod. He signed his name. We walked to the front of the house, and I rang the bell and we waited. I could see the silhouette of Mr. Jackson through the glass as he came over toward us. He opened the door, and I said, "Mr. Jackson, this is Dr. Murray. Dr. Murray, this is Mr. Jackson."

6

In the fall of 1979, after the success of *Off the Wall* made him independently wealthy, Michael Jackson began putting the pieces of his
solo career in place. His first move was to hire John Branca to serve
as his legal counsel. A corporate tax attorney with considerable
experience in the music industry, handling everyone from Bob Dylan
to the Beach Boys, Branca renegotiated Jackson's contract with CBS,
securing him a royalty rate equal to that earned by the top talent in
the business. Branca also succeeded in severing Michael's recording
contract from his brothers'. Now, Jackson would only have to record
or perform with his family if and when he chose to; the label couldn't
make him. In 1983, at the peak of *Thriller* mania, Joe Jackson's
managerial contract with his sons came up for renewal, and Michael
wanted a professional divorce from his father as well. Always averse
to dealing with conflict himself, to avoid having to fire his father
directly, Michael had severance papers drawn up and delivered to his
dad by messenger.

John Branca had drafted the papers; he was now Michael's
closest and most trusted adviser. Riding alongside Jackson and
Branca during these years was Frank DiLeo, Jackson's manager, hired
shortly after Joe Jackson was let go. DiLeo had been the head of
promotions at Epic Records during *Thriller*'s release, and Jackson
gave him considerable credit for the album's success. As Jackson's
manager, DiLeo served as executive producer for the full-length

movie *Moonwalker*, negotiated Michael's landmark endorsement deal with Pepsi, and managed the record-setting world tour for *Bad*.

Michael Jackson's team was, for a time, unstoppable. In 1984, John Branca negotiated Jackson's purchase of the ATV music catalog, which contained the publishing rights to thousands of songs, including hundreds written by the Beatles. Jackson purchased the catalog for $47 million, but it would soon grow to be worth considerably more, becoming the bedrock of the singer's vast personal fortune. Five years later, in the fall of 1989, Branca negotiated Jackson's contract renewal with Sony, the new corporate parent of CBS/Epic Records. Sony agreed to give Jackson a record-setting $15 million advance for each album. By contrast, Bruce Springsteen's advance was just $2.5 million. Billy Joel earned $1.7 million. Branca also negotiated for Jackson to receive a royalty rate of 25 percent; most acts earned only 12 percent. The new deal with Sony was the most lucrative recording contract in the history of the music business. At the peak of his success, Michael Jackson was worth an estimated $700 million.

Jackson's talent—and the unlimited earning potential it represented—served as a magnet, drawing the most powerful people in the business to his side. When the singer surrounded himself with the right people, he flourished. When he surrounded himself with the wrong people, he faltered. By the late 1990s, more and more of the wrong people started coming around. In 1989, Jackson had abruptly fired Frank DiLeo, accusing him of mishandling funds. As the decade progressed, Michael's relationship with John Branca went through ups and downs as well, and Branca would eventually get his walking papers in 2003. The accusations of child abuse that hit Jackson in 1993 left him emotionally devastated, vulnerable. A scrum of celebrity lawyers latched onto the singer, jockeying with each other to be the lead attorney on what promised to be the trial of the century. Those same attorneys would ultimately convince Jackson to settle the case, causing irrevocable damage to his life and career.

By the turn of the century, estranged from his family and the team that backed him during *Thriller*, Jackson had lost the anchors that kept him grounded. His affairs were being managed not by a recognized industry heavyweight but a little-known German businessman named Dieter Wiesner, who was steering the singer's career in odd directions, such as launching a Michael Jackson–branded energy drink in Europe. Jackson also launched a number of business endeavors with a financier named Marc Schaffel, who had a history as a producer of pornographic films—hardly the best association for a performer whose public image had been tarnished by allegations of sexual misconduct.

After Randy Jackson's brief spell as Michael's manager had torn the two brothers apart, Jackson turned to the woman Randy had hired to serve as his publicist, Raymone Bain. Bain, a relative outsider in the music business, was primarily known as the political crisis manager responsible for resuscitating the scandal-ridden career of former Washington, D.C., mayor Marion Barry. During the summer of 2006, Jackson put out a press release announcing that Bain would be taking over as general manager and CEO of The Michael Jackson Company, a new corporate umbrella that would consolidate the singer's increasingly disorganized empire.

Through all of this, Jackson's only constant was Grace Rwaramba, the children's nanny, who stayed with him for seventeen years. Rwaramba, a native of Uganda raised in the United States, started working for Jackson in 1992, handling personnel issues for his *Dangerous* tour, and the two became close. When Jackson's children were born, she was promoted to serve as their primary caregiver. But her real role in Jackson's life went far beyond that. Despite ongoing health concerns that caused her to be away at times, she was the gatekeeper through whom everyone else was granted access. Her relationship with the children gave her leverage that no one else in Jackson's universe enjoyed.

By the time Michael Jackson relocated to Las Vegas, this small

crew of people—Grace; Raymone Bain; his assistant, John Feldman—
were the only associates tending to his daily affairs. As the newest
members of that team, Bill and Javon tried their best to understand
the various personalities and office politics shaping their employer's
world. What they slowly came to realize, much to their own discom-
fort, was that the team around Michael Jackson was even more
dysfunctional on the inside than it appeared from the outside.

Bill: Mr. Jackson's manager, Raymone Bain, came out to Vegas in
February. She and a couple of her staffers drove out from D.C. They
didn't fly because she was bringing Mr. Jackson a briefcase that had
a couple hundred thousand in cash in it. You can't take that kind of
money through airport security without having to answer a lot
of questions. So she drove.

Her car pulled into the driveway; Feldman came out and got
the briefcase, leaving her in the car, and took the case into the house.
She and I sat outside and talked a little while. She kept saying she felt
she knew me from somewhere, but I didn't remember meeting her.
I think she was just trying to make me feel like we had a connection.

We were out there for a good thirty, forty-five minutes, and
by then it was pretty clear that Mr. Jackson wasn't going to ask her
to come into the house, that he didn't even want to see her. She
tried to play it off like it wasn't embarrassing. She was like, "Okay!
I guess I'm gonna get back on the road. You guys take care. Tell
Michael to call me if he needs anything." Then she left.

His own manager drives across the country to see him after
he's been overseas for months, and they don't even speak? That
made me wonder what the hell was going on with his business
arrangements. I thought it was strange. But at the same time, everything that was happening was new to me, so I just figured maybe
that's how their relationship was.

As Mr. Jackson's manager, Raymone was the point person.
She kept the schedule, organized his affairs. Most mornings, she

would send an itinerary over: go here, go there, call this person, etc. Sometimes Mr. Jackson would go through that schedule and follow it to the letter. Other times, he'd look at some appointment she'd made and say, "Oh, she has an ulterior motive for that. We're not going there."

We started to feel uneasy about their relationship. It was not a trustworthy one. He didn't speak highly of her, yet here she was handling his business. In the beginning, like that time we talked in the car, she was very nice to me. *Very* nice. Our security trailer? Like an oven. The air conditioning didn't work. She called me up on her own and said, "Bill, I'm gonna send you guys some extra money to get an air conditioning unit for the trailer."

She was always calling to make sure I had everything I needed. At the time, I thought, Hey, she's good like that. We're cool.

Javon: Ms. Raymone wanted to know Mr. Jackson's every move, but Feldman would never tell her anything. I'd think to myself, Damn, she's his manager. She should know what's going on. But Feldman would totally stonewall her, shut her out. So she wanted me and Bill there to be her reporters.

For a while, she'd call me or Bill and we'd let her know where we were going, what we were doing. We didn't know to do any different. But Mr. Jackson, when he found out we were telling her about his movements? He said, "Don't tell Raymone where we're going. I know you guys are just doing your job, but if there are things I want her to know, I'll call her and tell her." He was adamant about it. He told us, "You guys report to me. If you ever tell her where I'm going and I find out about it, I will fire you myself."

Every time Raymone came to town, I was the one who had to pick her up from the airport and bring her to the house. While we were driving, she'd ask, "How's the boss? Where have you guys been? What did he do today?"

I'd say, "We really didn't do much. I'm sure you can talk to Feldman and find out more."

She'd get upset that we didn't report everything to her, but we were just doing as we were told. It put us in an awkward position, because Ms. Raymone was the one who handled our paychecks. Our pay was never on time. If we were supposed to be paid on the 3rd and the 18th of every month, we might get paid by the 7th or the 23rd. Maybe. It was never consistent.

Bill: Mr. Jackson had several different corporations set up for various purposes. Sometimes we'd get checks drawn on MJJ Productions, sometimes we'd get checks drawn on The Michael Jackson Company. The money just seemed to come from wherever. There was no dedicated account for payroll. There were no systems in place.

Javon: You'd hear things in the media about his finances, but from where we stood, there was just no way a man like Michael Jackson could be broke. He had stashes all over the place, stacks of cash hidden away. Like that briefcase Ms. Raymone brought him. The same day our pay was late, we'd be going somewhere to spend twenty thousand dollars on something. He's flat broke and he's worth millions at the same time? That's what we never got.

Since he didn't trust Ms. Raymone, we just assumed that there was no way that she had access to every dime of his money. It seemed as if this one area of his finances, his payroll, was being mismanaged, but he was obviously still incredibly wealthy. That's what it looked like. I mean, how else was he paying all of these lawyers? These attorneys would call all the time, charging him six hundred dollars just to be on the phone with him for an hour.

Bill: It only took about a month for the lawyers to show up. Late January, this attorney, Greg Cross, started coming around. Greg was with Venable out of D.C. Big, high-end law firm. He was a tall, skinny white guy with glasses. Looked like Ichabod Crane.

We often took Mr. Jackson to meetings and depositions at hotels, but Greg was the only lawyer coming to the house. He visited maybe once a month. Greg was always cordial and respectful. I could tell Mr. Jackson trusted him. Feldman didn't seem to like him. There were times that Greg would call and he'd ask to speak to Mr. Jackson and Feldman would say, "He's busy right now. I'll have him call you back." If it was me, and the boss's six-hundred-dollar-an-hour attorney was on the phone? I'd check to see if he wants to take it. That was another power struggle there.

Javon: It was never really clear who was in charge. Ms. Raymone was the manager, but she was being kept out of the loop on purpose. Technically, me and Bill and the rest of security reported to Feldman, but he was always being overruled by Ms. Grace. Feldman presented her to us as the nanny, so at first that's all we knew about her. But we'd see her go shopping and come back with a lot of groceries, things for the kids, things for Mr. Jackson. She'd also handle things for him when it came to business. She used to set up shop with us inside the garage with her laptop and her printer, and she'd be in there handling some of his day-to-day business affairs.

It was obvious pretty quick that Ms. Grace was more than just the nanny. She was the closest to Mr. Jackson, hands down. She was the surrogate mother. The kids loved her. There was nothing about those kids she didn't know. Anybody on the outside looking in would have seen that she was untouchable.

Bill: Feldman and Grace were always at odds. Grace would come out and tell him, "Mr. Jackson wants such and such." And Feldman would say, "I don't trust that woman. I'm gonna check with Mr. Jackson and make sure that's what he really wants me to do."

There were times when Grace would go out and get bottles

of red wine for Mr. Jackson. Feldman didn't drink or smoke, so he would always hide the wine. Wherever Grace put the wine in the house, Feldman would go into the house, get it, and bring it into the trailer. "Mr. Jackson doesn't need to be drinking this," he'd say. "It's poison."

Then Grace would come out and go, "Bill, I'm going to run to the store. The boss wants some wine. I could have sworn I bought some, but he must have misplaced it."

"What kind of wine?" I'd ask. She'd tell me, and I'd say, "Feldman brought it in here." She'd get pissed and she'd take it back in the house.

A day or so later, Feldman would come looking around. "Where's that wine at?"

"What wine?"

"The wine I brought in here."

"I gave it to Grace."

"No! No! You can't do that!"

"What? Why not?"

"She's trying to *poison* him! Do you understand?!"

I thought the dude was crazy. At first, I thought he meant that she was actually trying to poison him, like she was putting real poison in the wine. Those two fought about everything.

Javon: Feldman stayed in a hotel nearby, and he went back there every night. Sometimes he'd go home on the weekends to his family in California. But even if he wasn't at the house, he wanted any orders for security to go through him to be filtered down to us. He wanted Grace to call him any time one of us left the property, but Grace wasn't going to do that. She'd come out to the trailer and she'd say, "The boss wants you to go pick up some cereal for Blanket."

I'd say, "Did you call Mr. Feldman?"

She'd say, "I don't have to call him, Javon. Michael's asking you to go. It's what he wants. He's just sending me down to tell you."

So I'd go to the store, and twenty minutes later I'd get this angry phone call from Feldman. "What's going on? Where are you?"

"I'm at Walmart getting cereal for the kids."

"You're at Walmart?! Why'd you leave the post?!"

"Don't worry. It's okay. Bill's there."

"Who told you to leave?"

"Ms. Grace came outside and told me Mr. Jackson wanted me to get cereal for the kids."

"Why didn't you let me know?!"

"Ms. Grace said it was okay."

"Javon, she's gotta stop this shit!"

Then Feldman would drive over to the house and come at Grace, saying, "Stop sending my guys off!"

And she'd say, "I don't answer to you! If Mr. Jackson asks me to do something, I'm going to do it!"

That's how petty it was. They'd tear into each other over who gets to tell Javon to go to Walmart and pick up Honey Bunches of Oats. It was constant.

Bill: Feldman was possessive of Mr. Jackson, big time. He'd become overly protective, like a parent. His style could have been a little more diplomatic. I tolerated Feldman. We had our clashes from time to time. When it came to doing the job, we did the job. But outside of that, I tolerated him. For a time, Grace didn't know where I stood with Feldman. Was I going to be loyal to him or was I someone she could maybe use in her corner? I told her, "Look, I'm my own man. I make decisions for myself."

After that, she and I started to talk more. I could go to her with some of my questions, and she felt comfortable giving me more of the background, like with Mr. Jackson's family and that whole Randy situation. He always had issues with Michael, especially financial. She'd share these things with me, and we established a rapport. Only thing I didn't feel comfortable bringing up with her was Raymone. Grace and Raymone talked. I liked Grace, but the two of them had their own thing.

Raymone would come into town from time to time to meet with the boss or do some business dealings on his behalf. Whenever she flew down, she would stay at a hotel close to Mr. Jackson, the JW Marriott, and usually one of us would pick her up and take her to her hotel from the airport. After her first few trips, she flew in and I was driving her to Mr. Jackson's house and she asked me, "Bill, do you know any housekeepers?"

There was a young lady who used to clean my house every couple weeks, so I said, "Yeah, I know somebody."

She said, "Oh good. Because I need my place cleaned at least once a week. I want to keep it tidy when I'm not here."

I was like, Huh? She has an apartment in Vegas? I only remembered taking her to the hotel. I was curious, but I didn't ask her anything about it. I just recommended my cleaning lady, who also happened to be a friend.

Couple weeks later, I was speaking to this woman about coming to clean my house and she said, "Can we change the date? I need to clean Raymone's place."

I said, "Where's Raymone's place?"

She said, "At the Turnberry."

"The Turnberry Towers?"

She said, "Yeah, the Turnberry apartments."

When she told me that, I was like, Wow.

Javon: Apartments in the Turnberry Towers are *nice*. They can run you a few thousand a month, easy. It's the kind of place that caters to celebrities and professional athletes. There's full-time security, valet parking, dry cleaning—all those perks you get for paying these high prices for these little condos. The Turnberry was where Ms. Grace had an apartment. So when Raymone first started asking us to drive her there, I thought I was taking her to visit

Ms. Grace's. I wasn't thinking at first that she had her own place.

When you pull in to the complex, they have a guardhouse right at the front. I was used to giving Ms. Grace's information to the guard. Then Ms. Raymone started giving her own apartment information, and pretty soon they were just waving her through. They knew her on a first-name basis. "Hey! How was your day, Ms. Raymone?" Everyone knew her, even the valets.

Bill: Having contacts here in Vegas, I can usually get certain kinds of information when I need to. So I looked into it. Both of them, Grace and Raymone, had apartments in Turnberry Towers, but Mr. Jackson didn't seem to know anything about it. He always talked like Raymone was still staying at the Marriott. He'd say, "Go pick up Raymone from the hotel." Stuff like that.

I didn't say anything to him at the time. I never felt comfortable going over those boundaries. His relationship with his manager? That was way above my pay grade. You don't go to Michael Jackson after two months on the job and start giving him advice on how he handles his affairs. But if things were this messed up down at our level, if there was all this drama with simple things like payroll or sending Javon to run errands, you could only speculate about what was going on at the top of the organization, at the billion-dollar level, where all his record deals and financial affairs were being managed. How was that being handled? You wondered.

It hadn't always been like this. That's one of the things Grace and I would talk about. She told me how well things used to run. At Neverland, back in the day, it ran like a machine, like a real corporate business. Everybody was paid on time. People knew their place, played their position, and that was that. There wasn't all this jockeying for control, because people knew who was in control. Michael Jackson was in control. Those days were over.

It was that trial. That trial destroyed everything, destroyed him. You could see it. He became very vulnerable, exposed. He got a lot of death threats. Like, a lot. He was terrified. He trusted no one. The fear and the paranoia consumed him.

It started in the early 1990s, the first time he was accused of child molestation. Things started to unravel then. But the second time he got accused? He was here in Vegas when it happened, staying at the Mirage the day the sheriff's department turned Neverland upside down looking for evidence. Grace told me, "Bill, they destroyed that house." Mr. Jackson saw it, too. He went back after they raided it. He went back, once, saw what they'd done, and then he just turned around and left. After they destroyed Neverland, he was never the same person again.

Javon: I'd actually been to Neverland, as a kid. I went with my church when I was fourteen years old. We had a program called Teen Fellowship, and Mr. Jackson would invite groups like ours to come and ride the rides and play with the animals and such. He actually wasn't there the time I visited, but one of his staff members gave us a tour of the house and the property.

I remember you had to get on a train to even get on the estate. You parked a few miles away and then you'd ride the train up. It was beautiful. We went to the zoo. He had monkeys. He had flamingos. He had a pond with all these exotic fish in it. I can remember riding the carousel and the mini roller coaster. He had the teacups where you spin and turn. There was unlimited ice cream and candy and popcorn, too. The vending machines didn't take money. You just picked whatever you wanted. No charge. It was real nice. It was a blast. We loved it.

Bill: My only trip to Neverland was that March. There were some things Mr. Jackson wanted, some pictures, a few personal items, so he sent me to pick them up. The house had been abandoned for a while. The only person there was a security guard stationed at the entrance. I drove out and he let me in.

I got there at night, so I couldn't see much, but you could tell that it was not being maintained. All the carnival rides just sitting there. Whole place dead quiet. Nothing lit up. No animals in the zoo. All the plants and trees overgrown. There was a lake near the house, a little pond, and it was dirty, real dirty, filled with algae.

The inside of the house looked ransacked. After the sheriffs went through there, nothing was ever put back into place. Drawers left open, boxes overturned, everything covered with dust. It was eerie.

I didn't stay long. I didn't want to be there. The whole time I kept thinking about what the guard told me at the gate on the way in. "Be careful," he said. "There's snakes."

"Snakes?"

"Yeah. Rattlesnakes. Lots of 'em."

PART TWO

WHY DON'T THEY JUST LEAVE ME ALONE?

7

In August 1968, the Jackson 5 made their industry debut at a private Beverly Hills party hosted by Diana Ross. Motown's PR department issued a press release heralding the band's arrival in L.A. In order to up the boys' cuteness factor with teenage fans, the announcement deliberately shaved two years off the age of each member of the group. Michael was ten years old at the time, just three weeks shy of turning eleven. Motown's press release said he was eight. The first thing America thought it knew about Michael Jackson was a lie.

From that very young age, Jackson learned how the public's fascination with celebrity could be exploited to fuel commercial success. For a time, he embraced his fame and happily used it to reach the top. Starting with a single white glove, Michael Jackson the man carefully crafted the public spectacle known as the King of Pop. He studied magicians and the way they manipulated audiences, using the buildup of mystery to create big, jaw-dropping revelations. He studied the lives of iconoclasts like reclusive filmmaker Howard Hughes and circus impresario P. T. Barnum. After *Thriller*, Jackson gave his handlers copies of Barnum's autobiography, telling them that he wanted his career to be the greatest show on Earth. Pretty soon, it was. In February 1993, to promote his *Dangerous* album, Jackson opened the gates of Neverland to television crews for the first time, granting a tour and interview to Oprah Winfrey. The singer discussed his personal relationships, his use of plastic surgery, and the skin condition he suffered from, vitiligo, which had caused the lightening of his appearance in recent years. Over 90 million viewers tuned in.

Six months later, Jackson lost control of his public image and never got it back. That August, during the Asian leg of the world tour for *Dangerous*, British tabloids broke the news that the Los Angeles police department had launched an investigation based on allegations that he had molested a thirteen-year-old boy, Jordan Chandler. In the days that followed, Jackson collapsed backstage before a concert in Singapore. Citing a variety of health reasons, he began canceling performances.

Raised a devout Jehovah's Witness, as a young man Jackson famously did not drink, smoke, or even curse. In 1984, while he was filming a Pepsi commercial, a pyrotechnic mishap set his hair on fire, causing second-degree burns to his scalp and nerve damage that left him in considerable pain. He started taking prescription painkillers and, in the years that followed, began using them with increasing frequency. The Chandler scandal pushed him over the edge. In November, Jackson canceled the remainder of his tour, checked into a London rehab facility, and issued a press release acknowledging his addiction to prescription pain medication. But rehab offered only a brief escape. Released the following month, Jackson was forced to undergo a strip search conducted by investigators looking for alleged "identifying marks" on his genitals that had been described by his accuser.

Jackson was humiliated, and the press gleefully reported his humiliation in every detail. The same revolution in broadcast technology that fueled Jackson's meteoric rise on MTV had turned on him with a vengeance. The rise of twenty-four-hour cable news outlets fused the tabloid media and mainstream journalism together into a new industry built on a never-ending stream of sensational "infotainment." The circus surrounding Jackson's legal troubles—and, shortly thereafter, the murder trial of O. J. Simpson—set a template for the obsessive, wall-to-wall coverage of celebrity scandal that has now, in the age of the Internet, become routine.

In 1994, *GQ* magazine published an article titled "Was Michael Jackson Framed?" that reported the results of an exhaustive investigation into the charges leveled against the singer. Reporters found that Jordan Chandler's father, Evan, had made attempts to extort Jackson prior to going to the police. Also, the statements Jordan made about Jackson were only given after much prodding from his father and under the influence of a powerful sedative. Evan Chandler, a dentist, had given his son a dose of sodium amytal before having him interviewed; patients under the influence of the drug are highly suggestible. Prior to that interview, Jordan had always insisted that Jackson had done nothing wrong.

But *GQ*'s debunking of the allegations didn't make for the same sensational headlines as the allegations themselves, and Jackson's decision to settle the case out of court was perceived as an admission of guilt. Almost a decade later, in a misguided attempt to repair his reputation, Jackson gave British journalist Martin Bashir an all-access pass to film the now notorious documentary *Living with Michael Jackson*. Far from rehabilitating the singer's image, Bashir's report focused heavily on the singer's relationship with thirteen-year-old Gavin Arvizo, a cancer patient whom Jackson had befriended and helped through treatment. The film sparked a new investigation by Tom Sneddon, the district attorney for Santa Barbara, and led, ultimately, to fresh accusations from the Arvizo family that Jackson had molested their son and had gone so far as to imprison them at Neverland to protect his secret—outlandish claims that directly contradicted previous public statements, all positive, that the family had made about their relationship with the singer.

When the Arvizo case went to trial in January 2005, it created a media firestorm unlike anything America had ever seen. Over 2,200 credentialed media descended on the tiny California town of Santa Maria, forming a twenty-four-hour encampment around the county courthouse. During each day's testimony, journalists reported every lurid and sensational claim about the singer, consistently failing to communicate that those same allegations were being routinely discredited by Jackson's attorney on cross examination. The public's perception of the trial bore almost no resemblance to what was transpiring inside, where it was gradually revealed that the prosecution's case rested on little more than the uncorroborated testimony of one family—a family whose own motives came under suspicion and whose members repeatedly contradicted their own statements under oath. But the media coverage was so slanted that when the jury voted unanimously to acquit, the verdict was seen by many as a travesty of justice rather than the vindication of a man wrongly accused.

On the day they began working for him, Bill Whitfield's and Javon Beard's understanding of Michael Jackson was no different than that of most people. They were in awe of his celebrity, but after a lifelong barrage of gossip and innuendo about the singer's personal life, those feelings of deference came with nagging questions. Who was this person they'd signed up to protect? Who was Michael Jackson, really? After three months on the job, that hadn't changed. The new security team had learned much about Jackson's world but very little about the man himself. They stayed at their post outside the house while Jackson, for the most part, remained a mysterious presence inside. Then, in April, Jackson made a change to his inner circle. The move would fundamentally alter Whitfield's and Beard's relationship to their new employer and allow them to see, up close and unfiltered, the real man behind the media hype.

Bill: Late February, one Saturday night, we took Mr. Jackson and the kids to dinner and then to see Lance Burton, a magician who performs at the Monte Carlo. After the show, the family went backstage to meet Burton, and as we were leaving through the side door of the theater, there were three quick flashes. Boom, boom, boom!

This photographer snapped three quick pictures and then took off down Las Vegas Boulevard. Kids didn't have on their masks or anything. Mr. Jackson freaked out. "He has pictures of the kids! Get him! Get him!"

Feldman turned to me and said, "Bill, *go!*"

I ran. Las Vegas Boulevard on Saturday night is packed with tourists. I was chasing this guy through all these people. I ran maybe three blocks and caught up to him and grabbed him from behind. It was a scene. People were stopping and watching. I grabbed his arm, wrested the camera out of his hand. Then I ran back to the car and gave Feldman the camera. I never saw what was on it. Mr. Jackson was so relieved. He kept saying, "Oh, thank God." That was his biggest fear: exposing the kids to the press.

I thought that was the end of it. Then about two weeks later, I was at home, sitting in the living room with my daughter. There was a knock at the door. We weren't expecting anybody. We looked at each other like, Who the hell is that? I've got cameras around my house, one on the front door. I turned and looked at the monitor and I could see these two dudes with a third dude standing in the background. Having been in law enforcement, I knew. They were cops. Plainclothes, but I could tell. I answered the door.

"Mr. Whitfield?"

"Yes, sir."

"I'm Detective So-and-so and this is Detective So-and-so. We're from the Las Vegas Metro Robbery Division. Do you work for Michael Jackson?"

"Yes, I do."

"We are subpoenaing you to appear before a grand jury. You've been identified as someone that robbed a man of his camera."

They hit everybody with subpoenas. Me, Feldman, Raymone, Greg Cross. This photographer had gone and hired a lawyer and told the police, "Michael Jackson and his bodyguards mugged me and took my camera." Feldman was freaking out. He kept saying,

"They're gonna indict the boss for robbery. He's going to go to jail!" Pretty soon he was freaking me out too, the way he was acting. The next day at work, we told Mr. Jackson what was going on. He said, "Get rid of it. Give him back his camera."

I figured it was simple. Erase the photos and give it back. But Feldman said he didn't have the camera. He said he'd destroyed it. Why would you do that when all you have to do is pull out the memory card? It was an expensive one, too.

Me, there's two things I'm not doing. One, I'm not testifying against a client. Two, I'm not lying under oath. So I was wondering if I was going to have to make myself scarce until this whole thing blew over. Raymone got in touch with a lawyer, this big-time celebrity attorney in Vegas. He started working out a settlement.

While all this was going on, in early March, Mr. Jackson had to go to Japan. His fans over there are some of the most devoted in the world. He was appearing at this event where people were paying thousands of dollars each just for the chance to say a few words to him and get their picture taken. Feldman told us that Mr. Jackson wanted me and Javon to stay and watch the house. He was going to reach out to a local team in Japan that had handled security for Mr. Jackson over there before.

It was very quiet once they left. We didn't have to do much except watch the house. I worked days. Javon came and stayed overnight. Mr. Jackson and the kids were away for four or five days. During the trip, Feldman called me from Japan, still worked up about the camera thing. He said, "It looks like the boss is going to be arrested as soon as we get back to the country."

I thought he was crazy. People like Michael Jackson don't get arrested because of things like this. Sued? Yes. Arrested? No. But Feldman was all hyper about it. They flew back into LAX a few days later, stayed a few days in Los Angeles, and then drove back and met us in Vegas. The legal situation with the photographer was settled soon enough. The lawyer worked out a deal and the guy agreed to go away for some amount. I think it was around $75,000. For a $3,000 camera. The guy said he was roughed up. I didn't hit this guy, nothing. I just got the camera. But this wasn't about me; it was about Michael Jackson. Whatever the final amount was, it got settled. But by then Feldman was gone.

Normally, Feldman communicated with Mr. Jackson every day, but after Japan and this camera business, his relationship with Mr. Jackson took a real turn for the worse. Feldman would come out with our schedules and tell us what we were doing. Then Mr. Jackson would come out and say, "Oh no, we're not doing that today. I'm staying home." They weren't communicating. Their relationship wasn't the same. You could tell.

Then one day Feldman was just gone. This would've been in early April. There was no word from him. No telephone call. We didn't know if he was gone for a week or gone for good. Nobody told us anything. After he left, three days went by without any sign of Mr. Jackson. The chef would come and deliver the family meals; we'd leave the food at the rear patio door and go back to the trailer. Then a few minutes later, on the security monitor, we'd see Prince come out, retrieve the food, and close the door behind him. For three days, other than that, we had no communication from inside the house.

You have to understand: Feldman was our primary contact with Mr. Jackson. With him gone, we were in limbo. We didn't really know what to do except show up to work and do our normal routine. Mr. Jackson didn't leave the house. We barely saw him. Grace became the go-between. She started sending us on certain types of errands, things that Feldman normally would've done— that's when we started getting the impression that he definitely wasn't coming back.

It went on like that for about three weeks. Then Grace came to me one afternoon and said, "Bill, you're going to get a call tonight. Somebody wants to speak to you."

She was very cryptic. But just the way she said it to me and the way she looked at me, we both knew who she was talking about. I didn't know what to think. Up to that point, I had never really talked to Mr. Jackson. There were "Good mornings" and "Good afternoons," small talk about the day's errands, things like that. But no real steady conversation. I didn't exactly have a relationship with him. Pretty much everything had gone through Feldman. Grace said, "Just be yourself and talk to him like he's a regular person. Don't be nervous." She made me nervous just by saying that.

Late that night, around eleven-thirty, my cell phone rang, but I didn't get to it in time and the caller didn't leave a message. It wasn't from the landline in the house, which was what I was expecting. It was a number I didn't recognize, so I dialed it back. After several rings somebody picked up and said, "Hello, who's calling please?"

The voice was real deep and heavily distorted, like someone talking through an electronic voice changer. I was thrown. "Who is this?" I asked.

"May I help you?"

"You called me first, asshole."

Then I hung up the phone, a little confused and pretty pissed off. Seconds later, my phone rang again. Same number I'd just called. I picked up the phone and said, "Who the *fuck* is this?"

"Bill, it's me! It's Mr. Jackson."

It was his regular voice, with no distortion. I froze. "I'm sorry, sir. I'm so sorry. I thought it was a prank call."

He kept apologizing too. He said, "Yeah, I get that all the time. I have to disguise my voice because people always get my number somehow, and they call and say very mean things. You have no idea how many times I've had to change my number."

He sounded like he was a bit nervous himself. He said, "Listen, I'm going to be taking a trip back east, and—you know that Feldman's no longer with us, right?"

"Yes, sir."

"Right. So what I need you to do is—Bill, I can trust you, right? I can trust you?"

"Yes, Mr. Jackson. You can trust me."

"Good. Okay."

He told me that Feldman was gone and that Grace had told him I was okay. She and I had built up that rapport, and the good things she told him about me must have been enough for him to believe that I could be trusted. He started telling me all these things he needed me to do. He never came out and said, "Bill, you're the new head of my security team." Those words were never spoken. He just started talking to me in a way that conveyed a sense of "You're handling this stuff from now on."

He asked me, "Do you have a computer here?"

"No, sir. I don't."

"Okay, I need you to go out and buy a laptop. I'll give you the money. How much do you think one's going to cost?"

"About five to six hundred dollars, sir."

"Okay, I'll leave you a thousand. Raymone is going to send you some pictures, and I want you to put them on the laptop and show them to me."

"Yes, sir."

He left the money in an envelope at the back door and I went to Best Buy and bought a laptop. Raymone emailed me some pictures. I gave him a call to let him know I was back. He let me in the back door and I opened up the laptop and we looked at the pictures together.

It was a strange feeling, being in there. This was my first time just being alone with him, talking to him. I've been around a lot of different celebrities. But this was *Michael Jackson*. This was the man that's done everything, been everywhere. It's like, I've never met the pope, but I figured this might be what it feels like. You'd get tongue-tied. You'd go to address him and you almost wanted to say, "Yes, your Highness!" The first time I met him, I didn't know whether I should bow down or shake his hand like a normal person. That's just how it felt. It took me a while to not be nervous around him.

We sat there going through this little slideshow. It was pictures of all these houses and mansions in Virginia, Maryland, Connecticut, New York. He'd look at one, nod, and I'd hit the button to go to the next. I was looking at the price of the houses going by: $6 million, $7 million, $12 million. We finally got through them, and he pointed at the screen and said, "Tell her I like this one."

I called Raymone and told her which house he liked, and she said, "Okay, I'm going to be arranging for you guys to come out here this summer. Mr. Jackson is going to be taking the kids on a summer vacation."

Over the next few days, Raymone started calling me more frequently to handle this or handle that. More and more, I'd hear Mr. Jackson on the phone with his lawyers and other people. He'd say, "Call Bill" or "Talk to Bill" or "Have Bill set that up." I started getting faxes, emails, things for him to read, things for him to sign, appointments that needed to be scheduled. All that started coming to me. I didn't ask for any of it, and I certainly hadn't expected it. Three months earlier, I was just a guy freezing my ass off in this man's garage. Now, all of a sudden, I'd become the gatekeeper for the King of Pop.

8

Estranged from his family, what Michael Jackson had long desired was a stable family of his own. When his life was engulfed by scandal in the fall of 1993, for solace and support he increasingly turned to one person, Lisa Marie Presley. The two had been introduced at the home of a mutual friend in Los Angeles the previous January. Soon after, they began seeing each other on a regular basis. Though they seemed an unlikely pairing, in some ways they were a perfect fit. The daughter of Elvis Presley, the King of Rock 'n' Roll, was one of the few people who understood the rigors of being the most famous person on Earth. In Michael Jackson, Lisa Marie saw a powerful, charismatic figure wrestling with many of the same demons that had troubled her father. She had no doubt that the allegations being made against Jackson were false, and she believed she could save him.

In May 1994, Jackson and Presley married in a private cere- mony in the Dominican Republic, but the marriage lasted for just eighteen months. Michael, who had focused on himself and his career so relentlessly for so long, was unable to share his world with someone else; his new wife kept her own house in Los Angeles and never lived at Neverland full-time. For her part, Lisa Marie, with two children from a previous marriage, wasn't interested in having more—a fact that Michael, who very much wanted a family, could not accept. The hasty union had been a mistake. Jackson and Presley amicably divorced in December 1995.

Less than a year later, Jackson married Debbie Rowe, a nurse he'd met in the office of his dermatologist, Dr. Arnold Klein. Rowe promised to give him the family he wanted. When they married in Michael's hotel suite in Sydney, Australia, during the world tour for *HIStory*, Rowe was already six months pregnant with their first child. Three months later, in February 1997, she gave birth to a son, Michael Joseph Jackson, Jr., nicknamed "Prince." In April 1998, they welcomed a daughter, Paris-Michael Katherine Jackson. Rowe and Jackson divorced in the autumn of 1999, and both children remained in their father's custody. Two years later, in February 2002, via an unknown surrogate mother, Michael fathered a third child, Prince Michael Jackson II. Jackson nicknamed his youngest son "Blanket," a term of endearment he often used, meaning to blanket someone with love and affection.

By the time Jackson settled in Las Vegas, his last studio album and his last concert performance were more than five years behind him. His children had become the sole focus of his day-to-day life. Shielding them from the media's harsh glare had become the overriding consideration in almost everything he did. Though their childhood would never be the same as anyone else's, he was determined to make a stable home for them and give them as normal a life as possible.

Javon: The schoolteacher, Ms. Ilean, flew into town right after the holidays. She was an Asian woman from Bahrain. Mr. Jackson met her while traveling overseas, and he'd hired her to handle the kids' schooling. He'd rented her an apartment about five minutes away from the house. Weekdays, one of us would go and pick her up at 7:30 and bring her to the house to teach.

Mr. Jackson was no joke when it came to the kids' education. School started at 8:00 a.m. *sharp*. A spare room on the first floor was converted into a classroom. Like, it was an actual classroom.

We helped the teacher hang chalkboards, set up computers, bookshelves, maps, educational posters with the alphabet and multiplication tables, all that. The kids each had their own desk. It looked like any classroom you'd see at any regular elementary school. It was the same whenever we were traveling and staying in hotels. A separate room was always reserved and we'd have the hotel set up desks in there, and that room would be used as the kids' classroom.

Bill: As up and down as their lives could be, Mr. Jackson insisted that there be structure and routine in the kids' educational environment. They even wore school uniforms. Prince and Blanket wore white shirts with black slacks and ties. Paris wore patent leather shoes and a dress, like a little Catholic schoolgirl dress. They were always well groomed. Hair combed, uniforms pressed. And Monday through Friday, every morning, the kids woke up, got dressed, came downstairs for breakfast, and then they "went to school."

The Nevada Board of Education has all kinds of requirements for homeschooling, which includes the children passing exams to make them eligible to move on to the next grade. Ms. Ilean organized her lesson plans to meet all of those benchmarks. She doled out homework, required book reports, instituted study hall periods. The quality of their schooling was as good as or better than what you'd see at any top-level private school. Those were some smart kids. They were constantly reading. Their brains were like little sponges, always curious, always asking questions.

When we drove them out to dinner or to go to the movies, Mr. Jackson would be in the backseat, quizzing them on whatever they'd learned that day. He knew exactly what they were studying. He sat down every week with the teacher to go over her lesson plans and keep tabs on what was being taught. He'd help them with their homework, too, in the afternoon and at night. They would come to him all the time. "Daddy, will you help me with my homework?" That was one of his favorite things to do.

Very little television was watched in that house. They'd have movie nights, watch DVDs together as a family, but it wasn't like a lot of households where you see kids just camped out in front of the TV. They'd do their homework, read books, play games, listen to music.

Javon: There were lots of extracurricular activities, too. The kids had PE every day. They'd jog laps around the yard, do jumping jacks, calisthenics. Sometimes we'd take them to this public park nearby. We set up a trampoline for them as well.

We took them on field trips. We took them to the Lied museum—that's the local children's discovery museum with hands-on activities and science experiments that kids can do. Paris, she loved going to art museums and galleries. The hotels on the Strip were actually good for field trips; they're constantly hosting exhibits and installations. We took the kids to the Bodies exhibit, the one with all the cadavers on display. That was at the Tropicana. We also did the shark exhibit at Mandalay Bay. There were IMAX movies at the Luxor, *Deep Sea 3D* and *Dinosaurs*. In class, the kids would read and study about the subjects, then we'd take them on these field trips and they'd have to turn in reports on them.

The first time we took the kids out on a detail without Mr. Jackson was some time in February. We took them to a playground with the teacher. We were still new on the scene, but she'd been with him for a while and he trusted her. She was able to report back to him how we handled ourselves. Her phone would ring, and we'd hear her going, "Yes, sir. No, they're okay." So we knew he was keeping an eye on us and how we were doing our jobs.

Bill: We relied on the fact that no one knew who they were. One of the first times we took them out was to the indoor amusement park at Circus Circus, with Grace. We got made by the paparazzi. Somebody must have followed us from the house. They took a few fuzzy snaps from far away but, fortunately for us, they didn't get a clear shot. You couldn't really tell who the kids were.

People have often wondered why Mr. Jackson kept his children's faces covered with masks and veils when they were in public. The tabloids said it was weird and crazy, but they didn't understand the reason for it. If no one knew what his children looked like, they could occasionally go to public places without him and have a somewhat normal experience. When they were away from their dad, they could be everyday kids doing everyday things.

For the first few months, any time we took the kids out, either the nanny or the teacher was with us. But starting around late April, he started asking me and Javon to take them out on our own, run errands with them, take them to the playground. When we first took the kids out without Grace or the teacher? That was a big deal. That's when we felt we'd really established a level of trust. He was so fiercely protective of his kids.

I remember one day we left the house to take the kids to go and get ice cream. Mr. Jackson stayed at home. This was in February, still cold out. We were halfway to the store, and Mr. Jackson called and asked if Blanket was wearing his hat. He wasn't. He'd forgotten it. Mr. Jackson said, "Turn around and come back and get it."

The kids weren't even really going to be getting out of the car where we were going, but he insisted. If it was cold out, his kids needed to have their hats and mittens on, period. We turned around, went back to the house.

Javon: People laughed at the idea of him being a father, laughed at the kids' names and the masks and all that. Like, how weird it must be for Michael Jackson to be a father. But the more you got to know him, you saw that being a father was the most normal thing about him. We were on post this one time, and he called down to say he'd run out of laundry detergent and could somebody run and pick him up some more. Before that moment, I'd never stopped to imagine Michael Jackson in the laundry room, washing his kids' clothes, but that's really how he was a lot of the time.

He didn't spoil them, either. There were the extravagant trips to FAO Schwarz and all that, but that was only for holidays and birthdays, or as a specific reward for doing well on a test or doing their chores. If they didn't do well, he was just as quick to take their privileges away. There was one time we were supposed to take the whole family to the movies. We'd run the whole pre-detail, rented out the theater for the afternoon, made all the arrangements. But that morning, one of the kids did bad on a test or hadn't finished some assignment, so he canceled it. We were downstairs, cars ready to go, and Prince ran out and said, "Daddy said we can't go."

You see all these celebrity kids on TV all the time, bratty and spoiled and arrogant. Michael Jackson's kids were the opposite. They never asked for much, and when they did, it was always "please" and "thank you" for everything. And when one of them did misbehave, it didn't take too much discipline to straighten them out. One little talk or one little time-out and they'd learn their lesson.

Bill: When Prince first got the dog, he didn't know how to take care of it, how to housebreak it and pick up after it and all that. So in those first few weeks, the dog got in the habit of using the garage to go to the bathroom—the garage we were working out of.

Javon: It stank. Place smelled like shit. We had to smell it while we were on the job. We were in brand-new suits and everything, and *we* smelled like shit. We had the trailer, but the garage was our post too; that was our working environment. That was where we washed and maintained the vehicles. We didn't want to be backing into the garage and driving in shit.

Bill: We thought eventually Prince would clean the shit up. Nope. He'd come out to that garage, step right over a pile of shit, go to his dog, grab a treat, give him a treat, turn around, hop over the same pile of shit, and run back in the house. Just leave the shit there.

Javon: We stepped in it a few times. Bill would instruct us to clean it up. He'd say, "Whoever's coming on shift, you gotta clean it up." So we were the ones cleaning it up. I'd complain all the time. I'd say, "We didn't sign up for this shit."

Bill: There were points where it came to a standoff. "I ain't cleanin' the shit." "Well, *I* ain't cleanin' the shit. *You* clean the shit." "No, *you* clean the shit."

Javon: So sometimes the shit would just stay there. But when Mr. Jackson stepped in that shit? That's when the shit got serious.

Bill: We were taking him to a meeting. Important meeting. He was all dressed up, nice suit, got his designer shoes on, and he came walking across the garage toward the vehicle and he just stepped right in it.

Javon: He chewed Prince out, big time. Hit him with the responsibility speech. "You wanted the dog, Prince. It's your dog. It's your responsibility. It's not the guys' responsibility."

After that, Prince walked a tight line. Anywhere the dog went, in the garage or out on the property, Prince would come behind with a broom and dustpan and clean up after it. Wasn't a problem anymore.

Bill: Prince was the big brother, for real. He was very bright for his age, very take charge. Mr. Jackson relied on him to help look after the other two, and Paris and Blanket always looked to Prince for guidance.

We always tried to run everything on a tight schedule. To make that schedule work, we always tried to leave at a certain time. But with Michael Jackson? It was *rare* that we left on time. His look had to be flawless before he'd go to any public event. There were times he'd get all the way to the car and say, "Wait, wait, I have to go back." And he'd turn around and go back in. He had a hair out of place or something—and this was after the stylist had worked on him for two and a half hours. Prince was the only one brave enough to literally grab his dad and say, "Let's *go*!" He'd go through the house, making sure his little brother and sister were dressed, putting them in the car. If we got somewhere on time, it was usually thanks to Prince.

Javon: All three of them were familiar with the nature of their father's life. It was like they were born ready for everything that he had to go through. The motorcade shows up at four in the morning, you get in, go here, fly there, have school in a hotel room. Ireland one day, Las Vegas the next. It was second nature to them.

In public, Mr. Jackson never called them by their names. He'd never say, "Paris, come here," or "Blanket, come here." He didn't want somebody in earshot figuring out who they were and snapping a picture. So all the kids had code names. Blanket's was "Kooco." Paris's was "Osh Kosh."

I actually can't remember Prince's code name because we never had to use it. He never got out of line. He knew the rules better than the other two. One time, we were at FAO Schwarz and Paris slipped and called Prince by his real name. He checked that real quick. He went up to her and said, "Don't call me that! You know not to call me that. Use our code names, sis."

Bill: I remember one night Mr. Jackson was having a business dinner with somebody and it was getting late, and he asked me to take the kids home. So I was driving them to the house, and Paris and

Prince were in the back where some of our gear was stored. Spare radios and such.

We didn't use our actual names on the radio. I went by "BB" for Big Bill. I had my earpiece on, and I'd just called the house— "BB to base. This is BB."—to let them know I was en route. A few minutes later, I heard somebody say, "Base to BB. BB come in."

I said, "This is BB. Go for BB."

The voice called back. "BB come in. Base to BB."

This went back and forth a few times, to the point where I was getting annoyed. I was yelling into the radio. *"This is BB! Go for BB!"*

Then I heard all this giggling. Paris was on one of the spare handsets in the back, disguising her voice. I didn't even know it was her. We all started laughing, and I said, "Okay, you got me."

Moments like that are what I really remember. You can imagine how if you were a kid and this was your world, code names and security guards, you'd be like any kid and use your imagination and have fun with the life you know.

Prince grasped who his father was. Maybe he didn't know the whole story, but he had seen enough to understand why all the secrecy was necessary. Blanket, I think he was too young to really get it. Paris, she grasped it a little. She knew the rules, but sometimes she'd get excited and forget them.

Javon: Paris was Daddy's Little Girl. She was this little girl surrounded by nothing but men. She had a big brother telling her what to do. She's got a little brother telling her what to do. Mr. Jackson telling her what to do. You'd think she'd maybe be a little tomboyish because of that, but she was always very much a girly-girl. Always smiling, always cheerful. She has these bright blue-green eyes that just light up a room. Loved playing with dolls, having little dresses. Me and Bill, we both have little girls, so we were total softies for her. The boys couldn't get away with much, but Paris could just look at you with those big green eyes and instantly you'd just want to give her whatever she wanted.

I remember this one time we were at Circus Circus. Prince and Blanket wanted to get on the Buccaneer. Bill went with them and I stayed with Paris, who was playing those little carnival games there, where you can win stuffed animals. She was playing the fishing game; it's this fishbowl filled with all these yellow magnets on the bottom with a few red ones sprinkled in, and you've got to hit a red magnet and pull it up. She wanted to win her daddy a teddy bear. She tried five or six times and looked back at me and said, "Javon, can you *please* help me get this bear?"

I knew what I was supposed to do. I'm supposed to stand back, keep watch, not get distracted. But she was just begging me, so I radioed Bill and asked if I could help her. He said, "Just go on ahead, as long as you keep an eye on her." I tried three or four times and finally got it for her. She was so thankful. She just wanted to win her daddy a teddy bear so bad. It was the smallest little bear, but she just *had* to win it for him. She started gushing, "Thank you, Javon! Thank you!" And she jumped up and gave me a big hug.

Just the way she said thank you, my heart *melted*. She was the sweetest little girl.

Bill: Any time we were on our way back from a detail with the kids, we would call Mr. Jackson to let him know that we were en route back to the house. We were driving back that night from Circus Circus, and Paris was so excited. She was like, "I wanna talk to Daddy! I wanna talk to Daddy!" She wanted to get on the phone to tell him she was bringing him this teddy bear she'd won for him. When she did that, Blanket almost lost it. He was suddenly real jealous. Now he wanted to go back and win one too. "Can we go back? Can we go back? I wanna win Daddy something!"

Blanket was an interesting little fella. When we'd get in the cars in the morning, Paris and Prince were always quick to speak up and say good morning. Blanket was very shy. Mr. Jackson would have to nudge him. "Say good morning to the guys, Blanket. Are you going to say good morning?"

He didn't say much, but you talk about mischievous? We called him "the Little Rebel." Feisty little guy. Mr. Jackson would always say, "Bill, keep an eye out for Blanket. He likes to run off." And he did. If we were in public, Prince and Paris followed the protocol; they held hands and stayed close. Blanket would try and slip out of sight, run off and do his own thing.

Javon: Any time we closed down a bookstore to go shopping, Mr. Jackson wanted everyone to go through the store together, section by section, so that they wouldn't get separated. They'd do the History section, then the Science Fiction section, and so on. Blanket? He'd take off for the Kids section immediately. You'd have to go chasing him through the store, and he'd catch a little attitude when you went and brought him back to the rest of the family.

Bill: One time we were driving past the New York–New York casino, where they have this big amusement park and all these rides out front. Blanket looked over at it and said, "My daddy's roller coaster is better than that one."

That was Blanket right there. There was this other time, I remember, he got in the car and he sat right behind me, where Mr. Jackson normally sat. I said, "Blanket, you need to move over. That's where your daddy sits."

He said, "I know!"

He didn't sit in that seat by accident; he did it on purpose. He was little, but he didn't see himself that way. "I'm gonna sit where my daddy sits!" Like that was going to be his seat one day.

Most of the time, driving with them, we kept the curtain between us closed. Being security, your job is to be as unobtrusive as possible to the client. It's very much a speak-when-spoken-to type of relationship. But more and more, the kids started to engage us. Mr. Jackson did too, from time to time. They got familiar and comfortable with us, and there was a lot more driving with the curtain open. One time, we were driving and Blanket started to say something, and Mr. Jackson kinda shushed him. The kids kept giggling and Mr. Jackson kept going, "Shhh! No, I didn't! No, I didn't!"

Blanket said, "Yes, you did, Daddy. You said that Bill looked like—"

"*Shhh!*"

So now I was curious. I said, "Bill looks like what?"

I looked in the rearview mirror. Blanket and Mr. Jackson were both staring at each other like, Who's gonna tell him?

Blanket looked at me and said, "Bill, Daddy says you look like the Thing!"

"The Thing? What's the Thing?"

"You know," Blanket said, "the guy from the Fantastic Four! Daddy said you look like the Thing from the Fantastic Four." And I was like, *Wow*. Okay. The brother's got jokes. Then Blanket said, "And Javon looks like Frozone from *The Incredibles*!"

We all had a good laugh about it. So I was the Thing now. Cool. Gradually, we started developing a rapport with them, seeing their sense of humor, understanding them better.

Javon: Mr. Jackson was always concerned that we were taking good care of ourselves. He'd always say to us, "Do you guys work out? Do you guys eat right? Don't eat a lot of junk food; it's not good for you." For the most part, he and the kids were very healthy eaters. He'd let them go to McDonald's sometimes, go get hot wings, ice cream, pizza, or whatever, but that was only as a treat.

In their cooped-up little world, just going to a fast food restaurant and ordering from the drive-through counted as an adventure. We'd pull up to the speaker box, and all three of them would climb over each other in the backseat, trying to be the one to get up to the window and place the order. "You ordered last time!" "No, you did! It's my turn!" Just to keep the peace, Mr. Jackson would let each kid place their own order themselves.

One time, after the boss, Prince, and Paris had all ordered, it was Blanket's turn. He had to stand up on the seat to be able to reach the speaker box. He got up there and said, "Can I please have two Krispy Kreme donuts with sprinkles?" We were at McDonald's.

Bill: Blanket loved Krispy Kreme. We were always looking for ways to let the children get out and see new things, so I made arrangements with the manager at one of the local Krispy Kremes to bring Mr. Jackson and Blanket in the back to see how the doughnuts are made. About two-thirty in the morning, we went in there and watched them. Workers showed him everything. Stayed there a couple hours, just walking around, learning how all the machines operated. We took home about five boxes of doughnuts.

They took their little excitements where they could get them. There were times we'd be driving somewhere and Mr. Jackson would say, "Bill, the kids are hungry. Can we just find a McDonald's?" We'd go to the McDonald's, grab some food, pull over in a parking lot somewhere, and me and Javon would get out of the car, let him and the kids sit inside and eat. He didn't tell us to get out of the car. We just did it. So he could have that moment with his kids. We knew how little privacy he had, so we gave him as much as we could.

The biggest indulgences for the kids were their birthday parties. For those, Mr. Jackson went all out. He'd come to us with a big list of everything he wanted. He'd say, "I want you guys to find a clown. A magician. A popcorn machine. A cotton candy machine. An inflatable jumper." He'd be real specific about it, too. "Make sure you find a clown that can make balloons into different animals." One time, the only clown we could find that did balloon animals wasn't available; she was booked. Mr. Jackson said, "Just do whatever you can to get her here." We ended up paying her more than triple. Her rate was $75 an hour and we paid her $250 an hour.

We'd arrange to have everything delivered—the jumper, decorations, big-ass cakes. We'd hire the clowns and the magicians, put them all through security checks and have them sign non-disclosure contracts. The paparazzi always knew when it was birthday time. Low-flying helicopters would hover over the house in the hopes of getting a photo of Mr. Jackson or the birthday kid. So we'd have to work around that too.

Javon: Whoever's birthday it was, we'd follow the same routine. We'd arrange to have FAO Schwarz closed down so they could shop undisturbed. Then we took them out to a special birthday lunch. Chinese food most of the time. The Wing Lei restaurant at the Wynn hotel, that was one of their favorites; there was a private room in the back they'd reserve for Mr. Jackson whenever he came. After lunch, he'd rent out a movie theater so the kids could go see a movie. And while they were out at the toy store and the movies, the house was being decorated. They'd come back and: "*Surprise!*" We'd have the magician, the clown with the balloons, the cotton candy. The whole place would be decked out for a party.

Bill: And there'd be nobody there. There were no other guests, no other children. It was just the clowns, Mr. Jackson, me and Javon, sometimes the teacher or the nanny. The kids didn't have any friends.

Javon: The only person who was ever there was Marlon Brando's son Miko; they were friendly because Mr. Jackson and Marlon Brando were tight. A couple times, Miko and his kids came by to celebrate, but it was usually just us.

Bill: It was hard to witness, hard to accept: nobody coming around, ringing the bell, and bringing gifts. No famous aunts and uncles calling to say happy birthday. Didn't matter if it was the kids' birthdays, his birthday, Thanksgiving, Fourth of July—there was nothing, nobody. It was just us. You kind of got used to it.

I remember we drove past a school once. Mr. Jackson and the kids were in the backseat. We were stopped at a red light. It was recess, and the schoolkids were out playing in the yard. We were sitting there, and Mr. Jackson whispered, "Bill, look."

I looked in the backseat. Paris and the two boys, their faces were *glued* to the windows. They were staring at these other kids, eyes wide open, this look on their faces like, Can you imagine what life is like out there? It was just a bunch of kids at recess, most normal thing in the world, but to them, it was like this whole other universe they weren't privy to.

Javon: That sort of thing happened a few times. It got to the point where I'd be driving along and I'd see a school with a bunch of kids playing outside and I'd feel bad. I'd purposely make a turn and drive around the playground, so Paris and the boys wouldn't see it.

Sometimes you'd feel sad about how they were so isolated, but they were always so happy just being together. When Mr. Jackson had to leave the kids behind at the house for a business meeting, they would always come to the door as a group to see him off. They'd follow him right to the car and they'd each say, "I love you, Daddy." And he'd say, "I love you more." That was their little ritual every time he left the house. And when he got home, didn't matter if he was gone for two hours or twenty minutes, they'd run to meet him, screaming, "Daddy! Daddy! Daddy!"

Bill: They were like this little unit, just the four of them. All they had was each other. There was roof access from inside his bedroom. There was a spiral staircase in there that went up to this private roof deck, where you could see the entire city and the desert around it, the mountains, the lights from the Strip. The times that we went up there, we'd see little candy wrappers and soda cans and cups, so we could tell they were spending time there. That was one of their favorite things to do as a family, to go up and watch the sunset or see the lights. Paris even mentioned it in this one interview she did not too long after he passed. They asked her what her fondest memories were and she said, "Going to the rooftop at the house in Vegas."

One Friday night, I was on post in the security trailer, monitoring the grounds on the surveillance cameras. All of a sudden, I heard a loud banging in the garage and a voice yelling, *"Open this door! Open this door!"* I thought somebody was trying to break into the house. I ran to the garage, turned the corner, and saw Mr. Jackson standing there in a blue shower cap and blue-and-white-striped flannel pajamas. He was banging on the door to the house with his shoe.

I said, "Sir, is everything okay?"

With this big grin, he said, "Oh, I'm fine. We're just playing hide and seek and they locked me out."

"Yes, sir."

That's how they were.

Javon: The Las Vegas Mini Gran Prix is this outdoor amusement park with go-karts, games, rides, and such. I had a cousin who was an assistant manager there. It was a couple miles north of the house. We'd pass it all the time, and Mr. Jackson would always say, "Man, I would sure love to go there one day with the kids. They'd love it."

Whenever he said that, I'd make a mental note of it, and finally I called my cousin and asked if we could come by the place after hours and just let Mr. Jackson and his kids play there. She called her district manager, and he called me back and we set it up.

Bill: We went back to Mr. Jackson and told him, "Sir, we made arrangements for you and the kids to go up to the amusement park one evening." When we told him that? He lit up like a kid on Christmas morning. He was like, "Really?! Oh my God! Great, great, great!"

The park closed at midnight. We got there around twelve-thirty. I got out of the car, went inside, walked around to make sure everyone was gone, and let the park attendants know I was with the people that were coming in. Then I went back to the car and brought the family in.

Soon as we got inside, Mr. Jackson and the little ones started running around like four crazy kids. First they went to the game room, raced from one machine to the other, playing against each other. Played pinball and won some prizes. Prince won a few things. Paris got a little upset. She didn't win anything. She started crying. I went over to the machine and tried to win something for her. Couldn't do it. Finally the manager came over, opened up the machine, and took something out for her. She was happy after that, running around with her little stuffed animal.

Javon: They rode the go-karts for a little while. At first it was just Mr. Jackson, Paris, and Prince out on the track. We stayed back and watched Blanket because he wasn't tall enough to drive. He was all upset because he wanted to get out there and race his brother and sister. Since no one else was there, the staff let him get in one of the cars and push the pedals a bit. He only drove about ten feet and ran into the side of the barricade, but that ten feet he got to drive just about made his little day.

Bill: There was also this giant slide, about a ninety-foot drop, that you'd ride down in burlap potato sacks. That was the last thing they did before they left. Blanket was so small that Mr. Jackson held him in his arms on his lap and he slid down, and Paris and

Prince each slid down by themselves. They all raced each other down to the bottom.

They had a ball. It was good to see. It was just different to see the excitement in them, because they didn't get out with this kind of freedom—they really didn't. Up to that point, it had really been all business with him. Lawyers, managers, meetings. We'd taken the kids to Circus Circus a few times but always without him. Being able to enjoy these moments with his kids, you could see that it didn't happen for him on the regular. So to see the excitement in his face, being free to do what he wanted to do with his kids at the park—he was just happy as hell. It was priceless.

Javon: The minute we got in the car, all of the kids fell asleep. They were knocked out. We drove them home all slumped over in the backseat and carried the three of them up to their rooms and put them to bed.

Me and Bill headed back downstairs while Mr. Jackson tucked them in. We'd just reached the bottom of the staircase when he came back out and called over to us in a whisper and said, "Guys, I want to thank you so much for doing this for my kids. They really appreciate it. And Javon, please give a personal thank-you to your cousin for closing the park down for free. It's rare that someone does a favor for me without wanting something in return. Make sure you remind me tomorrow to send her an autographed picture. Thank you. Thank you, and God bless you."

9

Michael Jackson first played Las Vegas in 1974, when he and all eight of his siblings put on a musical variety show at the MGM Grand. Joe Jackson had arranged the gig personally because Motown was against it; Berry Gordy felt it wasn't right for the band's image. But Michael wanted to play Vegas. He was a huge admirer of Sammy Davis, Jr., who'd broken the color line at many of the hotels and resorts in the 1960s. Michael thought it was important to continue that legacy, and so—as he did with everything—he threw himself into making their Vegas gig the best he could.

Though he was only sixteen years old at the time, Michael Jackson's tireless work ethic had already become legend in the industry. But in the decades since, as his life was beset by personal struggle, he became more famous for backing out of performances than for making them. In December 1995, Jackson committed to film an HBO concert special in New York. Three days before the event, he collapsed onstage during rehearsals and was rushed to the hospital. The concert had to be canceled. In 1999, contracted to perform two millennium concerts in Australia and Hawaii, Jackson pulled out of both events just months before they were to take place; the promoter sued and Jackson paid out $5.3 million to cover the damages.

Two years later, in September 2001, Jackson did follow through with his 30th Anniversary Celebration concerts at Madison Square Garden, but the album he was promoting with the event, *Invincible*, turned into a public relations fiasco of its own. Jackson had spent six years in the studio, on and off, to produce the record, repeatedly delaying its release and running up massive production costs in the process. *Invincible* debuted at No. 1 in the United States, the United Kingdom, Japan, and many other countries, but sales fell off quickly, and Sony halted the album's promotional campaign, sparking a bitter feud between Jackson and Sony Music chief Tommy Mottola.

After his 2005 trial, Jackson entered into a partnership with his host in Bahrain, Sheikh Abdullah, signing an ambitious contract that promised a wide range of projects, including new studio albums and a stage musical. In addition to providing Jackson with a palatial home and state-of-the-art recording facilities, Abdullah covered many of the singer's unpaid legal bills and advanced Jackson millions of dollars to cover his living expenses overseas. In April 2006, Raymone Bain issued a press release announcing Jackson and Abdullah's joint venture, Two Seas Records, saying that Jackson's first album for the new label would be out the following year. Less than three months later, Jackson reneged on the deal and departed for Ireland.

During all the time in which Michael Jackson "wasn't working," he was actually working all the time. In Ireland, he spent months in the studio with will.i.am of the Black Eyed Peas. Once back in the States, he collaborated frequently with producers and artists like Kanye West, Babyface, Ne-Yo, and RedOne, composing and recording dozens of new songs. Jackson still loved to work. He just wasn't following through on his professional commitments. He'd become a recluse. Once an admirer of Howard Hughes, Jackson had come to live much like him, holed up behind a gated wall in Las Vegas, behind a cordon of bodyguards.

And who could blame him? For years, going back to the Chandler scandal and even before, the tabloid backlash against Jackson had been unrelenting. Everything he did, every move he made, was taken and turned into yet another chapter in the crazy life of "Wacko Jacko." On a good day, he was called a weirdo and a freak. At the low end, a criminal and a pedophile. If spending millions of dollars to clear his name in court wasn't enough to change people's opinions about him, why engage with the public at all? Jackson withdrew. He buried himself in family life and creative projects and found some measure of happiness there. But the more he disengaged, the more his debts and his legal entanglements festered. To wipe them out, Jackson was being told he needed to go back onstage. To preserve his privacy and peace of mind, he mostly wanted to stay out of sight.

He couldn't do both.

Javon: Two days before the Tokyo trip, Feldman had told us that Mr. Jackson wanted us to outfit a music and dance studio in one of the rooms in the house while they were gone. We started making arrangements for all the equipment we needed to buy—the flooring, the egg-carton panels for the walls, all that. We went to a party rental place to buy the dance floor. Then Bill and I built out the room.

Bill: Up to that point, music-wise, nothing much had been going on. There was talk about Mr. Jackson doing one of these casino gigs. Jack Wishna, a promoter out here who recently passed away, he was involved in a lot of those negotiations; he was the one responsible for convincing Mr. Jackson to come here in the first place. We also took Mr. Jackson to several meetings with Steve Wynn, who owns the Wynn resort and casino. There were some discussions about building Mr. Jackson his own custom arena, like they did for Celine Dion at Caesars Palace. We took him to meeting after meeting on that. None of it ever went anywhere. There were times we'd be coming home from these meetings, and we'd hear Mr. Jackson on the phone saying, "They want me to do all these shows, but they don't understand that I'm not young like that anymore. I can't do what they're asking me to do."

Javon: These promoters were adamant about him performing five nights a week. That's pretty much standard for the major acts out here. He wanted to work three nights a week. That's one of the main reasons he wouldn't commit. He'd say, "Everyone wants me to do a show but they don't understand that when people come to a Michael Jackson show, they expect me to *perform* the whole show. I can't just be like the Osmonds. I can't just sit on a stool and sing 'Kumbaya' like these old Vegas crooners. People want me to dance from beginning to end."

He told us that when he was in his prime, he was like an athlete. He'd have to consume thousands of calories a day just to do one of his shows, and he'd lose three or four pounds every night from exerting so much. "That's a lot of wear on my body," he said. "My body can't take that anymore."

There was a small gym with a treadmill in the house. We worked out with him a few times. There were some days he'd come in and he could keep up with us for a while. There were other days he'd get on that treadmill and he couldn't go fifteen minutes without wearing himself out. But he wanted to give the same electrifying performances he gave twenty, thirty years ago. And if he did it on Monday, he wanted to do the same show on Tuesday. He'd say, "If people pay to see me, I have to give them a show."

Bill: The twenty-fifth anniversary of *Thriller* was coming up. That was another reason he'd come back to the country. There was talk about remixing the songs, reshooting the videos with new special effects. I overheard a lot of those conversations, and I could hear Mr. Jackson saying he was against it. He'd say things like, "There are some things you should never touch." But I believe Sony had more say in that than he did. They were dragging him into it. He was still under a lot of contractual obligations to them.

He hated Sony. That was another big problem. He didn't like a lot of the people he had to do business with. Artists always have problems and issues with their management companies and their record labels, but his hatred of Sony was on a whole other level. He hated Tommy Mottola, the head of the label. Hated him. Called him the devil.

One day, Mr. Jackson told us he wanted some headphones to listen to music while he walked on the treadmill. One of the other security guys went out and got him a pair. I was in the house less than a week later, and I saw that they'd been broken in half. These things weren't dropped. They were broken on purpose. I picked them up and saw they were Sony headphones. I wouldn't have bought him anything that said Sony on it, but whoever purchased them probably wasn't aware of the situation.

Careerwise, everything was just sort of static. You'd hear about deals coming up, such-and-such might be happening, then you weren't sure, then it was maybe back on again, then it wasn't. There was a meeting with Simon Fuller, the producer of *American Idol*. Mr. Jackson was supposed to make an appearance on that show. We started to plan the detail, organize the travel, the hotel. First he was going to appear on the show when they were filming in New York. Then it was supposed to be when they were in L.A. Then we just stopped hearing things.

Very seldom in Michael Jackson's world would you get definitive word that something was canceled. You'd just stop hearing about it. If he had something in the works, an event or an appearance, people would be calling you on the regular. "What time is he coming? What does he like? What does he want? Does he need such and such?" Then the calls would just stop. That meant one of his attorneys had stepped in to say that it wasn't going down.

Javon: It just seemed like he had no interest in work or business in general, but he still loved to create, to make music. There was a guy named Brad Buxer. He was a producer and engineer. He'd worked on the *Dangerous* album and the *HIStory* album with Mr. Jackson back in the day. Once we built the studio, Brad would come to Vegas on and off and stay for a few days at a nearby hotel. He would come to the house, bring some musical instruments, and they would just jam together. Once Brad started coming around, there was a lot more music around the house, and Mr. Jackson seemed rejuvenated and energized. They were working on tracks we'd never heard before.

Bill: There were several meetings with different artists and producers. Some of them working on remixes for *Thriller 25*. Will.i.am from the Black Eyed Peas, he was working on some of those tracks. There were meetings with Babyface, a couple of sit-downs with Akon. He was also doing one of the *Thriller* tracks, and they were collaborating on another song together called "Hold My Hand." We heard Mr. Jackson rehearsing a lot of the early demo versions of that. A lot of these meetings took place at the Palms. It's a hotel and casino complex that has a high-end, state-of-the-art recording studio. A lot of major artists come into town to record there.

Except for Brad, Mr. Jackson didn't spend a whole lot of time working with these guys face to face. They'd meet for a couple hours, collaborate, then go off and work on these ideas and concepts on their own. They'd talk and play him the tracks over the phone. Sometimes I'd get the songs emailed to me. I'd burn them to disc and bring them to Mr. Jackson, and he'd play them in the car. None of it was very organized.

There was always talk of assembling these bits and pieces into a big comeback album, but like most things in his world, that project never seemed to materialize. For the most part, he was just writing and creating music because he loved doing it. There were also choreographers coming to the house on a regular basis. They would be in the studio with him for hours, even though there was no show lined up. It was just for pleasure, for the love of doing it.

Javon: It wasn't just musicians and producers coming through at that time. Lots of people were anxious to visit with him because he'd been out of the country for so long. Andrew Young, the former mayor of Atlanta, came to visit him at the house. Jesse Jackson came to the house. Eddie Griffin, the comedian, he was a regular visitor. Chris Tucker came by; we took him and Mr. Jackson to see *Bridge to Terabithia* with their kids. Mr. Jackson talked to Nelson Mandela on the phone a number of times.

Bill: Dr. Murray visited on a couple of occasions, maybe once every six weeks or so, usually to check up on one of the kids. He was never there for very long, a half-hour or forty-five minutes tops. I honestly didn't pay him that much mind. There wasn't anything unusual about it. He was just another one of these people who came and went.

There were plenty of people coming through Michael Jackson's life, but there was nobody really *in* his life. He was friendly with these people who'd visit, but these meetings were business meetings, for the most part, like with Andrew Young and Jesse Jackson—that was to discuss some charity program in Africa. There was almost no one in his life on a personal level coming by to say, "Hey, let's go hang out." Never in the whole time I worked for the man did I hear anybody just call him up to say, "Hey, guess what movie I just saw?" There was nothing like that going on. It was business.

Javon: His main contact with the outside world was through the fans. He got tons of fan mail. Ms. Raymone's people would collect it and bundle it, and every few days it would arrive in these big sacks. It came from all over the world—Canada, England, Egypt, Japan, India, Ireland, Spain. He read all of it.

Every so often, early on Saturday mornings, we'd take him on long drives and he'd immerse himself in his fan mail. I'd drive. Bill would ride shotgun. We'd load up a few boxes of mail in the vehicle and then we'd head out into the desert and just drive for three, four hours. We'd drive up into the mountains, where there was still snow on the ground. We'd go all the way across the Hoover Dam, into Arizona, then turn around and head home.

Mr. Jackson would sit in the back, classical music playing, the curtain drawn. You could hear him opening envelopes, going letter by letter. Sometimes he'd say, "Hey, listen to this, guys. This is so sweet." And he'd read us something somebody had written. People would write about their children dying of illnesses and how much his music had meant to them. Some of it made him very emotional. You could hear him getting choked up. He'd say, "You guys may not understand, but this is where I get a lot of my inspiration to write my songs."

By the time we got back to the house, he'd have two separate piles of letters. He'd keep one, hand us the other and say, "These you can get rid of."

Bill: People would send gifts too—teddy bears, balloons, flowers, photos, personal keepsakes. A lot of this stuff was handmade. A collage or a card with a special message. He would mostly keep the gifts that were handmade. He liked that. Sometimes he'd get a package and it seemed suspicious to him or he just didn't feel right about it. He'd give it to us and want us to check it first. There was never anything dangerous, no bombs or anything like that, but a lot of teddy bears and music boxes wound up drowning in the pool for us to find that out.

There was so much of it that one of the bedrooms had to be designated as the fan mail room. The walls in there were plastered with handmade cards and letters, and the floor was covered with big stacks. And that was just what accumulated in Las Vegas over a few months' time.

Javon: Except for those letters and occasional visits from his mother or one or two other people, he really was just alone with the kids inside this little bubble. From the outside, you might think that Michael Jackson led this high-flying, glamorous life. But all the high-end restaurants and five-star hotels we went to? Never once did we go in through the front lobby, where everything's beautiful and pretty and clean. We were moving through underground parking structures, going through side entrances in the back by the dumpsters. We didn't ride in the nice glass elevators. We rode in the service elevators with trash bags stacked in the corner, waiting to be hauled down to the basement. That's the world Michael Jackson lived in.

Bill: There were times when you felt like a rat scurrying through a maze, going down all these dimly-lit corridors. The smell of the service entrances was horrible. I'd have on a freshly pressed suit, polished shoes, and we'd be stepping in filth, rotting food. I'd be thinking, Damn, it stinks in here.

Name me one other celebrity that has to go in through the back of the hotel every time. Not every now and then, every single time. There's only one occasion I can remember that we weren't sneaking around in the back of a hotel. Mr. Jackson had a meeting at the Bellagio, and we ran into Steve Wynn. He asked us to walk through the Bellagio's casino area with him, so we did. A few people were gawking, but it was mostly an older crowd. Wasn't too busy that time of day. We walked into the front lobby area and Mr. Jackson looked around and said, "You know, I can't even remember the last time I saw the lobby of a hotel. I forgot how beautiful they are. This is really amazing."

A lot of the time, hanging out, he was just a regular dude. But every now and then you'd get these reminders of how isolated his life had been. It would come at odd moments, like with some of the words he used. One of the times we had to stay at a hotel, they'd snuck Prince's dog into the room. They couldn't really walk the dog outside because there were supposed to be no pets at that hotel. Plus the dog wasn't fully house-trained anyway. You can imagine what it smelled like in there after a couple days. Mr. Jackson came to me and he said, "Bill, I need you to go out and get some smells."

"Smells? What's 'smells'?"

"You know, things to make the room smell good."

"You mean air fresheners?"

"Yeah, yeah. Stuff like that."

Sometimes he used words, I didn't know what he meant. One time he said, "Bill, I need you to go to the airport and pick up the governess."

"The governor's coming? What governor?"

He laughed. "No, Bill. The gover*ness*. Like, the person who watches the kids."

"Do you mean the *nanny*?"

"Yeah."

So why not just say that? He'd use these words, and I'd be like, "Mr. Jackson, I don't know what you're talking about."

He'd just shake his head. He'd say, "You guys need to read more."

Javon: That's how he filled all those hours by himself: books. He'd read anything and everything he could get his hands on. History. Science. Art. There were so many trips to Barnes & Noble. It was almost a weekly thing. He would go into bookstores and drop five thousand dollars like he was buying a pack of gum. At one point, he actually bought a bookstore—I'm talking about an entire bookstore. He paid cash for it.

Bill: It was on his way back from Tokyo, during those couple days he spent in L.A. He went to visit this used bookstore. It had a lot of rare books from the personal libraries of some pretty famous people, Hollywood stars. These were books that Humphrey Bogart had signed, books that Ingrid Bergman had signed. He asked the owner how much it would take to buy all of his books. The owner didn't take him seriously. So he made an offer of $100,000. Said he'd pay cash on the spot. Couple weeks after he got back from L.A., this U-Haul filled with all these books showed up at the house in Vegas.

Javon: When that U-Haul pulled up, me and Bill were like, "What the hell are we supposed to do with this?"

Mr. Jackson pointed out one of the rooms on the second floor and said he wanted to turn it into a library. He said, "You guys will need to build shelves in here."

So we went to Lowe's and bought some bookshelves, brought them back to the house, and set them up. Then we had to move all the books up in the elevator, box by box. At first, we tried to label and categorize them all, fiction or nonfiction, but it got so overwhelming that we just started stacking the books on the shelves in no particular order. But he was happy with it. He'd just go in there and get lost and find interesting things to read.

Bill: He never wore reading glasses in public, so whenever we'd go into a bookstore, he'd always go to that rack where they keep the glasses. He'd grab a bunch and he'd do a Fred Sanford, trying different ones on until he found a pair that matched his prescription. That's how I learned his eyes were messed up. When he read at home, he had one of those magnifying glasses that they use in doctors' offices, the kind with a built-in light that blows things up about a billion times bigger.

There's a newsstand in Vegas where you can get newspapers from damn near every country in the world. He wanted those, every week. He'd say, "Whatever foreign newspapers they have, bring those to me."

"Even ones in different languages?"

"Yes."

Whatever they had that was foreign, we'd pick up. Whether he read them all, what foreign languages he understood, I have no idea.

He read *The Wall Street Journal* every day. That was the only American media he'd consume, because the *Journal* was pretty much the only place he could get real news without running into crazy Michael Jackson stories. That's part of why he didn't watch TV, only DVDs. The man was a punch line on Jay Leno's show practically every night. It was like he couldn't risk turning on a television. He didn't want to see that stuff, and he didn't want the kids exposed to it.

That was a challenge just because we went to so many bookstores and newsstands. We'd get calls from Raymone. She'd say, "An article came out in such and such magazine. Make sure he doesn't see it." So we would walk into Barnes & Noble ahead of him, and we'd know which magazine to look for. We'd grab the whole stack, flip them around, or just take them off the shelf.

Sometimes there'd be a good article about him in a magazine. Raymone would FedEx it to me with a note to give it to Mr. Jackson. I'd go and bring him the magazine, and he'd reach for it and then jerk his hand back and say, "Is it okay for me to read?"

"Yes, sir."

"There's nothing bad?"

"No, sir."

"Oh, okay."

He never went on the Internet. Same reason. If he wanted something online, he'd tell me and I'd go look it up. He did do some eBay shopping, though. He tried that a couple times. Maxed out my damn credit card.

The man had a lot going on. Mental stress. Anxiety. On the one hand, that required us to be hypervigilant about everything in his world. Hiding magazines, keeping cameras away from his kids. At the same time, it was our job to try and make his life as normal as possible, and that meant backing off so he had the space to just be a person. He didn't want us crowding in on him, making him feel more like a prisoner than he already was. We had keys to the house, but we would always let him know if we needed to come in. We didn't really need to be in his living space. That belonged to him and his kids. So we made every effort not to be in there.

Javon: There were a couple times he invited us in to watch movies with him and the kids. He asked us twice, and we said no both times. Bill told him, "Sir, we can't look out for you and your kids if we're watching a movie." I think Mr. Jackson really appreciated that.

Part of the reason his security turnover rate was so high was because people would get too familiar with him. "Mr. Jackson, is it okay if my kids come over and meet you?" We didn't do that. He'd had security on him practically every day since he was ten years old. There were things about our job that he understood better than we did. So I'm sure he was evaluating us, studying us as much as we studied him.

Bill: Sometimes he'd ask to see our guns. He'd want to hold them and check them out. He wanted to be informed about everything we were doing, but I think it was also because he thought they were cool. One time I was showing him the piece I had, and he said he'd always thought about owning a gun himself, that it would be useful for protection, but that he would never have one with his children in the house. "Besides," he said, "there are probably too many people I'd want to shoot."

Javon: We were working nonstop. I was working fifteen-, eighteen-hour days. Sometimes I wouldn't even go home at all. I worked 7:00 a.m. to midnight and had to be right back in there at 7:00 again, and I lived about forty minutes away. So I'd bring some extra food along and sleep in the trailer.

I'd just had a newborn baby right about the time I started working for him. I hadn't told anybody, even my child's mother, who I was working for. I'd been telling her that I was working for a high-profile dignitary. After a while, she didn't want to hear that. It got to the point where she was like, "Are you really working? Are you having an affair on me or not? I don't know anybody who has to be at work this much."

She thought I was really doing some dirt, cheating on her. She said, "Here we are with a newborn baby. You're not about to keep going to work and not telling me where you work at. What's the big secret?"

So after about three months I had to give in and let her know. When I told her it was Michael Jackson, she said, "You lyin'!" She didn't believe me. She was like, "Of all the things you could say, you gonna tell me you're workin' for Michael Jackson?! How long did it take you to come up with that one, Javon?"

We went back and forth until I finally had to show her my pay stub. When she saw it said MJJ Productions, she was like, "Wow, you really work for this guy."

Bill: There was a pool house in the back; we'd use the shower in there. I'd call my daughter and ask her to bring me some clothes, bring me this or bring me that. Undershirts, razors, an extra toothbrush. We were hitting up Burlington Coat Factory on the regular, picking up clothes to keep in the trailer for when there was no time to go home and change. It got to the point where it wasn't that you wanted to stay, but you felt like you couldn't leave.

For the overnight shift, we worked out a signal with Mr.

Jackson. We put a lamp in one of his bedroom windows, and as long as the light was on, that meant he was up and might need us for something. When the lamp was off, that meant everything was okay and he was turning in. Whenever he couldn't sleep, we'd hear him in the studio. The way it was set up, we could see the studio windows from the trailer. It'd be three-thirty in the morning, pitch black outside, the whole neighborhood quiet. The light in the studio would come on. You wouldn't hear anything for a while. There was a TV in there; maybe he was watching videos or something. Then, about fifteen minutes later, you'd hear a bass line. You'd hear him adjusting the volume, the tempo. You'd hear his feet moving on the boards—and then that voice, that voice that sold millions of records. It would just come pouring out of him. Beautiful. Incredible.

Javon: It gave me goose bumps. How could you *not* get goose bumps, hearing Michael Jackson performing like that? In the dead of night, just sitting there and listening by yourself, no one else around? We never really got used to it. It was always amazing no matter how many times we heard it.

We'd get these little peeks at how his mind worked. We'd have some piece of music on in the car, a classical symphony or something, and he'd get hung up on a sound he heard in the background, some type of instrument or a tone, and he'd want to rewind it and listen to it again. He'd play it back and go, "Can you guys hear that?" He'd play it over and over, going, "Right there. That cymbal, right there, do you hear it?" We couldn't hear it. There were sounds in music that he'd hear and get obsessed with, things that we couldn't even pick up on.

It was like he had a musical soundtrack in his head, running all the time. We'd be driving along and he'd just start humming a melody or beatboxing some percussion. In the days after, you'd hear him working it out in his head. No words, just sounds. It was almost like it wasn't something he was doing consciously; it just happened. He told us that sometimes complete songs would just come to him, the melody, the lyrics, every instrumental part. He couldn't get the beat out of his head until he'd worked it out. It just took him over entirely. That's when you'd hear him in the studio late at night.

Bill: When you heard him in there? It was something you wanted to tell the world, especially if it was music that you knew nobody had ever heard before. Sometimes he'd play his old music and just dance to it. Other times he'd be working on a new track or a new melody. You wanted to grab your cell phone and call someone and say, "Yo, I'm listening to Michael Jackson singing right now. Like, *right now*." But you couldn't.

Javon: He would turn it up *loud*. Loud to the point where you'd be wondering if he was going to wake up the kids. You could tell he was pouring all his anger and frustration and energy into his dance moves and his music. Sometimes it would go on all night. I'd be on graveyard shifts, and he'd have that light on in his room till dawn. I'd think to myself, "When does he actually sleep?" I was working all these hours and I was dog tired, and he was in there wide awake.

Some nights, you'd think maybe he fell asleep with the lamp on, but then you'd see the kitchen light come on and you knew he was still up. That happened a lot. He was up at night more than he wasn't. If I worked the graveyard shift three times a week, three times a week Mr. Jackson would be up on my watch. If he turned in early and the light went off, it would almost come as a surprise.

But you always knew when he was sleeping well, because when you got to work in the morning, he'd be real engaging, real friendly. He'd come out before breakfast just to say hello. Then there would be times that he would go two or three days without communicating with us at all, like when Feldman left. We started getting used to it. Like, "Okay, he's going through his quiet stage again."

Bill: When he was in good spirits, we did what we could to keep him in good spirits. When he went into that quiet mode, or a loneliness stage, we knew. We felt it. Plenty of times, start of the day he'd jump into the car, happy and smiling and animated. "Morning! Everybody sleep well?"

"Yes, sir."

"Good. I slept like a baby."

Other times, he'd get in the car, wouldn't say a word. We'd know something was wrong. He'd got a phone call. Some kind of bad news. Something. We'd drive for a little bit. There would be total silence for ten minutes, twenty minutes. Then, out of nowhere, real soft: "Why don't they just leave me alone?"

Javon: There were many nights when he'd call and say he wanted to drive down to the Strip. Those evenings were not planned; a mood would just strike him. He'd call Grace and tell her to come over to watch the kids, and once they were asleep, he'd come down, jump into the ride, and we'd roll out.

"Anywhere in particular, sir?"

"No, just drive. I want to look at the lights."

We'd drive from the Sahara all the way to the Tropicana, bust a U-turn and head back the way we came. Sometimes he'd want to stop and see the water show at the Bellagio or the volcano at Treasure Island. But mostly we'd just circle around the Strip about six or seven times. He wouldn't say much; we wouldn't say much, either. We'd just drive slow. He'd crack the window a little bit, look at the lights, look out at the people. We must have done that at least twenty or thirty times.

There was one time we passed the big sign for Cirque du Soleil's *Love* show at the Mirage, the one based on the songs of the

Beatles, which Mr. Jackson owned the rights to. He saw the sign for it and said, "When did that start?"

I said, "That's been here for at least two or three months now."

He said, "What? Nobody asked me about that. They didn't get my permission for that." He was livid. He said, "I have to make some phone calls." Then he asked Bill to make arrangements so he could go see the show. We went. He said it was okay.

Bill: What he really wanted to be able to do was get out and walk around, so we had to figure out a disguise for him. "I've tried everything," he said. "I've been through two- to three-hour makeup sessions not to be recognized, but people always recognize me."

That's when I came up with the idea for the motorcycle helmet. We'd dress him up like a biker from head to toe and he could wear a motorcycle helmet with a tinted visor. He said he had never done that before. It would draw stares, but nobody would know it was him, and there are plenty of stranger things to see out on the Strip on a Saturday night. So I said, "Let's go for it."

That outfit must have cost about six hundred dollars, from the jacket to the pants to the boots. We drove down, parked at the Bellagio, he put the helmet on, and we walked. We kept our distance to give him space. We didn't wanna bring attention to him by our presence. Javon and I both had street clothes on. No earpieces. We just strolled. We walked from the Bellagio to the Excalibur, maybe six or seven blocks, which are long blocks on the Strip, maybe about a mile and a half. It was hot as hell out there. He must have been burning up in that thing. Every few minutes, I'd ask him, "You all right, sir?"

"I'm fine, I'm fine."

After we'd walked all the way down, Javon went back to get the car. We sat on a bench, and he came and picked us up. Mr. Jackson got in the car. When he took that helmet off, sweat just poured down his face. But aside from the heat, he loved it. He was almost giddy about it. "Nobody knew who I was!" He was amazed at that. It was very therapeutic for him. He said, "I needed that. I just needed to get out of the house and go for a walk."

Javon: One night, we were driving home from the Strip, and there was this on-ramp for the freeway that we had to pass to get back to the house. We were stopped at a red light by this ramp, and right off the road there was a homeless man and woman. They were arguing with each other about something. The man was sitting and the woman was standing with a sign; it's the kind of thing you see all the time out here, people with signs that say "Homeless, Please Help." Vegas is a hard town. You get caught up in gambling and all that? It'll ruin you.

Bill: Mr. Jackson saw these people and said, "Why are these people out there?"

"Those are homeless people, sir."

He was like, "Really? Wow."

He told Javon to pull over. We pulled over to the curb and we just watched for a minute. Mr. Jackson saw all the other cars passing by, and he asked, "Why isn't anybody helping them? Why isn't anybody stopping?" Then he said to Javon, "Call the woman over to the car."

Javon rolled down his window, waved her over. When she got to the car, Mr. Jackson rolled his window down just a little bit and said, "What's your name?"

"Amanda," she said.

They talked for a bit. He wanted to know her story. He asked her where she was from, where's her family at. She said she used to be a dancer, a showgirl. Then I heard him reaching around in the backseat for something. I heard the sound of paper. He was pulling out money. He pulled out three one-hundred-dollar bills, gave them to her and said, "Here. Take this."

She was floored. She was almost crying, saying, "Thank you, thank you, thank you."

Javon: After he gave her the money, she backed up a few steps and I started to drive off. The guy that had been sitting near her got up, came over to her, and tried to snatch the money away. She pulled back, but he kept trying to grab it from her and they started fighting again. She started yelling, "No! This is mine!"

Mr. Jackson saw that and said, "No, no, no! Javon, stop the car. Pull back over."

I pulled back over, he leaned back out of the window and called the man over this time, saying, "Don't do that! Here, I've got something for you too." He pulled out another three hundred dollars and gave it to the man. The lady started crying, like she'd been saved.

Bill: He told them to use the money for food. "Get something nourishing," he said. "Don't get any drugs."

"No, sir!" they said. "No, sir!" They were both gushing with thank-yous and God-bless-yous when all of a sudden the man stopped and looked in the car window and said, "Are you Michael Jackson?"

"No. No, I'm not."

I turned to the backseat. "Are you ready to go, sir?"

"Yeah, I'm ready," he said. And we pulled off. As we were driving, Mr. Jackson said, "Are there a lot of people like that in Vegas?"

"Yeah," I said. "There are parts of Vegas where a lot of homeless people live."

"Really? Can we go there?"

I hesitated a moment. "You want to go there tonight, sir? Tonight wouldn't be a good time."

"No, no," he said. "We can go another day. I just want to see."

The bad part of Vegas is on the north side, Main Street and Las Vegas Boulevard, over by Cashman Field. When he mentioned going there, I was hoping he'd forget about it. Sometimes when he made unusual requests, things I knew weren't feasible or just weren't a good idea, I'd wait a bit before following up, to see if he'd drop it. Sometimes he would. If he reminded me again, I knew he was very serious. This time, he remembered. A couple days later, he came to me and said, "When are we going to go to that side of town?"

"What side of town is that, sir?"

"Where the homeless people are."

"We can go there today."

"Okay, let's go."

So we took him to the other side of town, about twenty minutes from the house. We headed north up Main Street, and all of these people were out. You could hear in his voice that he was shocked that all of these people out here were homeless. He couldn't believe it. "It's just amazing," he said. "This country is so rich and these people are poor and living on the street."

He asked Javon to pull over, so we pulled over. I was a little antsy. I wasn't cool pulling over in a nice car with all these people around. We sat there on the side of the road for a bit. Then Mr. Jackson said, "I want to give them something."

I thought he meant he wanted to get out of the car. I said, "I don't think it'd be a good idea to go out there, sir."

He said, "No, no, no. I'll pass it out of the window."

He cracked the window and started waving people over. He had a fanny pack he was wearing. He opened it up and the whole thing was stuffed full of cash. They would come to the window and he would pass out a hundred-dollar bill through the crack in the window to each one. One thing I noticed was that he was trying to catch the attention of the women. He wanted to make sure they were the ones who got the money. He was like, "Come here. No, no, no. You. You come here." A lot of men got money too, but

I could hear him singling the women out of the crowd, calling them forward. People started lining up outside his window, like it was an ATM.

Javon: He gave away so much he ran out, and he got upset with himself. He was saying he should have brought more. We started to see another side of him, his compassion for others, and it was kind of amazing. There was no media out there, no cameras. There was only a crack in the window, so no one could tell it was him. It was just something that he wanted to do.

After that, we went and handed out food to the homeless a number of times. He'd say, "Me and the kids are not going to eat this. Let's take this down and give it away." One time, he wanted the kids to come with us and see it, so we brought them along.

Bill: He read the Bible a lot. Oftentimes, if he answered the door for some reason, he would have a Bible in his hand and his reading glasses on. That was common. I remember he'd say things like "God bless you" to fans, but he always used "Jehovah" when talking to the kids, like, "Jehovah wouldn't like that." There were these merchandising people who used to call him all the time to put his name and his image on slot machines. He wouldn't do it because of his religion. He'd say, "No, Jehovah wouldn't like that." But they've got Michael Jackson slot machines now. I see them all the time. Every hotel in Vegas has those same slot machines he said he did not want. Somebody signed off on it.

Javon: His favorite thing to do was go to the movies. He loved taking the kids, especially to the big action blockbusters like *Spider-Man* or *Transformers*. There's a big multiplex at the Palms, which is where we'd usually go. We'd call a day or so beforehand, talk to the manager, and they'd set aside a screen for a private viewing. The only time it was a problem was for *Spider-Man 3*. He wanted to go on opening day. We called the manager, and she said she didn't think they could close down a theater on short notice for opening day. Mr. Jackson said that was fine; he wanted to see it with a big crowd anyway. Sometimes he liked watching things with an audience. Whenever he wanted to do that, I'd go in and save the seats. Then we'd wait for the previews to start and the lights to go down, and Bill would radio me that he was walking in with Mr. Jackson and the kids. I'd light up my phone and let them know where I was at. They'd come and sit down, and me and Bill would walk out and stand by the door.

Bill: Any time we went to the movies, he insisted on bringing spray butter and hot sauce for the popcorn. *Had* to have them. *Would not* start the movie without them. Sometimes we'd get to the theater, and I'd be thinking that Javon had brought the spray butter and hot sauce, and Javon was thinking that I'd brought the spray butter and hot sauce. When we realized our mistake, one of us would have to run to the store to pick them up. Sometimes we'd have the managers hold the movie until we could get the spray butter and hot sauce safely delivered.

I don't care what anybody says about Michael Jackson trying to act like or turn himself into a white man. Anybody who insists on taking his own spray butter and hot sauce to a movie theater? That man is black, ghetto, and hood.

Javon: He had these particular fixations. Once he wanted something, he wanted it, period. There was no getting that thought out of his mind. He'd point to something and say, "I want that." That meant, Make it happen. Didn't matter what obstacles there were, how difficult it was to get. Just make it happen.

When *Spider-Man 3* was out, we were driving on Spring Mountain Road. We passed a Burger King and they had a promotion going on. They had these life-sized Spider-Man figurines attached to the lampposts outside of the store. Mr. Jackson said, "Javon, you see that? I need one of those. Stop the car."

I pulled the car over. Mr. Jackson said, "Do you think you could get up there and get that?"

This was in the middle of the day on a major street, in broad daylight. I said, "Sir, I don't think that would be a smart idea."

"I think you can do it," he said. "I think you can."

"Sir, I don't think so."

"You look like you don't want to do it."

"I kinda really don't, sir."

"Well, do you think you could come back and get it?"

"I can try. But I still don't think it would be a good idea."

But he wanted that Spider-Man figurine. There was nothing I could tell him. I tried to go back at night and get it. I was up there, trying to jimmy it down with this little knife, cut the strings from the pole, but it was way too high. I would have needed an eight-foot ladder. It was crazy. I went home and told him it was a no go. He was really disappointed. He said, "Can you do some research to see where I can buy one?" We did. We couldn't find it.

Bill: He wasn't used to being told no. This one time, his attorney called me up and said, "Bill, Mr. Jackson is upset because he said that you yelled at him."

That was another thing about him. He didn't deal well with confrontation. He'd never tell you directly that you'd upset him. You'd just get a call. I know, because I made a lot of those calls myself, telling people, "Mr. Jackson didn't like when you did such and such." So I got this call from his attorney saying I'd yelled at him. And maybe I had, but it was only because he'd asked for something that was impossible. There were times Javon was off handling something, and Mr. Jackson wanted to go somewhere with just me, him, and three kids, with no pre-detail. I didn't feel comfortable with that. I didn't feel it was safe. So I told him no. We told him no a few times. Sometimes he respected us for telling him no. Sometimes he really didn't like it.

I'm sure at one time, at the height of his fame, he'd snap his fingers and things would magically happen for him. And he honestly felt that the world just operated that way. He'd go into a store, pull a piece of candy off the shelf, open it up, throw the wrapper down, and eat it. Like, don't even worry about it. He also had a thing for umbrellas. We went to a store once, we were in a Staples, and he went by this rack of umbrellas, pulled one out, took the tag off, popped the thing open. We walked around the store like that. And he wasn't stealing. He'd grab the candy, pop the umbrella, and say something like, "Make sure I pay for this."

Javon: There was a helicopter flight simulator at FAO Schwarz. Blanket loved to ride in it. We were shopping one day, and Mr. Jackson said, "I want that. Find out how much that is." Me and Bill were like, what? This thing was the size of an actual helicopter cockpit. I don't think it was even for sale. It was just a ride they had for kids to play with in the store. We asked the manager, who said it cost something like $75,000. But this thing was so big, you couldn't even get it inside a house. Fortunately he kind of dropped it after a few days. We just got used to those kinds of requests.

Bill: The thing he wanted most was the thing he couldn't have. There was a house in Vegas that he'd wanted for years, going back long before we worked for him. It was this sprawling estate, right off Durango near the Spanish Trail Country Club, this massive place owned by some Middle Eastern prince who'd built it but never actually lived in it. It was the largest estate, I believe, in all of Las Vegas. Mr. Jackson always wanted to go and visit that house. He was constantly talking to realtors about buying it.

We set up a number of appointments to go see it. The caretaker for the property would meet us at the front gate and let us in.

The first time I was in that house, I walked around with my jaw on the floor. Indoor pool. Walls painted in gold leaf. A kitchen like you'd find in a hotel. It was amazing. Mr. Jackson and the kids went around the grounds like they had been there before, almost like they already owned the place. The kids would run around and say, "This is my room! This is my room!" Mr. Jackson would point and say, "We'll need more trees over there. We're going to need guard dogs."

He showed us the guesthouses on the property. He showed us this other building where he said we were going to stay; that was going to be the security center, he said. It was a hell of a lot nicer than the trailer we had at Monte Cristo. He said he was going to buy a fleet of mini golf carts and have a garage for them. If you lived there, you'd need a golf cart just to get around the place. It was that big. He wanted a property so huge that he could go outside and feel like he was free. He could go and climb a tree, do whatever. He said he was going to buy it and call it Wonderland.

Javon: We found out this place was on the market for something crazy, like $55 million. Part of us was thinking, How can he possibly afford this? How? But at the same time, he was so convincing in the way he talked about it. He talked about the house like it was already his, like the deal to buy it was basically finished, and there were a couple of formalities holding things up and that was the only reason he didn't live there already. If we were going to the movies or the bookstore, he'd want to drive by it just to take a look. He'd say, "Let's drive by my house."

Bill: He'd visit nearly every chance he got. Sometimes it was once a week, usually on Sunday. This one time, we couldn't reach anybody to make an appointment. We pulled up out front, and there was a chain on the gate. We sat there almost thirty minutes trying to reach somebody to let us in. Finally Mr. Jackson said, "I wish we could just get in there somehow."

I looked at Javon, and Javon looked at me. We both knew what he was asking us to do. Back of my mind, I wanted to say to the guy, "Don't you think you've got enough lawsuits against you without adding a charge for breaking and entering?" And me, I wasn't keen on going to jail. But Michael Jackson wants what Michael Jackson wants. He just sort of sat there with this sense of expectation.

Javon: We had a toolbox in the back with a pair of bolt cutters in it. I didn't want to volunteer that I could break into someone's house for him. But he stayed on it. He was like, "Don't you guys have something to get that chain off the fence?"

I said, "We do, sir. But I don't know if that's a good idea."

He said, "It's no problem, Javon. It's going to be my house. The realtor knows. It's okay, I'm telling you."

And he wore us down. He was that convincing. He *believed* that this house was his, so much so that he made *you* believe it was his and it was okay for him to do what he wanted with it. I got the bolt cutters and got out. This was right off a busy street, broad daylight, cars going by. The whole time Mr. Jackson was giddy. It was like this little adventure for him. Not me. I was too busy looking around for the police and thinking, How the hell we gonna explain this shit? I popped the lock and got the gate open and we went onto the property. The door to the house was unlocked, and they all went in and walked around and ran through the kitchens and the bedrooms like they always did.

Bill: Michael Jackson's reality was unlike anything I've ever experienced. That's what made this job so different. I always considered Mr. Jackson to be different. Never weird, just different. Every day with him was a different direction of thinking. Every day was different from the day before. There was always something new you'd find out, whether it was a request, something he would say. I didn't understand a lot of the things he did, a lot of the choices he made, but I also could never begin to understand the life he'd lived, which had led him to be that way. That's what made it so impossible to judge a lot of his actions, one way or another.

There was this one time we went to a magic shop. He was a big magic buff. We went and saw nearly every magician who played on the Strip. He had a bunch of those take-home magic kits, too, for doing tricks with coins and cards and stuff. Around May or June maybe, he wanted to go to the magic shop at the New York–New York casino. So we started planning that detail.

The morning we were supposed to go, he called down and asked me to go pick up some gauze. I asked him how much. He said, "Get as much as you can." I was worried that somebody was hurt. I went out, picked up a couple of bags of medical gauze from the drugstore, and I brought it to him. About half an hour later, he called down again and said, "Bill, I'm ready."

Javon got the cars ready to roll. I was out in the driveway, waiting for Mr. Jackson to come around the corner. He came around, and when I saw him, he had on a green coat with a hoodie underneath. But his hands were all wrapped up with gauze. His entire head was wrapped in the stuff too, with little slits for his eyes. He was dressed like a burn victim or something. He looked like the Mummy. At that point, I thought I'd seen everything with Michael Jackson, but this floored me. I called Javon on the two-way radio. I was whispering into the microphone, "Yo, Javon. You ain't gonna believe what the boss has on."

Javon: Bill was trying to call me, but my radio was off. I was in the security trailer, still getting ready to go. So when I stepped outside, I had no idea what was going on. I walked out and I saw what looked like this weird guy, all bandaged up and disfigured, wandering around the property. This alarm went off in my head. I thought, Intruder! and I ran. I booked it across that driveway and I grabbed this guy and I slammed him against the car, yelling, "*Who are you? What are you doing here?*"

Then Bill started yelling, "Javon, no! Javon! That's the boss! That's the boss!"

I realized who it was, and I backed off and I panicked. I mean, I'd shoved him *hard*, and he was so skinny and fragile. I was scared I'd broken his arm or something. I started gushing, "I'm so sorry, sir. I didn't recognize you at all. I'm so sorry. Please forgive me. I'm so sorry."

Bill: Javon probably apologized about a thousand times, but Mr. Jackson just started cracking up. He thought it was hilarious. I thought for sure he'd be livid; for a minute, I thought that this was going to be the last day we ever worked for the man. But Mr. Jackson thought it was great, that his disguise had actually fooled someone. He just climbed in the car, laughing and saying, "Did you guys really not know who I was?"

Javon: We got in the car and drove out to the casino, like it was any old regular trip, with him dressed up in this mummy costume in the back. We took the back entrance into the casino, but the magic store was still a few hundred feet from where we entered, and the place was packed with people. Soon as we walked in, they started turning and noticing me and Bill wearing these black suits, following this guy who's dressed like a mummy. You could hear the whispers, people going, "Who's that? What's going on?"

It was obviously drawing more attention than it was avoiding. If you looked at him even for a minute it wasn't hard to figure out who he was. He'd gone to all this trouble, wrapping up his face and his hands, but he was wearing the white socks and the hiked-up pants with the slip-on loafers. That's his signature look. Everybody knows that. Plus he just had a way about him—the way he moved, the way he walked, the way he'd pick something up off a shelf—that was unmistakably Michael Jackson. Everyone on the planet knows how Michael Jackson moves.

Bill: At one point, as we were walking through the casino, this lady walked up to him, middle-aged woman. She walked right up to him and stood next to him in this mummy getup. Then she sort of gave him this look and said, "I know who you are."

Mr. Jackson said, "Hmmm?" He did it in his high-pitched tone, acting like he didn't know what she was talking about. "Hmmm?"

She said, "I know who you are. You're not fooling anyone."

Then she just walked off and let him be.

We finally made it to the magic store, and Mr. Jackson was browsing. The store manager walked up to him two or three times and asked him if he could help him with anything, and he'd just shake his head no. Didn't really say anything. They had a lot of these kits and magic tricks. Mr. Jackson was picking things up, looking at them, playing with them, putting them back down. I was watching the store manager's eyes, and I knew exactly what I would have been thinking if it had been my store. I watched this guy pick up the phone, quietly say something, and then hang up real quick. About five minutes later, two police officers walked in and they went over to the manager. They talked for a minute and then he pointed at Mr. Jackson. I was just shaking my head, thinking, No, no, no. Please no. This isn't happening.

One of the officers came up and addressed Mr. Jackson. He said, "Excuse me, sir? Do you have an ID?"

"Hmmm?"

"Do you have an ID?"

The second time he said it, he kind of grabbed Mr. Jackson's arm, like he wasn't messing around. I stepped up and politely tried to get between them and explain the situation. I told them that I was personal security for this man, a high-profile dignitary, and he was in this disguise in order to remain anonymous. "This man is very famous," I said. "And it would really be best for everyone if we could keep his identity a secret and quietly exit the store."

The cop said, "Famous? Who the hell is he?"

By now a crowd was starting to form. The manager had come over. The other police officer was stepping in behind me. I was reluctant to identify Mr. Jackson, but I felt the only way we were going to get out of there was to be straight with these officers and get them on our side. So I leaned in to the guy and I whispered, "It's Michael Jackson."

"Who?"

"Michael Jackson."

"Get the fuck outta here."

I said, "Look, we'll just leave."

Then this cop turned to his partner and he said—and he said it real loud and arrogant, like I was some jerk—"Hey, this guy says he's doing a security detail and that guy in the bandages over there is Michael Jackson."

Out of the corner of my eye I saw the first camera flash pop. *Shit.* Then I heard this murmur of voices start to ripple through the crowd: "Michael Jackson?" "Michael Jackson?!" *"Michael Jackson?!"*

I grabbed him and said, "Mr. Jackson, this way." I ushered him quickly toward the back of the store, moving his body through the aisles, left, right, as fast as I could hustle him. I looked around, found the door to the stockroom, and rushed him in there. The manager followed us back, and I asked him, "Is there another way out of here?" He pointed me to a back door that led to a little service hallway and out to the parking lot. I radioed Javon and told him to get the truck and meet us outside.

You could hear the crowd outside. It was intense. I was really worked up, agitated. Like an idiot, the store manager had even gone back out and confirmed that it was Michael Jackson. Now he was all excited about it. Now he was like, "Hey, Michael Jackson is in my store!" It was turning into a mob scene. We could hear people screaming, "*Mi-chael! Mi-chael! Mi-chael!*" The two officers were stuck out front doing crowd control, dealing with what they'd started.

I stayed in the back with Mr. Jackson. I was on full alert. My pulse racing. Looking this way and that. Watching the door, listening to this crowd, trying to figure out what was going to happen next. Was there going to be more trouble with the police? The paparazzi? Meanwhile, Mr. Jackson was just chilling, like this was any other day. The crazed mob of people screaming his name outside the door? Like it wasn't even happening. He was just wandering through the stockroom shelves, casual as you please, checking out these little magic tricks. Dude was still shopping. He pulled this one thing down and brought it over to me and said, "Bill, can you find out how much these are?"

I wanted to say to him, "Really? We've got a couple hundred people breathing down on us, and you want me to stop and do a price check on some Houdini tricks?"

But he just shrugged the whole thing off. "This is what happens all the time," he said. "They should have left us alone. People should mind their own business."

Finally, Javon radioed me to say that he'd pulled the car around. The two cops came back into the storeroom to escort us out. Just as we started to leave, one of the officers came over to me and he leaned in and said, "Hey, one more thing."

"Yes?"

"Do you think maybe he'd mind signing an autograph?"

I turned to Mr. Jackson. "Sir, the officers would like to know if you could sign an autograph."

"Oh, sure," he said. "Just give me a pen."

The officers gave him their report pads and he signed each one and then we left. We just bounced. He didn't even buy anything.

It was times like that we'd be left scratching our heads. But it wasn't our place to say anything. I felt like the only person who really understood Michael Jackson was Grace, the nanny. The way they'd go at it with each other, you'd think they were a couple sometimes, or brother and sister. But Grace had some health issues. Nothing too terribly serious, from what I understood, but she would leave from time to time. After those first couple months, it got to the point where she was not around as much. She'd be gone for a week and be back in town for a day or two and then be gone again. That was happening with more frequency.

Javon: When he had Neverland, he had dozens of people to run the place. Now, except for the teacher and Ms. Grace, on and off, all his domestic work had basically fallen to me and Bill. We were personal assistants, couriers, handymen. We did the grocery shopping, took the dog to the vet, babysat the kids. Bill was even holding the family's medical insurance cards and their passports.

I was just hired to be a foot soldier, you know? Drive the car and watch the gate and go home. But this was something else. To say we had no idea what we'd gotten ourselves into would be a huge understatement. There were days I'd walk around thinking, How the hell did I end up here?

Bill: With Feldman gone and Grace away, I felt this huge sense of added responsibility. Some days, I really couldn't believe that this was *the* Michael Jackson and I'd basically become his point man. Everything started coming to me. I was getting documents, faxes, emails. Someone had to get these documents to him. Michael Jackson doesn't exactly come down to the gate to sign for packages.

I never opened his mail, but a lot of this information was faxed, so I could see it plain as day. There were a lot of numbers floating around. A lot of numbers. I'm talking about $35 million here, $100 million there. I saw the words "a billion dollars" on one of these documents.

Whenever payroll was late, Raymone would always give us these vague excuses. "Mr. Jackson's money is tied up." Now, being put in this point-man position, I was starting to see things. I knew I was only looking at a couple of pieces of the puzzle, but I was starting to get a glimpse at the bigger picture of his finances.

That June, the first iPhones came out. He wanted one. Javon went and stood in line for two and a half hours to get it. When I first brought him the phone, he came back to me and told me it didn't work. He said, "It doesn't do anything."

I said, "Sir, you have to get it set up, create an account."

He said, "I thought you already did that."

"No, sir."

"Oh. Can you?"

I had all his personal information, so I said sure. I first tried to set it up in his name, but after running Michael Jackson's Social Security number, AT&T wanted a $1,500 deposit. Just to turn on a cell phone. That's how bad his credit was. I went ahead and set up the account in my name. Then he wanted an iPhone for his mom, so he could send her pictures of the kids. I set up his mother's cell phone in my name too.

But it was strange. Even as I was doing that, I still never thought of him as being broke. The King of Pop, as a business, was still a thriving concern. Between the publishing rights that he owned, his album sales, he never stopped earning millions. It was a question of what was being done with it. He spent lavishly. Trips to FAO Schwarz and buying bookstores. The tabloids always focused on those things, like he was toy-shopping his way into bankruptcy. But to be honest, the money I watched him spend on those shopping trips was nothing. It was nickels and dimes compared to the figures I was seeing in these documents. There was a ton of money changing hands all the time. Lawsuits, creditors, bank loans, attorney's fees. Millions of dollars would come in and go right back out.

Javon: The lawsuits were constant. It seemed like a new one was filed against him every week. I can't even tell you how many times we'd be on shift, standing out at the front gate, and somebody would come up with one of those envelopes, trying to serve him papers.

One time, I was walking the dog, and this gentleman was parked outside. We thought he was a fan or something. I circled the block with Kenya, and right as I opened the gate to go back in, he came up and said, "Is this the Jackson residence?"

I said, "I don't know what you're talking about."

He said, "Take this."

He tried to hand me these papers. I jumped back. "I'm not taking nothing," I said.

He threw it at my feet and said, "You've been served. Make sure he gets it."

I just left it on the ground. You've got to put that envelope in somebody's hand. Doesn't count as long as it doesn't touch you. People would come up and drop these things through the gate, onto the driveway, and we wouldn't go near it. We'd just go get the water hose, wash it right back out into the street.

I'll never forget this other time, this one lady. The gate was open because we were loading some stuff into the house, and she walked right up the driveway, waving this envelope, trying to hand it to me. "You've been served," she said.

I didn't touch it. I said, "Ma'am, you need to get off this property. I ain't taking nothing from you."

This woman was pissed. She started screaming, "You better fucking take them, 'cause you're gonna wind up in line to get paid just like everybody else! He's not going to pay you, neither!"

I said, "Lady, what are you talking about?"

Her face got all twisted up. There was just this crazy anger in her voice. "*Tell him to pay his fucking bills! He's not gonna fucking pay you guys like he hasn't fucking paid us! Just you fucking watch!*"

Bill: I'd hear Raymone and Greg Cross bickering back and forth with Mr. Jackson on the speakerphone about business. Oftentimes they would call me and I would hold the speakerphone toward Mr. Jackson in the backseat. He would only put it to his ear and talk if the conversation turned to sensitive information. This one conversation, from what I could tell, Raymone was trying to get him to take out a loan with this one bank, and Greg Cross was advocating for a different one. They each were giving their reasons why. Then it turned into a screaming match.

That was not the beginning of Raymone and Greg disagreeing about Mr. Jackson's affairs. That was going on when I got there. The two of them were always at odds. Late that June, we were at the house, and I was asked to set up a conference call for the three of them. I arranged the call on my phone, got Raymone and Greg on the line, put them on hold, and then went around to the back of the house where Mr. Jackson was waiting for the call. I knocked on the glass door to the kitchen area. He was sitting at the breakfast counter, this huge marble countertop that could sit fifteen people. I handed him my phone and walked back to the security trailer.

About half an hour later, I heard this crash. Plate glass shattering. Loud. I jumped up and ran around the corner to the kitchen and I saw Mr. Jackson. He was sitting in the same chair as before, and the glass door was smashed in a million little pieces all over the ground. My phone was lying in the middle of it, cracked. I asked him if everything was okay. He just quietly looked up at me with this blank expression on his face. Then he looked down at the glass and he sort of sighed and said, "I'm sorry, Bill. You're going to need a new phone."

I asked him again if he was okay. He didn't really answer. He'd buried his head in his hands, kind of exasperated. "They're all devils," he said. "I should call my father and tell him to come kick their asses."

I told him I'd get it cleaned up. We had a new door installed a couple of days later and that was pretty much it. We didn't discuss it again. That was shortly before we left for Virginia.

It had been discussed for a while that he was going to be taking a trip back east; that's why I'd been sent for the laptop, to look at the pictures of houses in Maryland and Virginia. Now those plans started to crystallize. Raymone called me and said, "The boss wants to take a vacation." The kids were out of school. It was their summer break. Mr. Jackson wanted to take them and get outdoors, get out in the middle of nowhere, where they'd have room to move around. We were going to fly to D.C. and stay at a place called the Goodstone Inn near Middleburg, Virginia. Raymone and Greg were both based in D.C., too. I think they wanted him closer to them, to try and get some of these business issues settled.

Javon: The lease on the Monte Cristo house was up at the end of June. That was in the middle of this trip they were proposing. We knew he hated that house, and he'd been talking nonstop about this huge estate on Durango. So were we coming back to this place? Was he going to move? It never came up. The whole issue of where he was going to be living was just up in the air.

We couldn't get any answers about how long the trip was going to be, either. We needed to plan for our families if we were going to be on the road. I asked Mr. Jackson how long we were going to be gone, and he said, "Just a little while."

"How long is 'a little while'?"

"Oh, it's not going to be that long."

Bill: I'd assumed that Javon and I would both be going. Mr. Jackson spoke as if that was the case, too. But when I saw the itinerary Raymone had set up for us to fly out, I noticed Javon wasn't on it. I asked her about it and she said, "Mr. Jackson will be coming back to Vegas after the trip, and we need Javon to stay with the house."

She said she was going to arrange for a team to look after Mr. Jackson in Middleburg. These were her people, some police officers who'd worked security for Marion Barry, the former mayor of D.C., who was also a client of hers. She told me that like I was supposed to be real impressed by it, like, This is the *personal* security team of D.C. Mayor Marion Barry.

I thought, That's nothing to brag about. We weren't comfortable with any of it. I wanted Javon with me, and he wasn't too cool with being left behind, either. But we went with the flow. Raymone was still the manager, so we had to respect what she told us. We got Mr. Jackson and the kids ready to go. The whole trip felt very thrown together, like it hadn't really been thought out. There was no clear agenda. When we left, all I knew was that we were going to Virginia for a couple of weeks. That was supposed to be a two- maybe three-week adventure. We were gone for five months.

10

By the middle of June 2007, Jackson's children had finished their school year, passed their final exams, and were ready for summer vacation. Their father's time in Las Vegas, however, had not been nearly as productive. The studio work for *Thriller 25* was dragging along with no end in sight, despite the fact that the album's anniversary was just five short months away. Countless attempts to work out a deal to headline on the Strip had also gone nowhere; event promoter Jack Wishna and resort developer Steve Wynn—two of the players responsible for bringing Jackson to Vegas the previous December—had both issued press statements on the futility of trying to reach a deal with the indecisive performer.

In late spring, Raymone Bain had also set up a dinner for Jackson with Randy Phillips, CEO of AEG Live, the live-performance division of the Anschutz Entertainment Group. Phillips wanted to discuss the idea of putting on a series of comeback concerts at AEG's O2 Arena in London. Jackson wasn't interested.

After six months in Las Vegas, Michael Jackson was no closer to resolving the financial and legal problems that had brought him back to the country in the first place. So he chose to deal with them the same way he'd been dealing with everything of late: by leaving.

Bill: The night before we were supposed to take off, Mr. Jackson came to me and said, "Bill, I want you to get me in touch with the pilot."

I said, "Is there a problem, sir?"

"No, I just want to talk to him about what flight path we're taking, what kind of weather he's expecting."

That was another one of those moments I had with him where I was like, Who does this? He wants to discuss flight paths? But I called Raymone, and she had the pilot call me and I put him on the phone with Mr. Jackson. I heard them talking. He was asking all kinds of questions. What altitude we'd be flying at. How long the flight would be. He was asking questions about aviation so detailed it was like he was a pilot himself. Whatever they discussed, I guess it was enough to make Mr. Jackson comfortable, because the next day we left for the airport. It was me and Mr. Jackson plus Grace and the kids and the dog. Since the kids were out of school, the teacher didn't come along.

Javon drove us down to the executive terminal at McCarran. We boarded and got all of our luggage stowed away. It was a small private plane. I don't particularly enjoy flying, but this was a damn nice plane, that's for sure. We were on board, all buckled in, ready to take off. The engines started up, and then, all of a sudden, the power went off and everything shut back down. The captain came over the intercom and said there were some technical issues they had to check out. About forty-five minutes went by. Then Prince ran up the aisle and said, "Bill, Daddy wants to talk to you."

I went to Mr. Jackson. He said, "What is the problem? Why haven't we left yet?"

I went and asked the pilot. He said they had a part that went bad, a fuse or something. They were waiting for someone to bring a replacement. I went back and told Mr. Jackson. He was not happy about that. "No," he said. "Tell him I want another plane. I'm not taking my kids on this plane. If something happened to them, I'd lose everything."

So I went up to the pilot and told him the client wanted a new plane. He told me we couldn't get a new plane until tomorrow. Mr. Jackson said, "Fine, we'll leave tomorrow." So we called Javon, and he came and got us. We spent an extra night in Vegas and went back to the airport the next day.

The next morning, they put us on a different plane and we flew out. This time everything went smooth. The little ones, they were running up and down the aisle like they'd done this a million times. Mr. Jackson was in the back, listening to music and sleeping, his seat all the way back and his feet up. He finally looked relaxed.

As we were landing at Dulles Airport, I looked out the window and saw these five SUVs lined up. When we got off the plane, the security team Raymone had hired was waiting for us. I walked down and introduced myself. I brought the kids and Grace down and put them in a vehicle. Then I brought Mr. Jackson down, escorted him to the vehicle and put him in the backseat. Meanwhile, those other guys were taking care of the luggage.

We were just about ready to go when I saw a stewardess from the plane, waving and yelling like crazy. "You forgot the dog!" I ran back to get Kenya, and as I was bringing her back down, the cars pulled off. They just drove off and left me there. The motorcade got about twenty-five, thirty feet and then it came to a screeching halt. Mr. Jackson leaned out his window and said, "Bill, what are you doing?"

I yelled across the tarmac, "I'm getting the dog, sir."

Then I ran, caught up, hopped in one of the vehicles with Kenya, the whole time thinking, What was that about?

We drove about forty-five minutes from the airport out to the Goodstone Inn, which was made up of several different buildings across this large estate. There was the main house, where Mr. Jackson and the kids were staying. Surrounding it on the property were several smaller houses where Grace and I and the other security would be staying.

When we pulled up in front of Mr. Jackson's house, Raymone and about a dozen people, all the maids and service people, were standing out there in the driveway. They were lined up, standing next to each other as we rolled in. Like a receiving line. Like we were visiting royalty or something. I knew Mr. Jackson wasn't going to like that. He didn't want fanfare. He didn't trust strangers. The cars stopped and I got out of my vehicle and walked up to his. He said exactly what I was thinking. He said, "Bill, who are all these people? Why did Raymone do this?"

"I don't know, sir."

"I don't want all these people here. Get rid of them."

I went and found Raymone and told her, "The boss doesn't want all these people here."

So she went and said something to somebody, and all these folks started disappearing. Mr. Jackson pulled me aside and asked me if I'd brought the countersurveillance kit. He wanted me to check for bugs and hidden cameras. He said he wanted the locks changed on his room and the kids' rooms too.

We'd just arrived, so all the housekeepers were still in the rooms, making the beds. I had to go into the house and tell everyone to clear out. "Everybody has to leave this house right now." I started going through, moving room to room with this device, wearing these headphones. I'm sure these people were looking at me like, This dude's crazy.

Raymone came and found me and said, "Bill, what's goin' on?"

I said, "I have to sweep the house."

She said, "Oh, there's nothing to worry about. There's nothing here."

I said, "Do *you* wanna tell Mr. Jackson that?"

She paused for a minute. "Okay, scan the house."

It took me about an hour, start to finish. Didn't find anything. We finally got the kids settled in their rooms, got him settled into his room, and carried in the luggage. I brought Mr. Jackson's personal belongings upstairs to his bedroom. Once we got up there and we were alone for the first time, he said to me, "Bill, did you see what happened at the airport? I had to tell them to stop the car. They tried to leave you."

It had been bugging me the whole drive out. I wanted to think it was just an accident, but at that point, I was starting to feel his paranoia, where it came from. I was starting to understand better all the animosities and conflicting agendas in his world. Back in Vegas, whatever was going on between Raymone and Greg Cross, I stayed in the wings. I was there to do a job, and that was it. But with the access I had to Mr. Jackson, I couldn't help but be a player in that now. With millions of dollars at stake in all these deals, people could be trying to push me aside to get what they needed. I didn't know if I was getting sucked into his paranoia or what, but the more I thought about that moment, the more it didn't sit right with me. Mr. Jackson recognized it too, and it wasn't good. But he was like, "Don't worry, don't worry. I'll be making some changes soon." Whatever that meant.

Once I got him settled, I asked the other security team where I was going to be staying. They told me they'd be staying in the house right next to Mr. Jackson's, and I was in a place farther down the road. I wasn't feeling that. But I didn't want to make too many waves. I was still surveying the situation. It was late anyway, almost midnight. I went to my room, called Javon and told him what was going on. He was pissed too. He was still camped out on Monte Cristo with no word about if we were going back to that house. Or going back to Vegas, period. It was all up in the air.

Out of nowhere, Mr. Jackson called me and told me that he needed to see a doctor. Like, he wanted to see a doctor that night. He said his wrist had been bothering him since he fell in his studio in Vegas and it was causing him a lot of pain. I didn't know about this fall; he'd never mentioned it before. So I called Raymone and said that Mr. Jackson wanted to see a doctor. She said, "Right now?"

I said, "Yeah, right now."

She said, "I don't think we can find a doctor to come out here this time of night."

I went and told Mr. Jackson this, and he said, "Why can't I just go to the hospital?"

I was like, Wow, he's serious. Raymone talked to her people and found out that the nearest hospital was forty-five minutes away. Mr. Jackson said, "Okay, let's go." So we went. The security team drove us down.

I wouldn't say this hospital was creepy, but it was a quiet-ass country hospital. Middle of the night, a few people in the waiting room. I went in first to talk to the doctor, pulled him to the side and let him know who I was about to bring up in there. He said no problem. I brought Mr. Jackson in, they did some X-rays, he talked to the doctor a little bit. They put one of those Velcro braces on his wrist and gave him a prescription for some pain medication. We were there for maybe an hour and a half. The next morning, I had one of the guys take me into the city, I filled the prescription, and brought it back to Mr. Jackson up at the main house.

This farm was huge. You could see a lot of deer, cows, horses. All you had to do was walk out of your back door. But even with all that room, Raymone's guys still didn't know to give Mr. Jackson his space. They parked their cars right in front of his house. Early in the morning, he and the kids liked to walk outside, enjoy the scenery, but every time they'd walk out of the house, these security dudes would get out of their cars and walk wherever he walked. I would have known to stand back. They didn't. Mr. Jackson called me and said, "Bill, I don't want them parked in front of my house. Tell them to go down the street somewhere."

I went to the guys and said, "Mr. Jackson doesn't think it's necessary for you to park that close to the house. He wants you guys to pull back."

They paid me no mind. They stayed right in the front of the

house. Mr. Jackson called me back. "Bill, didn't I tell you to tell these guys that they don't need to be that close to the house?"

I said, "Those are Raymone's people, sir. They don't listen to me."

I could tell he was pissed about it. I was getting uneasy about those guys, too. We carried wireless cameras, tiny little pinhole cameras, which we used whenever we took Mr. Jackson to a hotel; we'd set them up outside his room so we could monitor the hallways and keep an eye on the hotel staff. Without those guys knowing, I took two cameras and set them up, hidden and tucked away, outside the front and rear entrances to Mr. Jackson's house. That way I could keep an eye on them from my laptop.

In the meantime, Raymone called to tell me they were going to let the lease expire on the Monte Cristo house. She didn't say if we were going back to a different house in Vegas or what. She just told me the house needed to be packed up and everything put into storage. I called Javon, told him he needed to get a crew and start boxing everything up. I was going to leave him to handle that, but then Mr. Jackson came to me and said, "Bill, I want you to go back to Vegas and help Javon to make sure all of my stuff is safe. Then both of you fly back and meet us here."

I was hesitant about leaving. "We don't know these guys," I said, about Raymone's people. "I don't trust them."

He said, "Bill, I've had security all my life. Don't worry, I'll be fine."

"Are you sure?"

"I'll be fine. I need you to go because I need you to do me a favor. It's very important. There's something that I want you to bring back for me. In my bedroom, to the left side is a walk-in closet. Inside the closet there's a small hidden door. Inside there you'll find a silver metal briefcase. I need you to bring me that briefcase."

I stood there a moment, curious, thinking he was going to tell me what was in it. He didn't. I didn't want to pry, but I needed a general idea of what I was going to be carrying. I asked him if it could be checked in at the airport. He said, "Oh no, you have to carry it with you at all times."

The next day, I made the arrangements with Raymone and flew back to Vegas to start packing.

Javon: The house was messed up. A lot of wear and tear. Crayons on the walls. You could tell Blanket had been busy with that. Mr. Jackson's room was cluttered with fan mail, books. There were half-opened boxes everywhere, like they'd never really unpacked.

There wasn't a lot of furniture to deal with; the house was furnished when he got there. But there was a lot of personal stuff from all his shopping trips. The library was the biggest hassle. There were so many damn books. Then there were all the little presents and cards that had been sent in by fans; there were boxes of that stuff. We had a good ten of us packing everything up; pulling up the wood floor in the studio; breaking down the kids' trampoline in the back; unplugging all the equipment he had in the house, all the stuff that he'd bought at The Sharper Image. He loved that store. Gadgets, he loved gadgets.

When I went to pack up the kitchen, I opened up the pantry and that's when I found the Tabasco sauce. A shitload of it. I stepped inside and there were just shelves and shelves of Tabasco sauce. There must have been a few hundred bottles in there, no lie. The green and the red. I couldn't believe it. When I saw it, all I could think about was all the times we'd gone to the movies and forgot the Tabasco sauce, and how me and Bill would be running around like chickens with our heads cut off trying to find some. And he had crates of it in his pantry the whole time. Why would he not just bring it with him?

Bill: I remember Javon calling me from across the house. "Bill! You ain't gonna believe this!"

"What?"

"Just come to the kitchen."

I went over and looked in the pantry, and the whole thing was nothing but hot sauce. You'd see things like that and it just made you stop and wonder.

Once the management company found out that Mr. Jackson wasn't coming back to the house, they were pissed. That night, I got home and got a call from Raymone telling me that we had to have Mr. Jackson's belongings out of the house by 5:00 p.m. the next day or he'd forfeit his fifty-thousand-dollar deposit. She said if we weren't done on time, she'd be sure and tell Mr. Jackson that we were the reason the deposit was lost—like it was our fault this was all down to the wire. I knew we had to get back to that house the next morning and make it happen.

Javon: There's a place in Vegas called All Storage. It's huge. We took the biggest units they had, car-sized units, big enough to put a mobile home in. That's where we put the security trailer, the Bentley and the Rolls-Royce. It took us two days, all day, with a dozen or so guys, but we got it done. All told, we had five units worth of stuff. We were exhausted by the end.

Bill: The silver briefcase, I retrieved that from his closet and kept it with me. It was heavy. I took it home, put it on the table in my living room. All night, I just kept looking at the thing. Mystery briefcase. Like out of the movies or something. I wanted to open it. I was dying to know what was inside. At the same time, I wanted no part of whatever it was. But if I was going to be going through airport security with this thing, crossing state lines, I decided I had to find out. I opened it.

Inside were two Academy Awards. At first, they just looked like generic Oscar statues; I'd never seen one up close. But then I looked more closely at them, and they both had *Gone with the Wind* on them. One was for Best Picture. I looked it up online.

Apparently, these two statues were the most valuable Oscars ever bought at auction; Mr. Jackson paid $1.5 million for them back in 1999. It's in the *Guinness World Records*.

I sat there staring at these two things, like, *Damn*, I got a couple million dollars sitting on my coffee table. I didn't sleep too well with that in my house. My brain kept turning over, wondering, What the hell does he want these for? The only reason I could think of was that they were collateral. The way he talked about the briefcase, he said he *needed* it, like he needed it "just in case." His finances, something wasn't right, and these statues were a hard asset. Why else would you need your *Gone with the Wind* Oscars with you at a horse farm in Virginia? I imagined I'd find out when I got back.

Raymone was supposed to make the arrangements for us to fly back to Virginia, but her office was not returning my calls. All I got was, "She's not here. I'll have her call you right back." Then she'd never call. Two days went by like that. I called Mr. Jackson to tell him everything was wrapped up in Vegas, and we had a few conversations about Raymone's security team. He sounded very concerned. He said, "Every time I'm outside with the kids, I hear them calling Raymone. I can tell that they're reporting everything I do to her. I don't like that. You know I don't like that." He said he felt that they were taking pictures of him. He said, "I don't trust these guys. When are you going to be back here? You're flying back, right?"

I said, "Yes, sir. I'm trying. But Raymone won't return my calls."

He told me to call Greg Cross, but I didn't. I just didn't like the sound in Mr. Jackson's voice, him being so urgent about when I'd get back. I could hear it on the phone, his anxiety about having his kids surrounded by people he didn't trust. When I was with him, if he said, "I need this," boom, I could make it happen. But here I was, stuck in a situation where I could not make things happen. It was frustrating. So I just decided. I went to Javon and said, "You know what? We're gonna do what we gotta do. We're driving, man."

Javon said, "Yo, I'm with you."

We loaded up, hit the road. We took both SUVs, drove about sixteen hours a day. We'd get a motel room in whatever little town we were in, get up at 5:30 the next day and do it again. I never even told Mr. Jackson how we were getting back. I just told him that I would handle it. A day into the drive, I got a call from Raymone, being all apologetic. "Oh, sorry I couldn't get back to you. We've been dealing with some financial matters. Let me give you an itinerary." She started giving me all these details about flights. She didn't know I was already on the road. I was just driving and saying, "Okay. Yeah, yeah, yeah. Sounds good."

I was done. Between the thing at the airport, bringing on all these new people, jerking me around about making plans to get back— I knew that us driving back like this, bringing Mr. Jackson's vehicles, when she found out, it wasn't going to be pretty. But we weren't going to sit back and do nothing. So we got in the vehicles and we drove.

Part of it was our loyalty to Mr. Jackson, certainly. That was a huge motivating factor. But another part of it was that we just weren't going to be treated like that. The safety and well-being of this man and his children, that was our responsibility. We had a professional responsibility, and we took that very seriously. So when she tried to push us aside, I just felt like . . . no. Uh-uh. I'm not going to let that happen. This is not where it ends.

11

Situated an hour west from Washington, D.C., Middleburg, Virginia, has long been a favorite retreat for the wealthy members of the East Coast elite. The rolling hills that surround the tiny village are dotted with idyllic farms and country estates. Its residents still enjoy rarefied sports like fox hunting and steeplechase. Promotional materials for the area proudly declare it "The Nation's Horse and Hunt Capital."

About a ten-minute drive outside of Middleburg sits the Goodstone Inn, where Michael Jackson had decided to spend his summer vacation. A former plantation, the Goodstone is a massive 640-acre estate of open pastures and forested walking trails bordered by a beautiful, winding creek. At the center of the complex is the plantation's former carriage house, which now houses the inn's restaurant and main offices. Radiating out across the property is a handful of historic homes and cottages, beautifully restored and converted into freestanding guest suites. The singer and his children were in the stately, four-bedroom Manor House, tucked away in the north corner of the complex.

For Michael Jackson, the best part of his new retreat was not the luxurious accommodations but the fact that he'd managed to disappear. When he left the Monte Cristo house, local papers reported that he'd moved into a different Vegas home. Other rumors spread that he was maybe somewhere on the East Coast. Random sightings were reported here and there in the D.C. area, but no specifics about his location leaked out. He was completely off the map, which allowed him, finally, to relax and enjoy time with his family.

Bill: We hit Middleburg around eleven-thirty at night. Normally, I wouldn't call Mr. Jackson that late, but I called him and told him that we'd arrived. He said, "You're back? Great. How was your flight?"

I said, "We didn't fly, sir. We drove back, and we brought your vehicles."

"You *drove* back?! Wow. That is so great."

Javon: The next morning, we went over to the main house. We drove up and Raymone's security team was sitting outside in their trucks. When they saw Bill and me, they were clearly not happy. We went into Mr. Jackson's house. He called the kids into the room and said, "Look who's back!"

The kids all ran over and gave me and Bill big hugs, saying, "Welcome back, Javon! We missed you!"

"I missed you guys too!" I said. And I really had. I'd been worried about them.

Bill: We'd brought the kids a lot of their favorite toys, some of the boys' action figures, some of Paris's dolls. So they were excited about that. I had the silver briefcase with me. That was the first order of business I wanted to take care of. All morning, I'd been thinking he was going to be really excited about getting it, but when I handed it to him, he acted like it was nothing. He just put it down, off to the side, like it was no big deal. He didn't even check to see if the contents of the case were inside.

We talked about the trip. I told him how I'd decided to drive when I hadn't heard from Raymone. That set him off. "These guys tell her everything," he said. "I had them take me to the magazine store and they were on the phone telling her my every move."

Now that we were back with Mr. Jackson's vehicles, he suggested that we didn't need Raymone's people anymore. He said, "Tell her they're dismissed."

I didn't want to have that conversation with her. I really didn't. I knew she was going to be furious about my upsetting her arrangement here. So when he asked me to do that, I kind of hesitated. He said, "You want me to tell her?"

"I'd prefer that, sir."

"Okay, I'll tell her."

Javon: We watched as her guys left the house. Those dudes walked off with an attitude; I tried to chat with them, but they wouldn't speak to me. They went down and packed up the house they were staying in and left. Then me and Bill moved over to that house, and we went back to work. Simple as that.

Bill: The Fourth of July celebration was just a few days away. There were fireworks stands on the side of the road, all throughout the county. Mr. Jackson was really excited about buying some, and he sent me out to get a bunch. I went and bought about five-hundred dollars' worth. On the night of the Fourth and for several nights after, we'd see Mr. Jackson and the kids out in the fields after dark, setting off firecrackers and bottle rockets and Roman candles. We'd watch them from our house down the way.

Javon: Most days, they didn't do much. The kids would play outside in these big, open fields, and Mr. Jackson was taking it easy inside. We ate most of our meals in the restaurant, spent our mornings and afternoons patrolling the area, keeping everything straight, running errands or planning details whenever he wanted to go somewhere.

Bill: The people at the Goodstone gave us a list of activities and points of interest in the area, things to do with the kids. There were several Civil War battlefields nearby that offered tours. We weren't too far from Hersheypark, the amusement park in southern Pennsylvania. That was on the list along with a few other things, including a hot-air balloon ride. When I first saw the list, I figured the balloon ride was the last thing in the world that Michael Jackson was going to want to do. Turned out, it was the first thing he picked. He called and said he wanted to take the kids up in the hot-air balloon. I couldn't believe it. I turned to Javon and said, "Hot-air balloon? He knows brothers don't do that, right?"

Javon: Bill let it be known he wasn't going up in any hot-air balloon. I said, "I ain't going up there neither. No way. Nuh-uh." Neither of us wanted to do it, but one of us was supposed to be with Mr. Jackson at all times. So the whole time leading up to the trip we were thinking, Who's it going to be? One of us was going to have to submit.

Bill: We had to leave the house at five-thirty in the morning to get to the launch site by six-thirty. It was a husband-and-wife team operating the balloon ride. Per usual, they didn't know who they were going to be taking. They thought it was just going to be a family of regular tourists. We arrived and they went through the whole drill, telling the kids about how the balloon worked, safety precautions, that sort of thing. There was a little breakfast spread arranged for them before the ride started.

When it came time to take off, the kids were so excited they couldn't get in that balloon fast enough. They ran over and jumped right in with big smiles. Me and Javon sort of shuffled and stood back, and Mr. Jackson said, "Aren't you guys coming?"

I looked at Javon, like, I think Javon's got this one, sir.

Javon said, "Nah, I'm good. I'm good."

There was a bit of an awkward pause. Mr. Jackson said, "What, are you guys afraid?"

I wasn't about to tell the man I was scared of riding in that damn balloon. I said, "Nah, we ain't afraid. It's just . . . you know—"

"It's okay if you're afraid. You can just say so."

"Nah, nah. It's not that. It's just, you know, we just feel like—"

He said, "Okay. Why don't you just stay down here and follow us in the truck? I think we'll be fine."

I said, "I think that's a good idea, sir. We'll keep an eye on you from down here."

So we followed the balloon in the truck. They were pretty high up. It was a nice summer day, not much wind blowing. Still, I was glad I wasn't up there.

When they finally landed, Mr. Jackson came over to me and said, "Bill, the guy who flew the balloon, I think he took a picture."

Sometimes you'd think that he was being overly paranoid about that sort of thing—and sometimes he was—but just as often he'd be proven right. I went over to the guy and said, "Hey, I need to see your phone." He had one of the new iPhones. I went through the photos and, sure enough, this guy had tried to snap a picture on the sly. All he got was the back of Blanket's head, but it was the breach of privacy that mattered to Mr. Jackson. Even just relaxing and trying to have fun on vacation, he couldn't trust anyone. That picture got erased.

Javon: It was one thing to keep Michael Jackson hidden in Las Vegas. The town is practically built for it. Lots of high rollers with personal security, restaurants with private rooms that cater to A-list stars who want total secrecy. It was a very different challenge moving the man around suburban Virginia. He didn't exactly blend. We didn't blend, either.

Bill: One day, he decided he wanted to go to Walmart to do some shopping. It was just me and him; Javon was off with the kids. We went in the store, he had the veil on, dressed in all black. He went in first and I was five feet behind him in plainclothes. There was a security guard at the entrance, an older guy. Mr. Jackson walked in with that veil on, and this guard looked at him as we went by. I heard him say, "Did you see that guy? He's dressed like he's gonna rob the place."

We went inside. Mr. Jackson grabbed a cart and went strolling through the aisles. He was looking at stuff—clothes, DVDs— just shopping like a regular dude. We'd been in there for about twenty minutes when I heard a radio and looked over and saw a cop coming our way. This was soon after the magic-shop incident in Vegas, so I immediately thought to myself, Oh, shit. Here we go again.

The officer came over and approached Mr. Jackson and said something to him. People began to stop and stare. I went over to the cop and tried to intervene, giving him the usual spiel. I'm doing private security for a high-profile dignitary, etc. Same as before, the cop wanted to know who the guy was. I did not want a repeat of the magic store. I did not want to say it was Michael Jackson, but this guy was pressing me for a name, being real persistent. "Who is it?"

I made a snap decision. I said, "It's Prince."

"Who?"

"Prince."

"The guy from *Purple Rain*?"

"Yes, sir."

"Why is he all covered up?"

"He's trying to be incognito."

"Oh. We thought he was here trying to rob the place."

"No, sir. We're just shopping."

So the one cop told the other cop and he told the floor manager, and as word started to circulate, the crowd dispersed. If it was

Michael Jackson, it was a mob scene. If it was Prince, people didn't seem to care. That's just how it was.

When we got back into the car, Mr. Jackson said, "What happened back there?"

I said, "I told them you were Prince."

"Prince?"

"Yeah."

He just laughed and said, "No wonder they left us alone."

Javon: Once a week, the kids got to pick a special place to go, and one of their favorite places was Chuck E. Cheese's. Since Middleburg was in the middle of nowhere, the nearest one was forty-five minutes away in Alexandria, south of D.C. We took the kids there maybe three times. Two of those times, Bill and Mr. Jackson just dropped the kids off with me and Ms. Grace. We stayed at the restaurant while they drove around and went shopping. But this one particular time, we took the kids to Chuck E. Cheese's, and Mr. Jackson wanted to go in too. He wanted to watch them play. I escorted the kids in first. Mr. Jackson came in about ten minutes later with Bill.

The kids were playing, and Mr. Jackson was sitting in the corner with a hat and a black veil over his face. The kids knew that whenever their daddy was in a public place, they couldn't run up to him or approach him; that was against the rules. Can you imagine having to learn to stay away from your own father when he's sitting just across the room? That's what they had to do. It was a precaution, like using their code names. But Paris? She loved her daddy. There was no telling her, "Don't talk to your daddy." She wasn't having it. She was going up to the top of these slides, yelling, "Look, Daddy! Daddy! I'm going down the slide! Look!"

I'd just reminded her not to do that, but she was so excited she was up there doing it anyway. It wasn't really a big deal. There were lots of fathers in there; she could have been yelling at anyone. But a few minutes later, she was playing with this other girl in that big pool of plastic balls they have. All of a sudden, Paris ran over to her dad, gave him a big hug, and pulled his veil down and gave him a kiss on the cheek and then put the veil back and ran back to the play area.

The little girl Paris had been playing with watched this happen. She just stood there, in the middle of all these plastic balls, with this stunned look on her face, staring at this man in the veil. It was like she lost her breath for a minute, like she was too excited to speak. Then she finally got her breath and she pointed and screamed as loud as she could, *"Mommy! It's Michael Jackson! It's Michael Jackson, Mommy! Mommy! Michael Jackson!"*

Bill: The whole room got quiet. All these heads turned to look in our direction. Mr. Jackson shot straight up and walked out the door. He didn't run, just a fast-paced walk, but he was out of there in a hurry. I walked out right behind him. I gestured to Javon to stay with the little ones. When I got outside, Mr. Jackson had gone over to the truck, but he couldn't open it, so he'd sort of crouched down between the cars. I ran over there, and he said, "Bill, open the door."

I couldn't open it, either. Javon had the keys. I was on the driver's side and I saw his head going away from the car and heading toward the street. He ran across the street and right into a Staples. I was nervous, looking around, thinking people were going to start coming after him any minute. But the amazing thing was nobody followed us out.

Javon: Inside the restaurant, people were looking around, and you could hear them talking. "Michael Jackson?" "Did she say Michael Jackson?" "No way. Couldn't be." It didn't cause a scene because no one believed it, because who would believe that Michael Jackson was hanging out at a Chuck E. Cheese's in Alexandria, Virginia, on a Tuesday night? This poor little girl, everyone thought she was making things up, but she was dead sure she'd seen what she'd seen. She kept insisting on it to her mom. Finally, she walked over to Paris and said, "Is Michael Jackson your dad?"

Paris was like, "Yeah, I *wish!*"

She was pretty quick on her toes with that one.

Bill: One afternoon, Mr. Jackson called me and said, "Paris wants to ask you something. Can you come to the house?"

I went over. Paris was sitting there with him, and he nudged her. "Go ahead, ask him."

She said, "Prince has Kenya, but he never lets me play with him. So I'd really, really like it if you could find me a kitten."

A kitten? I thought, Who buys a kitten when they're traveling? But Paris would just look at you with those big green eyes, and you couldn't tell her no. And I couldn't just go buy one, either. Mr. Jackson said it was important to adopt, to help all the unwanted animals out there. So I went back to Javon and said, "Yo, we gotta find a kitten."

We both got online and started searching. We found a pet store in Chantilly, this small town outside D.C.; it was about forty-five minutes away. There was a pet store there that did adoptions. I printed out a list of all the kittens they had, with color photographs of each one. Must have been close to a hundred. I brought it to Paris and said, "Go through this and see which one you like." About an hour later, she called me back and told me she knew which one she wanted: a little golden-brown one with white stripes.

The next morning, I ran some errands, grabbed breakfast, got off to a bit of a late start. When I got to the pet store, they told me, "I'm sorry, sir. That kitten has already been adopted." Someone had picked it out the day before and the website just hadn't been updated.

Paris was already calling me, asking if I had the kitten yet, saying, "Make sure you get lots of toys and lots of food!" She was so excited. Hearing the anticipation in her voice, how happy this was making her, I knew I could not go back there without that kitten. I looked at all the kittens to see if there were any that looked similar to the one she wanted. There weren't. I said to the guy at the store, "Yo, listen. My daughter really, really wants this kitten. I need to know who got this kitten."

He told me he wasn't at liberty to divulge that information. I said, "Maybe you could call them, give them my number." They said all they had was the person's address. I begged them to give it to me, saying I wanted to go and offer this person more money than what they paid. Finally the guy gave me the address. I put it in the GPS, and it was a ways away, close to an hour. What the hell. I was on a mission. I got on the road and went to the person's house.

Finally got there. It was an older man, a single dude. Strange. I explained the situation. He didn't seem particularly attached to this one cat; he'd only had it for a day. I asked him, "What can we do for me to get this cat from you?"

He said, "Well, I guess you could just give me what I paid for it."

"How much did you pay?"

"Twenty-five dollars."

I gave that man three hundred dollars in cash. I used my own money, too. I got that cat, hopped in the truck, and started flying back to the Goodstone Inn. I was at least two hours out. On the way back, my phone started blowing up. Paris was calling me. "Are you close? Are you close? When are you going to be here?" She called me so much that I just stopped answering my phone. I got to the house and pulled up in front. She must have been looking out the window, because the second I pulled up, she ran out with this huge smile on her face and snatched that cat out of my hands and ran back into the house with it.

Then, as I was getting back in the truck, she ran back out of the house yelling, "Bill! Bill!" I stopped and she ran up to the window, climbed up on the doorstep, gave me a kiss on the cheek, and said, "Thank you for bringing me Katie."

If that's all it took to make her happy, it was worth it.

Javon: The biggest surprise Mr. Jackson gave the kids was taking them to D.C. for three days to visit the Smithsonian and the National Zoo. We arranged with the museum and zoo officials to have guided tours in the morning, before they opened. We did the Air and Space museum, the Natural History museum, the Museum of the American Indian, and on the last day we went to the zoo.

Bill: We were escorted through the zoo by security. One of the head zookeepers was guiding the tour. There was a D.C. city council member there too. This had all been arranged through Raymone, with her political connections.

They drove us all around the zoo, to the monkey house, the reptile house. The funny thing was that Mr. Jackson had owned and operated his own zoo. We'd be walking through the tiger exhibit and Mr. Jackson would be talking in depth with the zookeeper about conservation efforts for tigers in the wild, the best ways to handle them in captivity. At one point, the zookeeper asked if we wanted to go and see such-and-such animal, and Mr. Jackson said, "No, I don't need to see that. I've got plenty of those."

Half the time the zookeeper just looked confused, like, Why am I even here? Why don't we just let him run his own tour?

Javon: When we were at the hippopotamus exhibit, Bill was walking a few feet ahead with Mr. Jackson, Prince, and Paris. They'd all seen the hippopotamus and moved on. I was hanging back with Blanket. He was straggling a bit because he was just so amused by this hippopotamus. He thought it was the greatest thing. Prince already had his dog, and Paris had just gotten her kitten, so Blanket thought he should get a pet too. He called out, "Daddy, I want one of those as my pet."

The zookeeper and everybody, they all laughed. But I knew that little guy wasn't joking. If they still lived at Neverland? I'm sure a hippopotamus wouldn't have been entirely out of the question. With all the other crazy things we'd been asked to do, I half-expected Mr. Jackson to say, "Guys, I need you to find Blanket a hippo." Instead, Mr. Jackson just humored him. He said, "We'll have to see about that."

The zookeeper said if Blanket liked the hippo, he could help feed it. They gave him some apples and he tried to throw them in, but he couldn't get them over the fence. I picked him up so he could get high enough to toss one over. After he did that, I put him back down and turned around to follow the others. I didn't take my eyes off him, but half a second and he was climbing up that fence, trying to get up on the railing so he could keep throwing apples in there. He was slipping around and trying to pull himself up. It was about a ten-foot drop down the other side. I had this whole scenario flash through my head. I could see the headlines: Michael Jackson's Son Eaten by Hippo. I grabbed him by the shirt collar, saying, "Get your little ass down here before I lose my job lettin' you get eaten up by a hippopotamus."

Bill: If Blanket had actually fallen in there, we'd have had to shoot that hippopotamus.

Javon: There were some days Mr. Jackson just wanted to take the kids and go for a ride, see the hills and the countryside. We'd get in the car and go for hours. We did end up going by a few of those Civil War battlefields when we were out driving around. Manassas. Bull Run. Whenever we passed one of those historical markers, Mr. Jackson would be in the backseat, educating the kids about it. He'd point and say, "This is where the Union Army did such and such." Or, "That's where over five thousand Confederate soldiers were killed." When it came to history, he knew his stuff. Prince was really into it. He was curious, asked a lot of questions. Paris and Blanket, not so much.

Bill: The little three-week stint that we were supposed to be on vacation? That came and went, and we just stayed. There was no house to go back to in Vegas, no discussions about going somewhere else or moving into a new place. We didn't know what to tell our families about when we were coming home, if we were coming home, nothing. It was sort of like, Okay, we live on a horse farm in Virginia now. This is just what's happening.

We had to buy all our clothes on the road, because we hadn't packed enough. We lived at the Burlington Coat Factory. Him, too. He'd say, "I need more clothes for the kids." He'd give us a set of clothes for each one so we'd know the sizes, and we'd go shopping for them. For himself, all he wanted was pajamas. He's Michael Jackson. He's not wearing anything else if he doesn't have to.

Javon: The errands were the worst part of it. In Vegas, he'd send you out any time he had a whim for something. You didn't get a list. He just sent you out for that one thing he wanted at that moment: an iPhone attachment, a snack, whatever. It wasn't such a big deal, because there were stores and restaurants five minutes away. Here, the closest place with any real stores was Chantilly, and all Chantilly had was one pet store, one Blockbuster, one McDonald's. There were places out there that weren't even on the GPS. Me and Bill, we're not country people. We got lost damn near every time we went somewhere.

One night, Mr. Jackson called and said that he and the kids were watching a movie, and could we find them some movie theater popcorn. He didn't want regular popcorn. He wanted movie theater popcorn. It was almost midnight on a Wednesday in the middle of backwoods Virginia. We called every movie theater in the eastern suburbs of D.C.; they were all closing down for the night. Then we just went through the phone book and started dialing. Finally, we found this country store that sold Jiffy Pop, the kind you hold and shake over the burner on the stove. We raced over there, picked up a bunch of that, popped it in our little kitchen and brought it to them in these large Tupperware bowls.

The next morning, Mr. Jackson said, "Guys, where did you get that popcorn?"

We told him it was Jiffy Pop, and he let out the loudest laugh. He said, "If you couldn't find any real popcorn, it's okay. You could have just told me."

Bill: He was a huge fan of *The Simpsons*. He owned every season that was out on DVD, and that summer, the last week in July, *The Simpsons Movie* came out. He was ecstatic about seeing it. As we were walking through the theater, he noticed this big Simpsons display that was in the lobby to promote the movie. He said, "Ooh Bill, I want that. Get that for me."

Of all the strange requests we got from Mr. Jackson, that one had to be in the top five. This display was huge. It had life-sized figurines of the whole family. Each one was as big as a person, and they were heavy. And where the hell was it supposed to go? We couldn't ship it back home. There wasn't any home to ship it to. Did he want me to assemble this thing in his house at the inn, which we expected to be leaving at any given point? Was he going to take it to the next hotel with him? What would he do with it then? Didn't matter. He wanted it. I called the theater manager. She said she'd take one thousand cash for it.

Javon: It was too big to fit in the back of the SUVs. We had to rent a U-Haul. We loaded it into that, brought it back to his room at the Goodstone. When we showed up? He was like a kid on Christmas morning, all this excitement in his voice. As we were bringing it in, he said, "You guys might think I'm crazy for buying this, but do you have any idea how much this will be worth in twenty years?"

Bill: When we first flew out to Virginia, there was talk of setting up a recording studio at the Goodstone Inn and having will.i.am and some of those guys come in to work on some tracks for *Thriller 25*. That deal was still grinding along. But like all the other talk about deals and projects, it didn't go anywhere. He didn't want to work on any music while he was out there. What he really wanted to be working on, the only thing he seemed excited about, was movies. He wanted to make films.

His dream project was to do this big movie about King Tut. It wasn't going to be a live action film; it was going to be computer-animated. Less like a Pixar movie and more like *Avatar*, made with motion capture and green screens. This was back when that technology was just taking off. He'd always talk about it in the car. He'd say, "I'm going to be doing this animated film about King Tut. All the kids are going to love it." Even back in Vegas he was talking about it. Only now that he was out here he really started focusing on it more and more. That's when Michael Amir started to come around.

Michael Amir Williams was in the Nation of Islam. Mr. Jackson knew him through Feldman. They had met in L.A., during that time he was on his way back from Japan and he bought that used bookstore. Michael Amir was also in film school at the University of Southern California in L.A. He wanted to get into the movies, and he and Mr. Jackson had struck up a relationship around that. While we were in Virginia, Mr. Jackson came to me and told me that Michael Amir was going to come out to help him with his film projects.

Javon: Mr. Jackson took a liking to Michael Amir, and he started coming out more and more. He'd fly in for a few days, they'd work, and then he'd go back to L.A. Mr. Jackson started sending us on errands to buy a bunch of high-end film equipment, laptops with editing software, fifteen-thousand-dollar cameras, this two-thousand-dollar green screen. Mr. Jackson wanted to learn how all of this stuff worked. They had it all set up in his house. I'd walk in and they'd be using the cameras, shooting little films.

There was a film professor from USC who would come and visit too, a Chinese gentleman, one of the teachers in Michael Amir's program. He was supposed to be an expert on a lot of this motion-capture technology. Mr. Jackson flew the both of them out to Virginia to discuss these different projects. They must have come out at least five or six times.

Bill: Michael Amir wasn't the only visitor he had in Virginia. There were two other people who came out to see him, and they were a complete surprise to us. A couple weeks into our stay, he came to me and he told me that a friend was coming to visit.

I asked, "Is this someone that I need to vet?"

He said, "No, no, she's okay."

Over the next couple days, whenever we discussed making arrangements for this person, he only referred to her as "Friend."

Javon: Bill came to me and said that we had to go to the airport and pick somebody up. "Who is it?" I asked.

"A lady named Friend."

"Friend? That's her name?"

"That's all Mr. Jackson told me."

I knew right away that it was an unusual situation. Typically, any time anyone came to visit, Ms. Raymone would plan the itinerary and give us instructions. Mr. Jackson didn't get involved. This time, he was giving us the flight information and telling us what hotel we'd be taking her to and such. It had to mean that no one else was supposed to know about it.

Bill: We drove in and picked her up at Dulles. She had my number and called me from the terminal to tell us where to pick her up. She had an Eastern European accent, maybe German. We pulled in outside the baggage claim, she flagged us down, and we helped put her luggage in the back of the car.

Javon: This woman was drop-dead gorgeous. She had dark, curly hair that sort of hung in her face a bit. Petite, about five foot four. Nice body. Real slender. She barely spoke, though, was very quiet. We introduced ourselves and she didn't say two words. On the way back from the airport, she got on her phone and called Mr. Jackson and said, "I'm here. The guys are driving me to the hotel." That was another sign to me that she was important. He'd only had that new iPhone for a couple weeks. Nobody had that number yet, so the fact that she knew it told me she had to be very close to him.

She was staying at this hotel in Chantilly, a Hampton Inn, about forty-five minutes from where we were in Middleburg. We got her checked in and let Mr. Jackson know. Bill and I were wondering why she was staying in a hotel. Usually, Mr. Jackson had us bring guests to the house, but not this time.

Bill: I did think it was all a little strange. She just stayed at that hotel by herself. She was in town maybe two days before Mr. Jackson went to see her.

I would take him on these little rendezvous. Late at night, after the kids had gone to bed, Javon would stay back to keep an eye on them and I would drive Mr. Jackson to this Hampton Inn. We'd sneak in through the emergency exit. I'd escort him to her room, then wait outside for him to call. The first time we went, he was there for maybe four hours. He never spent the night. He was always back at the house by the time the kids woke up for breakfast. And he never brought this woman around his children.

We went back the next night and a couple more times after

that. One night, I brought a DVD player and helped him hook it up; he said they wanted to watch some movies. She was in town about a week.

Javon: Friend was the first to visit. Flower came second. Just a few days after Friend left, Mr. Jackson came to us again. Same deal. All the travel arrangements were secret, and he never used her real name. She stayed at the Red Fox Inn, which is actually in Middleburg, a little closer to where we were staying.

Friend, she was pretty. She really was. Flower was okay. She had dirty-blond hair and freckles. There was something more exotic about Friend. Flower was more of a normal, around-the-way girl.

Bill: Flower lived overseas too, but she didn't have an accent. Both of them had curly hair. I knew that he liked women with curly hair. There was a fan back at the Vegas house, a woman with curly hair, and he'd always comment on how cute she was. So I figured that was his thing.

I didn't get the impression that he cared for Flower as much as he did for Friend. When Friend came to town, it was a big deal. He sent us out to go and buy nice presents; I had something engraved for her at Tiffany's. They would hold hands, sit very close together in the car, hug, kiss. They were definitely more flirtatious, more intimate with each other.

Flower, we never did or planned anything for her. He just went and visited her at the Red Fox Inn. She was more aggressive with him, too. She obviously wanted more from him than he was comfortable giving. I heard her say things like, "Let's take a picture together." And he'd say, "I don't think that would be a good idea." She was pressing him, and he didn't care for it. Flower only came that once, and then we didn't see her again. Friend flew back for another visit just a couple weeks after that.

Javon: When Friend came back, one night Mr. Jackson said he wanted to take her into D.C. He wanted her to see the Lincoln Memorial and some of the sights. So we got the truck ready. It was around midnight. Grace stayed back with the kids, and me and Bill took Mr. Jackson and picked Friend up from her hotel and headed into the city. While we were driving, they were in the back, talking and whispering. The curtain was closed and we had the radio up to give them some privacy.

We parked the car about a block and a half from the Washington Monument. From there, we had to get out and walk. When we pulled up, I turned the radio down to tell Mr. Jackson we'd arrived, and all we heard was smackin' lips behind that curtain. I knew exactly what that sound was. They were making out back there. I didn't want to interrupt them, but I just coughed a bit and said, "Uh, Mr. Jackson? Mr. Jackson, we're here."

"Oh! Okay, great. Let's go."

Bill: Before we got out of the car, Mr. Jackson asked me if I thought it was safe. I looked around. It was late. There weren't many people out. It didn't appear like we'd been followed. So I felt it was okay. He put a scarf on, wrapped it around his head. He was covered up but not to where it looked like he was trying to hide.

We walked up to the Lincoln Memorial. It was dark in the shadows of the trees and they could just stroll without being bothered. They just walked around, talked, took in the sights. Even late at night, the memorials are all lit up. She took some pictures. You could tell that it had been discussed that they weren't going to take pictures of each other, just of the monuments.

After that, Mr. Jackson said he wanted to see the Vietnam Veterans Memorial. We walked over there, and they went up to the wall. They were talking and reading some of the names, and he was saying, "It's a shame, just a shame. This is ridiculous. All of these innocent children dying." He asked if she knew the song "What's

Going On" by Marvin Gaye. She didn't seem familiar with it. He sang her a few bars as they walked along: "*War is not the answer, for only love can conquer hate.*"

From the Vietnam memorial we went back to the car. Mr. Jackson wanted to drive around, see some more of the sights, take her to see the White House. You can't drive directly in front of the White House anymore, but we drove around the side, looked at the gate where you go in, circled around Lafayette Park, and just took them around that whole area.

It was really late by that point. Mr. Jackson was ready to go home. We were about to head back toward the highway, when all of a sudden, we heard a siren and saw all of these flashing blue lights behind us. Javon moved to the side, hoping the car would pass, but then it pulled in behind us. Then another car coming toward us in traffic pulled over and blocked us from the front.

I looked in the rearview mirror, and I saw a guy getting out of the car. He had on tactical gear: the boots, automatic weapon, bulletproof vest. Another guy posted up at the rear of the vehicle and a third guy was standing in front of us at the corner. They'd taken up strategic positions around the car. This wasn't the police. This was the Secret Service. This was some kind of anti-terrorism thing. I didn't know what they could possibly want with us, but I was nervous. Mr. Jackson and Friend were in the back behind the curtain. Javon was sitting in the driver's seat, telling me, "Bill, you gotta handle this. Man, you gotta handle this."

I put the window down. One of the agents came up to my side of the car. I said, "Evening, officer."

He said, "Good evening. The reason we've stopped you is that you got Nevada plates and we found it somewhat suspect that a black SUV with tinted windows and Nevada plates is out here, circling the White House this time of night."

"We're just down here doing some sightseeing."

"Uh-huh. I also ran your plates when I pulled you over. Are you aware of who this car is registered to?"

"Yes, I am."

"Computer's telling me it's registered to . . . Michael Jackson?"

"Yes, sir."

"At Neverland Ranch?"

"Yes, sir."

"Okay, what's that about?"

Javon piped in and said, "We're doing a detail for a high-profile dignitary." But I already knew these guys were having none of that. The agent looked at Javon, looked at me, and said, "Can I see your insurance and registration, please?"

"Yes, sir."

I pulled it out of the glove box and gave it to him. He asked who was behind the curtain. I said, "My client is back there."

"Who is your client?"

I paused. "May I get out of the vehicle, sir?"

"Sure."

I stepped out and explained the whole thing to him, from A to Z, who was in the back, that we were here on vacation. He said, "You're telling me that Michael Jackson is in the back of this car?"

"Yes, sir."

He walked over and talked to the other agent for a minute. I was left there, standing on the side of the road, thinking about all the bad ways this could go, this woman in the backseat who no one on Earth is supposed to know about. I wasn't feeling good about it. Then the agent walked back over, handed me the registration, and nodded for me to get back in the car. The other guy must have said something to him. It looked like they were going to let us leave. I climbed back in the car and, just as I did, he gave me the hand signal to say hold up. "One more thing," he said.

"Yes, sir?"

"Do you think he'd mind giving us an autograph?"

"I'll see." I pulled the curtain back a bit. "Mr. Jackson, these gentlemen would like to know if you'd give them an autograph?"

"Oh, sure," he said. "Just give me a pen."

The agent gave me a pen and pulled off a piece of paper from his pad. Mr. Jackson opened up the curtain and took the paper and pen. This guy was totally starstruck. Mr. Jackson signed the paper and gave it to the guy. Then the other agent ran up, saying, "Whoa, whoa. Can I get one too?" The back window went down. Mr. Jackson said hello to the other guy and signed an autograph for him. They told us thank you and good night, and as they walked away, the second agent turned to the first and said, "Holy shit, man. We just met Michael Jackson. That was better than meeting the president."

12

In the 1980s, as one of the wealthiest entertainers in the world, Michael Jackson spent money extravagantly—because he could. But even as he lavished enormous sums on building his own amusement park and other endeavors, Jackson was famous for watching every penny. He checked over invoices to make sure no one was taking advantage of him, and he fired anyone he felt he couldn't trust. Somewhere along the way, that Michael Jackson ceased to exist. He stopped paying attention, started trusting the wrong people, and his fortune began to disappear.

After the Chandler scandal in 1993, Jackson's income began to shrink, but his outsized expenses did not. In addition to the annual upkeep of Neverland, Jackson continued spending several million dollars a year on chartered planes, antiques, paintings, hotels, and other personal expenses. If extravagant spending had been his only vice, he likely could have afforded it. But the singer also continued to make significant investments in his own career.

To achieve his artistic vision in the short films for "Thriller" and "Bad," Jackson had financed large portions of the projects himself— investments that had paid off in spades. In the 1990s, he continued the practice, sinking tens of millions of dollars into various film and video endeavors. Only now, with his record sales contracting, those investments no longer provided the same return. Various handlers and financial managers began inserting themselves more and more in the singer's affairs, using his money in questionable deals that yielded more legal entanglements than profits. Though Jackson was still worth hundreds of millions of dollars on paper, he quickly found himself in a severe cash crisis.

In 1995, Jackson sold Sony a 50 percent stake in the ATV music catalog for $100 million. In 1998, his debts still growing, Jackson took out a loan from Bank of America for an additional $140 million, putting his stake in what was now the Sony/ATV catalog up as collateral. By 2000, Jackson's line of credit with the bank had been upped to $200 million, and he was also deeply in debt to Sony, which had continued to advance him large sums against his future earnings—earnings that continued to decline.

By the time Jackson's trial started, the payments to service his debt—never mind his living expenses or his legal fees—were costing him over $4 million a month. As the trial dragged on, Jackson missed several of his monthly installments to Bank of America, and the lender sold his loan to Fortress Investment Group, a hedge fund that specialized in distressed assets. By the end of 2005, Jackson was already delinquent on his newly refinanced debt, and Fortress threatened to call the loan, which worried executives at Sony. If the singer defaulted, his share in the Sony/ATV catalog—now worth close to $1 billion, by some estimates—would be put up for auction and sold to the highest bidder, saddling the record label with a potentially unwelcome partner. That crisis was averted, momentarily, the following April. Fortress agreed to restructure the debt in order to allow Jackson to stay afloat. As part of the refinancing, he took out a $23 million mortgage on Neverland.

Even as he scrambled to cover his debt payments, Michael Jackson was still earning millions of dollars a year, mostly through the sales of his lucrative back catalog. But because his record label was one of his primary creditors, the money that Jackson earned was being withheld to cover what he owed to them. That left Jackson's other creditors to go unpaid, setting off a daisy chain of legal actions that further crippled his financial standing. Producer Marc Schaffel, who loaned Jackson millions in cash during their partnership, sued the singer in the fall of 2004, eventually winning a settlement of $900,000. Prescient Capital, a financial group involved in brokering Jackson's refinancing deal with Fortress, had recently sued, claiming it was owed fees from the transaction. Jackson settled with Prescient for $3 million in June 2007, just before leaving Las Vegas.

Other suits followed him to Virginia. Dieter Wiesner, Jackson's manager in the years before the trial, had filed a suit claiming he was owed $30 million for deals he'd arranged while handling the singer's affairs, forcing Jackson to spend days attending depositions at the offices of Venable, his law firm in Washington, D.C. Sheikh Abdullah of Bahrain, meanwhile, was threatening to sue over the $7 million he'd invested in Jackson during his time overseas.

For over a decade, Jackson's creditors and handlers had enabled his excessive spending and his penchant for bad investments. Everyone endeavored to keep the singer propped up so they might continue to profit off him for one more day. But those years of mismanagement had finally brought Jackson to the brink. His billion-dollar financial empire was collapsing, being picked over by scavengers even as it decayed from within. Much to his new security team's distress, Jackson was doing nothing to stop it.

Bill: Back in Vegas, our paychecks were slow in coming. They'd be late by a couple of days, maybe a week. But the minute we got to Virginia? They just stopped. From that day on, our payroll was completely cut off.

For the first couple weeks, it seemed like the normal delay. Then it was three weeks, a month, five weeks, six weeks. We'd call Raymone, and every time it was the same excuses. She's waiting for some deal to close. Mr. Jackson's money is held up right now. She doesn't know how she's going to pay her own staff. And so on.

But to us it felt personal. Other people were being paid. Grace was being paid. The security at Neverland was being paid. I saw a lot of his financial documents moving back and forth, and his lawyers never stopped taking their five-figure retainers or collecting their six-figure fees. I found out later on that Raymone was paying herself something like thirty thousand dollars a month, plus the apartment she had rented for herself back in Vegas.

So there was money for all these other people, just no payroll for Bill and Javon, and here we were working around the clock for Mr. Jackson on the road. And the little bit of back pay that we were owed? It was nothing compared to what these other people were taking from the pile. Javon was a little more hot-tempered than me, quick to get agitated. He'd see these documents with these huge money transfers, and he'd say, "Shit, and we can't get our bread? Our punk-ass money?"

Javon: All we had coming in was our per diem. It was seventy-five dollars a day, and that was supposed to cover the cost of our daily meals on the road. So you know what we'd do? We'd take that and we'd go buy Top Ramen, hot dogs, some sandwich bread. We'd get a bunch of that and live on that, and send the rest of the per diem home. It was all we could do.

Bill: The per diem wasn't enough. By the middle of August, I had my daughter calling me up, saying, "Daddy, the lights got turned off."

I had family and friends who stayed with her at the house whenever I traveled for work; they were taking care of her. But I also had a security system with cameras set up around my house so I could check online to make sure everything was okay. But with the power out, there was no visual. That worried me. There was also no air conditioning, and the temperature in Las Vegas was hitting 115 degrees. I told her, "Okay, baby, I'll take care of it." I called in some favors, did what I had to do.

Javon: My lights got cut off too, right after Bill's. I had my newborn at home. By that point, Raymone had stopped answering our calls. It took me days just to get through to her. When I finally did, she said she could give me a credit card number to get the lights turned on, but there was nothing she could do about payroll. When I went to call the power company to turn the lights back on, the card she gave me was declined. A couple weeks after that, my car was repossessed. When I couldn't make the payments, the bank came and repo'd it right out of my driveway.

Bill: When we drove back from Vegas and displaced Raymone's team, I knew she was going to be pissed off. I got messages from Grace to that effect. She said to me, "Raymone's not happy that you made those other guys leave; those guys took time off from their jobs to do security for the boss."

I told her, "Too bad."

Raymone never said, "Hey, I'm not paying you guys because you made me look stupid." But we thought it was obvious that our pay stopped for that reason.

Javon: In Vegas, Mr. Jackson was always adamant about not reporting his movements to Raymone. Now, in Virginia, he was telling us to ignore her completely. He said, "If there's something I want to tell Raymone, I'll have you call her. Don't answer her calls."

She started trying to manipulate us with scare tactics. She'd call and say, "I'm getting a call from a radio station saying that Mr. Jackson was seen walking around in Chantilly in his pajamas. Why is he wearing pajamas? I need to know where you are so I can respond to this report."

She'd be saying all this, and meanwhile I'd have Mr. Jackson in the car right next to me. He wasn't in pajamas, and we were nowhere near Chantilly. She was just trying to get a reaction, to see where we were. I think she was always afraid that Mr. Jackson was taking business meetings without her.

Bill: Maybe me and Javon didn't rank as high as Raymone, but she treated us like we were an obstacle to her being in control. All these petty games came down to one thing: whoever has Mr. Jackson's ear is the person who controls the money.

So it was obvious to us what she was trying to do. We felt like she was trying to starve us out by not paying us. That was the leverage she had; she could make it so uncomfortable for us that we'd have no choice but to leave. She wasn't even subtle about it. After a couple weeks of giving us her standard excuses, she came right out and said it. I called her about payroll, and she said, "You know, Mr. Jackson's really putting you guys in a terrible situation. He's put himself in so much debt. There's no way in the world I would go this long without being paid. If I was you guys, I would just quit."

To hear her say that? That we should just quit and walk away from him? I took that to mean that she wanted to get her own people back in. I told Mr. Jackson right away. He knew that our pay had been erratic in the past, and he'd always been very apologetic about it, but I don't think he grasped the urgency of the situation, and we were reluctant to press the issue directly with him. Celebrities? They don't sit down with calculators and go over time sheets. That's what managers and accountants are for. You don't talk money directly with the client. In a healthy organization, everything should have been handled between us and Raymone. Clearly that wasn't working, and I felt that Mr. Jackson needed to know. One day, I was driving and I turned the radio down and said, "Sir, do you mind if I tell you something?"

"Sure, Bill. What is it?"

"We spoke to Raymone about when she thought we'd be getting paid, and she told us that you got yourself in some financial mess, and if she was in our position, she would just quit."

He got *real* nervous. He said, "Bill, don't do that. You can't do that." He said it with a sense of anxiety, like he thought we were actually thinking of leaving. He said, "You guys just hang in there. I'll make sure you get paid." It was quiet in the car for a few minutes, and then he started up again. "How *dare* she?! How *dare* she tell you to leave me and my kids?!" I watched him in the rearview mirror, shaking his head. He was livid.

That wasn't the end of it. I'd receive emails and FedEx packages for him. A lot of this stuff, I didn't look too deep into what it was. Whatever stuck out on that first page, I might scan it to see who it was from, so I could inform him of what it was. I'd see packages from Raymone on the regular, and while we were in Virginia, I got this one document from her, a loan application. It was for something like $300 million. She'd sent it to me to have Mr. Jackson sign off on it. She called me and said, "If you can get him to sign this, I can get you guys paid."

When it came to things that required Mr. Jackson's approval, he'd sign his name to whatever was put in front of him. His lawyers would say, "Mr. Jackson, this needs to be executed to do such-and-such for so-and-so." He'd sign it. Didn't matter what it was. It was rare that he asked who it was for or what it was about. I never once heard him say, "No, that's wrong. I want to handle it this other way." He'd just sign his name wherever he was directed. He wanted whatever they put in front of him to go away.

Out in Middleburg, nobody had access to him except me. I started to feel like Raymone was using our back pay as leverage to get me to try and influence Mr. Jackson's business decisions in her favor. She and Greg Cross were still having the same loan argument they'd been having with Mr. Jackson at the Vegas house. I started getting documents from both of them, applications from different banks. Greg would send me something, and Raymone would call and tell me, "Don't let him sign that, make sure he signs mine."

At the same time, Greg Cross was calling me, saying, "Whatever Raymone sends, don't have him sign it. I need to look over it first." Greg didn't have direct control over our pay, but he would always say, "I'm trying to get you guys paid."

As I understood it, this loan package was something necessary to resolve Mr. Jackson's financial problems, and whichever one of them got him to sign their package was going to control the flow of these funds, millions of dollars.

This dragged on for weeks. In the middle of August, I got an email from Raymone saying that Mr. Jackson had authorized a $25,000 bonus for both me and Javon to make up for our troubles, and we'd get it as soon as "several major transactions" were finalized. It felt like a bribe. Here's me and Javon, living on Top Ramen and hot dogs, and she's all over me, saying, "Get him to sign this and everyone gets paid, and you get a $25,000 bonus."

Javon: One day, Greg and Ms. Raymone would be arguing with Bill, then the next they'd be trying to butter him up. I stayed out of it. I was always raised to keep my mouth shut. Bill had to tolerate the bickering, but he's not the type of guy to let you play with his integrity. He stayed out of it as much as he could too. These documents from Greg and Raymone? Bill would just take them and give them to Mr. Jackson with a sticky note on the front: This one's from Ms. Raymone, and this one's from Greg Cross. He didn't try and influence the boss to sign one or the other. We always took the position that Mr. Jackson was a grown man. Let him decide which one to sign.

Bill: This issue of the loan kept dragging on, and it finally came to the point where I had to reach out to somebody to ask, "What's going on? What am I supposed to do?" I talked to Grace. She agreed that I didn't need to be in the middle of it. That's when I was introduced to Peter Lopez.

Peter Lopez, he and Mr. Jackson went back some time. Lopez was a big-time attorney in the music business, married to actress Catherine Bach, who was Daisy in *The Dukes of Hazzard*. He was friends with Arnold Schwarzenegger, who appointed him to the California State Athletic Commission. Mr. Lopez was another one of these attorneys handling various parts of Mr. Jackson's business. They would talk from time to time, but their relationship was more like a friendship than an attorney-client relationship. Their conversations were very personal, a lot of "How's the kids? How's the family?"

I knew Mr. Lopez was someone Mr. Jackson trusted, so I reached out to him and told him about the situation. Talking to him, I got the impression that this was not the first time something like this had happened in Mr. Jackson's world. He said, "Bill, I know exactly what you're going through. The best thing to do is to talk to Michael."

But I'd talked to him already. We'd hinted at the problem to Mr. Jackson and nothing had been done.

Javon: He started to see that our morale was down. We were driving one day and he said, "Guys, is there anything you want to tell me? You don't seem like yourselves right now."

We opened up to him completely. We said, "Mr. Jackson, we've got bills stacking up. We're loyal to you, we're here for you, but this is taking a toll on our families back home."

He said, "What? You guys *still* haven't been paid?!"

"No, sir."

"But I told Raymone to pay you. I told her! Bill, would you please get Raymone on the phone?"

He called her right there in front of us, put her on the speakerphone. She answered, and he said, "Raymone, my guys' morale is down. What's going on with their paychecks? When are you going to pay these guys?"

He really tore into her. She started getting all flustered, stammering her way through the same old excuses. "I'll take care of it. We're just waiting for some things to come through. I'll take care of it."

He started shouting over her. "Raymone . . . Raymone . . . *Raymone!* You have to pay these guys. These guys are protecting me and my family. Without me, this machine doesn't run."

She said, "I'm gonna pay 'em. I'm gonna pay 'em this week."

"When this week? I have the guys right here, Raymone. They're on speakerphone. When this week?"

This was on a Tuesday. She said, "I'll pay 'em Thursday."

Thursday came and no pay. We were like, *Wow.* Are you kidding me? That's when we knew that Mr. Jackson really had no control over his own money. He was giving her direct orders and she was blowing him off. He'd apologize for it all the time. He'd say, "Guys, you know it's not my fault."

"Yes, Mr. Jackson. We know."

"I told her to pay you. She says she's going to pay you real soon. But you know it's not my fault, right?"

Bill: He really meant it, that it wasn't his fault. But on the flip side, I don't think he understood the depth of the problem, what happens when people like us don't get paid, the lights getting turned off, the phone getting turned off. He didn't understand that.

Javon: You can tell when somebody's bullshitting you and when they're being sincere, and he was being sincere in that it really was out of his control. But we were still upset. We wanted to grab him and say, "But it *could be* in your control. Why don't you *take* control? Why aren't you in charge of your own people?"

Bill: At one point, he said to me, "It's done. They're closing a big deal, and you guys are getting paid this week." That deal came and went. No paycheck. He called me and said, "Bill, I'm sorry. You guys would have gotten paid, but there's something about my balance with Greg's firm was bigger than I thought it was, so it applied all that money to the bill."

I thought, What the fuck? The lawyers work for you. How does that money not come to you first for you to make the decision about how you want to use those funds? Greg did a job and he expected to be paid. I understood that. But we were in the same position, and we were flat broke.

Michael Jackson was a billion-dollar enterprise, running 24/7, and there was nobody in charge. There was no organization, no actual company, just different people in different pockets all jockeying for different agendas. He didn't even have an office. His office was wherever he stood at. His business phone was whatever phone you put in his hand. Didn't have an email address. Most of his correspondence would go to Raymone. People would send her stuff and she'd overnight it to me wherever we were. Fans who knew who I was would even send mail to my house.

Mr. Jackson thought that Raymone was running an official office for his company in D.C. One day when I had to go and pick up a package from her and I pulled up in front of her address. It was a house. She was running his business out of her house. I heard him talking one day about how Raymone managed his office for him. I said, "Sir, Raymone doesn't have an office."

"Yes, she does. She runs my office in D.C."

"No, Mr. Jackson. She lives in D.C. She works out of her house."

"You mean I don't have an office?"

Not only did he not have an office, he didn't *know* that he didn't have an office. That's how disengaged he was from his own affairs.

Greg and Raymone were the two people that I had the most interaction with, but there were lots of other people: lawyers, accountants, flunkies, assistants. Some of these people had the authority to write and sign checks. There were people out there entering into agreements and signing contracts on his behalf. But who reported to whom, who was accountable for what, it was never clear. It never made any sense.

Part of it, I think, was misplaced trust. He trusted the wrong people, and he wanted to believe in them and they took advantage of him. But part of it was apathy. He was so beaten up by that point. He wanted to be with his kids, do his creative projects, and beyond that, he'd checked out of a lot of it. I'd been handling his correspondence for months at that point. Nothing went to him that didn't go through me. So I know for a fact he wasn't getting any monthly statements or financial reports or anything like that. He didn't have a checkbook. He wasn't sitting down with his accountants on any regular basis, keeping tabs on what was being done.

He'd been so rich his whole life that I don't think he really grasped the idea that he could go broke. He just thought there would always be more. He always had cash on him. He had hundreds of thousands of dollars stashed away in that house in Vegas, in little hiding spots, and I knew he had some of that cash with him in Virginia. To him, that was real money, money he could put his hands on to get whatever he needed right then. And as long as he had that, it was like he didn't think about the rest of it, all his investments and publishing rights, none of it. And I got the impression that his handlers knew that, that if they kept a couple hundred grand in easy reach for him, he would never pay too much mind to what was going on with the rest. And he didn't.

I was driving him in D.C. one day, and he was on the phone with Peter Lopez. I could hear parts of their conversation, and I heard Mr. Jackson say, "Peter, I don't know where my money is. Or how much money I have. Can you help me?"

The fact that those words could even come out of his mouth was terrifying to me. And by ignoring his financial problems and trusting others to handle them, he'd created all sorts of legal problems for himself, too. Michael Jackson was like flypaper for lawsuits. At any given time, there were hundreds of lawsuits pending against him, literally. Some of them were frivolous. Paternity suits from stalkers, that sort of thing. But a lot of these suits were serious, multimillion-dollar claims. With his business coming apart and nobody in charge, people weren't getting paid. Deals were being reneged on.

There was a whole cast of characters. Former managers and associates who claimed they were part of this or that and they hadn't been paid or they were owed a piece of something. People who'd worked on his albums and music videos, claiming they weren't getting their royalty payments. It was one problem rolling over into the next. I'd get these legal documents FedExed to me for his signature, so I saw how much money was going out the door. He'd settle for a quarter million dollars, half a million dollars, whatever it took. People usually sue when they think they can get something. And everybody knew that if you sued Michael Jackson, you'd get a settlement. He'd challenge the frivolous ones, like the paternity nonsense. He'd get those thrown out. But if you had any kind of claim that could justify going to trial? He'd just pay you to go away, because after what he went through in 2005, he was never going to set foot in a courtroom again.

Javon: While we were in Virginia, we took him to depositions at Greg Cross's office in D.C. We'd done several of them back in Vegas, and there were a couple he had to do here. He dreaded going.

These depositions were all-day marathons. They'd put him in the chair, and the opposing attorneys would grill him for hours. There'd be a team of Mr. Jackson's guys in that room too, all of them billing him at hundreds of dollars an hour for hours on end. Usually they'd provide lunch at these things, because they kept you there for so long. They'd take a conference room and lay out a bunch of sandwiches and snacks and fruit. At one point, Greg came out and offered us some food, and me and Bill went up to this room to grab something to eat. We were going through, making our sandwiches and talking. "Man, how long is this going to be? I'm ready to get the hell up out of here." Then we heard a sound from the back of the room. We looked over and it was Mr. Jackson. He said, "Hey, guys."

"Oh, hey! Mr. Jackson!"

I was caught off guard. They'd just left him in this room, sitting by himself, like a little kid off in the corner. It was like he was on a time-out. I swear that's exactly how it looked, like his lawyers had put him in the corner for a time-out. Then, once lunch was over, they took him back to the conference room, put him back in the chair, and grilled him some more.

When we got in the car to go home, he just went off. He vented to us the whole way home. "I'm so tired of all of this shit. I'm tired of it. I'm tired of giving depositions. These guys are asking me the same stupid questions over and over again. I just wanna go home to my kids."

Bill: You could tell when it got to be too much for him. The insomnia would get worse. In Middleburg, we did patrols around the property at night. There were no streetlights, just the light from the houses. His house and our house were pretty much the only ones in the immediate area, so it was usually pitch black. This one particular night, I was on a patrol around two-thirty in the morning. It was practically a full moon, so there was more light than usual. I was driving the property, and I saw someone walking. Couldn't tell who at first. He was wearing a green jacket with a hoodie and pajamas underneath. I was thinking maybe a neighbor, someone who lived in the area. I drove along behind him for a minute, and then I put on the portable spotlight on him. Didn't even turn around. He just kept walking with his hands in his pockets. So I pulled up alongside him and said, "Hello?"

The guy looked up from under his hoodie, and I saw it was the boss. Took me by surprise. I said, "Hey. Mr. Jackson? Everything okay?"

"Yes, I'm fine."

I said, "You want a ride?"

"No. I'm okay," he said. "This is good for me."

I wasn't sure what to do. I was surprised, certainly. But he was acting normal, so I figured he was fine. I said, "Okay, sir. Good night."

I turned off the light and dropped back and watched him, just kept an eye on him until he got back to the house.

Javon: He always used to say to us, "You guys don't know how lucky you are." Or, "You guys don't know how good you have it." In the beginning, we'd hear him say that and we'd think, Huh? You're Michael Jackson. But over time we saw what he was talking about.

We were driving outside Middleburg one day, and the kids saw a playground. They got real excited. They wanted to go play, and they begged their daddy to stop the car and come play with them. We said we didn't think it was secure; there were a few kids and parents in the area, and we didn't have masks for the kids and someone might snap a picture. Mr. Jackson told us to go ahead. He said he'd wait in the car so his kids could play and no one would recognize them. So we took the children and they went and ran and played in the park. Mr. Jackson stayed in the backseat, watching them from inside the car.

Bill: When you're a father and you see that? When you think about having to watch your kids from behind tinted windows while they go and play with strangers? I wouldn't trade what I have with my daughter for that. I wouldn't have switched places with him for all the money in the world.

Javon: We were Michael Jackson's personal security team. We're supposed to be these big, macho bruisers, right? Just be tough. Don't
show your emotions and this and that, but it was hard sometimes. It was hard not to feel the pain he was going through. If I
never knew him, and I heard somebody on the radio saying that
Michael Jackson was complaining about how he couldn't go to a
playground with his kids, I probably wouldn't care. I'd probably
think he just needed to get over himself. But it was different seeing it firsthand and knowing what he was talking about.

It would always be the littlest things, too, that you'd notice
about his life. We were in D.C. one day and we had some time
to kill between appointments, so he asked us to drive him around
to look at the city. We went out to Georgetown and wound up
stopped at a red light in front of this bar, this Irish pub type of
place. It was happy hour, everybody getting off work. Mr. Jackson
was watching the people going in and out of the bar, and he said,
"One day, I'm gonna walk into one of these places and sit down
and say, 'Bartender, give me a beer!' One day, I'm just gonna do
it. I'm just gonna walk in and do it."

He said it the same way a twelve-year-old kid would talk
about growing up to be an astronaut. Like it was this impossible
dream and someday he was going to get there. After he said it, Bill
and I were like, "It's no problem, sir. We'll grab a beer with you. No
reason you can't. Your money says 'In God We Trust' just like everybody else's. You want to loosen up, let's go. We've got your back."

We were encouraging him. But he was too scared to go in.
He said, "Those people in there won't let me."

Bill: He didn't trust strangers. Whenever he got caught in a crowd,
he'd be real frantic and nervous. We were at a shopping mall in
Virginia one afternoon. Javon had gone to get the car. I was waiting with Mr. Jackson by the exit with mall security. Somebody had
recognized him and a small crowd had formed. He was signing a

few autographs, waving to folks. It was a friendly situation, not a mob or anything. As Javon pulled up and opened the door for Mr. Jackson, this guy from the back of the crowd yelled out, "Fuckin' child molester!"

I heard it, plain as day. I looked at Javon; he'd heard it too. We were just praying that Mr. Jackson had missed it. But after we got in the car and drove for a bit, he leaned forward and said, "Guys, did you hear somebody say something back there?"

"No, sir," I said. "I didn't hear anything. You hear anything, Javon?"

Javon shook his head. "No, sir."

Mr. Jackson said, "I thought I heard someone say something very mean. I could have sworn. You guys aren't lying to me, are you?"

"No, sir."

We didn't want to lie to him, but we knew what would happen if we confirmed it. Hearing someone call him a child molester? That would completely shut him down. He'd close the door and vanish into his room for at least a week, and we didn't want that to happen.

We drove on with nobody saying anything for the next ten, fifteen minutes, and then out of the backseat he said, "I would *never* hurt a child. I would slit my wrists before I ever did anything to hurt a child."

For me, I never believed any of that about him. As a lifelong fan of the Jackson 5 and of him, I just didn't believe it. Growing up, I related to that family. His siblings, his father, were very similar to what my family was. They just seemed like the typical black family that was making it out of the ghetto, which is what we were all trying to do back then. I think a lot of black families felt that way about the Jacksons. We identified with them.

That started to change a little after *Thriller*. You still loved Michael, but he was on a level now where you couldn't identify with him as much. You started to see him doing all these things. Odd things. He's hanging out with Webster. He's hanging out with Brooke Shields. Dude's got a monkey. You knew that he was different, but I never thought he was different in a way that he would do anything to hurt a child. I never believed it the first time. I didn't believe it the second time. But by the time that second accusation and the trial came about? It didn't matter what you believed anymore. In the court of public opinion, it was already decided. He was looked upon as a freak, a weirdo.

Javon: If you were an up-and-coming comedian and you needed some easy material, you just mentioned Mr. Jackson's name and little kids and you'd get the first five rows to laugh, for sure. People didn't realize just how sensitive he was about that sort of thing.

Growing up in South Central, I would have laughed at those jokes same as everyone. I wasn't part of that same generation as Bill, where people had more reverence for the Jacksons. I was more of the hip-hop generation. We loved Mr. Jackson's music, but we only knew him as this eccentric rock star. You loved his songs, but you'd laugh right along when it came to his personal life. But now? When I heard stand-up comedians joking about the boss, it wasn't funny anymore. It made me angry. It was like hearing someone passing jokes about your friend or your mom.

Bill: Javon was quick to get angry, quick to want to lash out. We caught a clip of Katt Williams making fun of Mr. Jackson one time, and Javon started yelling at the TV. He said, "If I ever see Katt Williams, I'm gonna slap the taste out his mouth for talking shit about the boss." And that day at the mall in Virginia, when the guy yelled out "child molester"? The second it happened, Javon was in my ear on the two-way radio. "I can see the guy who said it. I see him. You want me to take him out?"

I had to say, "No, Javon."

He was serious. And it was frustrating. That perception of him that people had was something beyond our control. It's like with Friend and Flower. With anybody else, if you heard stories about a guy sneaking into hotels with hot European models, you wouldn't even ask what that was about. But because it's Michael Jackson, people still want to believe it's something weird. But that's not what I saw. What I saw was that beneath all the eccentric behavior, there was a regular guy desperate to get out and be a regular guy. Once you were around him on a personal level, you realized that all those rumors and allegations, it just wasn't possible. As a father, if I ever thought he'd done anything harmful to a child, I'd have kicked his ass myself.

Javon: Your perspective changed completely once you knew him up close. It was the same with his relationship with his own kids. The question we always get is, "Blanket looks more like him than Prince and Paris. Do you think they're all his?" And when we first started working there, we'd ask ourselves a lot of the same questions. "What's the deal? Are those really his kids?" But once you spent time with them, and you saw the way he was with them, you just stopped thinking about it. Those were his kids. He was their father. They were a family, end of story.

Bill: Every day, all over the world, couples use surrogate mothers, donor eggs, frozen embryos. People go to all different lengths to have families, and nobody questions the legitimacy of those families. Nobody points a finger at those families and says, "Those aren't really your kids." But with Michael Jackson, people questioned his right even to be a parent. But from everything I saw, they were a better, more loving family than a lot of families I've seen. There's really nothing else to say.

On one of the weekends that we took the kids to D.C., we decided to stay overnight at the Four Seasons rather than drive back out to Middleburg. Mr. Jackson called me and said the kids wanted to go in the pool. So I contacted management and they agreed to close the pool for a couple hours so that Mr. Jackson could use it. Following protocol, we did a sweep to make sure the area was secure. There were three hotel security cameras around the pool. We went through and made sure all of them were unplugged and disconnected. Then we escorted Mr. Jackson and the little ones from their room and led them down a back staircase. The kids had their bathing suits, flip-flops, and flotation devices. Grace was with us too.

We got to the pool. Prince and Paris jumped right in; they knew how to swim. Blanket was waiting for Grace to blow up his floaties so he could get in too. While the kids swam, Mr. Jackson was walking around. He was singing, lost in a tune in his head. There was something about him that seemed a little odd. He seemed a little more excited than normal, a little more upbeat. He started out singing low, just humming a little bit. Then he was tapping out a little percussion and singing louder. I looked at Javon. Javon looked at me. We figured he was in his comfort zone and doing his thing. I left to make a pass through the locker room and the exercise room, just to make sure they were still empty and no one had accidentally walked in.

Javon: Everything was fine until all of a sudden Mr. Jackson looked up and saw one of these security cameras. He completely lost his mind. He started yelling. "I told you guys about this! I fucking told you!" It was like something in him snapped. He ran over to this camera and he jumped up and grabbed it and started yanking on it, like he was trying to tear the thing down.

Bill: I heard Grace screaming, "*Bill! Bill!*" and I came running around the corner. Mr. Jackson was literally halfway up the wall, hanging off this camera, jerking it and pulling on it. I ran over toward him, yelling, "Mr. Jackson! It's disconnected! It's not on! It doesn't work!"

"I don't care! I don't care!"

He'd torn the bracket loose and this camera was only hanging by a few wires, and he jumped up one more time and gave it one more snatch and he just ripped the whole thing right out of the wall. Just ripped it out with his bare hands and then took it and hurled it down and smashed it on the floor. He was yelling at it, screaming, "*I hate you! I hate you!*"

I ran over to him. He looked up at me. His eyes were blood-shot red. There was blood on his hands, deep lacerations in his fingers from where these metal wires had cut into him. He started screaming at me. "You guys have to watch for this! You guys have to take care of this! These are my children! I don't want people taking pictures of my children!"

I tried explaining again about the camera being off. Nothing I said mattered. It really freaked me out, the way he was acting. My immediate thought was that maybe he was on something. His demeanor was very different from anything I had ever seen before. This was new to me, and kind of scary.

Javon: Everybody got quiet and shut up. We were speechless. We didn't know what to do, how to respond, how to handle it. He eventually calmed down and decided to stay at the pool. Bill went and brought the first-aid kit down to get some gauze and peroxide and a Band-Aid for his hand. The hotel ended up charging him eight thousand dollars for the camera.

We felt bad at times like that. We actually felt bad a lot of the time. Because it was our job to protect him, but we couldn't protect him from the things that had already happened, the things that had already hurt him.

Bill: There was this one night he called me while we were in Virginia. Earlier in the evening, he'd asked me to bring him a bottle of wine. I'd brought it up to his room, and that was pretty much the last thing I did for him before I turned in. Then, around three in the morning, my phone rang. It was Mr. Jackson's room number on the caller ID. I answered it, thinking there might be some kind of emergency. He said, "Bill, are you asleep? I hope I didn't wake you."

"I'm fine, sir. Is everything okay?"

He said he was just calling to talk, so we talked. About his kids, about Raymone. He said, "Sometimes I just get sick of it."

"What's that, sir?"

"All of it," he said. He sounded like he was trying not to cry, like he was choking back tears. "Why can't people just leave me alone? I'm not a circus act. I'm not an animal at the zoo. I just want to be left alone. Why can't people understand that?"

It wasn't really a back and forth kind of conversation. He spoke. I listened. A lot of the things he was saying, I didn't really have responses to. I'd never dealt with most of the things he was dealing with, so I wasn't going to sit there on the phone and pretend that I could relate to him on that level. And I knew he wasn't really calling me to get my thoughts and opinions on any of it. He was calling to vent.

"I just want my kids to have a better life than me," he said. "I never want them to go through what I had to go through. How would you guys feel if your kids asked you for something and you had to send someone out to get it? I appreciate what you guys do for my kids, but *I'm* their father. I should be the one doing those things, but I can't just get in the car and go. There are so many things I can't do for them because those people out there won't let me. You have no idea how that feels. You really don't. I just wanna live my life with my kids."

I said, "I understand, sir. You deserve that."

I can still remember standing there in my room, looking at myself in the mirror and not really believing that this was happening, that I was listening to Michael Jackson unburden himself to me on the phone. It was hard for me to hold back my emotions. It was a good thing we were on the phone, otherwise he'd have seen his security having a weak moment.

I was just feeling the weight of everything he was going through. By that point, guarding him had become my life. I wasn't in Virginia because I wanted to be in Virginia. I was there because he was there. If he wanted to go to Maryland tomorrow, we'd go to Maryland tomorrow. I went where he went. His reality had become my reality. And I can't say that it was a pleasant ride, his life. It was not fun. We had fun moments, but it was not fun. It was not joyful. There was a lot of turmoil, a lot of tug of war. The constant anxiety. Never knowing who to trust.

The fact that he was calling his security guard at three in the morning says a lot about it. If he was calling me, then he really had no one else to call. Javon and I felt that, too: the isolation. He and I could at least talk to each other, share our frustrations. But we couldn't talk to our families, to our friends. We had to make excuses about why we weren't getting paid. Everything had to be locked up, kept secret. You carry that stuff around inside you and it just eats at you. So when he was talking about how he was sick of it, I understood where he was coming from. I'd only been living like this for seven, eight months, and it was already wearing me down. He'd been doing it since he was ten years old.

We talked a little while longer. He kept apologizing for having called. He said, "I don't mean to bother you with this, Bill. I'm sorry. I'm really sorry."

"It's okay, sir."

"Thank you. I'm going to go to sleep now. Good night."

13

By the end of August, Michael Jackson's handlers were engaged in a frantic, behind-the-scenes effort to stabilize his finances, and Jackson himself was busy leaving Virginia for New York. Raymone Bain had arranged for the singer to do photo shoots for two different magazines, Italian *Vogue* and *Ebony*, the *Ebony* shoot was to be part of a cover feature to commemorate *Thriller*'s upcoming twenty-fifth anniversary.

For his time in the New York area, Jackson decided to stay at the New Jersey home of his close friends Dominic and Connie Cascio. Dominic first met Michael Jackson in the early 1980s, when the singer was a regular guest at Manhattan's Helmsley Palace Hotel, where Cascio worked as general manager. The two became friends, and soon the singer was a regular visitor at the Cascio home, dropping in whenever he made appearances in the city. He also invited the Cascios and their children out to Neverland for Christmas and other holidays. Frank Cascio, the family's eldest son, grew up to work as Jackson's personal assistant in the late 1990s. The second-oldest, Eddie "Angel" Cascio, encouraged by Jackson to pursue a career in music, had become a record producer; he'd built his own recording studio in the family rec room in the basement.

When Jackson arrived in the fall of 2007, the family added a dance floor to the studio and curtained off a corner of it to serve as the singer's bedroom; Prince, Paris, and Blanket took the guest bedrooms upstairs. Being at the Cascios offered Jackson something he had nowhere else: a window onto a normal life. Over the years, their home had become one of his favorite retreats, one of the few places he could truly be himself.

Bill: Late August, I got a call from Raymone telling me she'd rented a luxury van with a driver to take Mr. Jackson and the kids to New York. Javon and I would follow them up in the SUVs, and the two of us would be staying at a hotel about a mile or so from the Cascios. Grace wasn't with us. She met us later in New Jersey. The teacher met us there too. Summer vacation was over, and it was time to start school again.

Before we left, we had to pack up the house in Virginia. All of this movie equipment he'd bought. At least four- or five-thousand dollars' worth of books. That giant *Simpsons Movie* display. We packed all that up and put it in a storage unit. Michael Jackson had things in storage all over the world. He had stuff in London, stuff in California. He had four airplane hangars in New Jersey full of props from his short films and live shows. There were the units we packed up for him in Vegas, now Virginia. He'd just buy too much stuff. I guarantee you, there are still people with stashes of Michael Jackson's belongings all over the world, because he would just buy stuff here and there and then leave it.

When we got to Jersey, there was no word on how long we were going to be there, if we were headed back to Vegas, nothing. But by that point, it had just become our routine. This is where we're going today. Tomorrow, whatever.

Javon: The Cascios lived in this little town called Franklin Lakes, right off Route 4. Just your typical suburban family house. They were real warm, real nice. We'd met Angel before, in Vegas, but this was our first time meeting the whole family. We brought the kids and Mr. Jackson in, unloaded the little bit of luggage they'd brought.

Mrs. Cascio offered us a meal. We declined. Mr. Jackson said that he'd be fine alone at the house, so we went on to our hotel.

Bill: There was this one night before we left Virginia, late, maybe around two-thirty in the morning, I saw two cars drive up to the house where Grace was staying. It seemed odd, so I jumped into one of the trucks and drove over. By the time I got there, I could see people walking into the house. I called Grace and said, "Grace, what's up?"

She said, "Nothing."

"Everything cool?"

"Everything's fine. Why?"

"I see a couple cars here."

"Oh, I have some friends coming through."

She sounded a little defensive, but I didn't press it. The next morning, Javon and I were eating breakfast in the restaurant, and I saw this tall, white dude in there, eating by himself. I'd never seen him before. He looked out of place. Didn't really look like a guy who'd be on vacation out in horse country. I just made a mental note of it.

Couple weeks later, when we got to New Jersey, Mr. Jackson came to me and said he knew we'd been under a lot of strain lately, and Raymone had suggested bringing on a third team member, this guy named Mike LaPerruque. He used to work as security at Neverland. Mr. Jackson said it wasn't going to be like those other guys in Virginia. He said, "Mike's not coming to take over. He's coming to help you. He used to work for me and he knows how I like things."

I didn't think we needed it, but if it's what Mr. Jackson wanted, okay. I said, "No problem, sir."

When this Mike LaPerruque guy got in, he called me and said he'd like to meet. So I went to go meet him for breakfast, and he walks in and damn if he's not the same tall, out-of-place-lookin' white dude I'd seen hanging around the Goodstone Inn. I didn't tell him that I'd seen him in Virginia, and he didn't mention that he was in Virginia, but I knew it was him.

What I later pieced together after talking to Mr. Jackson was that, unbeknownst to myself and Javon, Raymone had been waging a verbal assault against us since the day we pushed her security guys out. Mr. Jackson said that she was constantly in his ear, telling him that he couldn't trust us, and she had brought Mike LaPerruque out to Virginia that night to meet with Mr. Jackson. She wanted to convince him to get rid of us and bring this guy back on as head of security, overseeing her team of guys. Mr. Jackson said he told her no. But he did think it was a good idea to bring Mike on to have an extra set of hands around.

Once we started working together, I could tell this guy had been told a lot of stuff about Javon and me. He talked as though he was there to fix things. If he was there to fix things, then someone must have told him that things were broken, and again that had to be Raymone. If he was there to spy on us, he wasn't very subtle about it. He would say things like, "You know, managers are so important. They need to know when the client is doing certain things so they can keep it out of the media."

Whatever. I'd tolerate the guy if Mr. Jackson insisted on it, but this whole time, we still hadn't been paid. How Raymone explained hiring a third man when she couldn't pay the first two, how she could pay to fly him out to Virginia while Mr. Jackson's money was "tied up," your guess is as good as mine. In the meantime, Javon and I were still living off our per diem.

Javon: Then the per diem got cut off. Three days after we checked into the hotel in New Jersey, it just stopped coming. We called Raymone and said, "What's going on? How do you expect us to eat?"

She said, "Don't worry about it. If you need anything, just charge it to the room."

But we weren't in some extravagant hotel with room service. It was more like a Marriott Courtyard–type hotel. The only food they had was soup and sandwiches. That's it. That's all we had to eat every day, soup and sandwiches and cold cereal for breakfast.

Without the per diem, we didn't even have petty cash on hand to do our jobs right. We used to take the trucks to get them professionally washed and detailed every week. Didn't have money for that anymore. We started going to those little do-it-yourself car washes where you pump in a bunch of quarters and wash and dry the car yourself. Some weeks, we couldn't even do that. Mr. Jackson and the kids would get in the car and there'd be dirt and food crumbs in the seats. We couldn't get our suits cleaned and pressed, either.

Bill: Tempers were running short. We were tired, frustrated, hungry. I tried to be the Buddha in the situation, tried to keep spirits up and keep calm. To me, having done this longer, it was all part of the business. But a lot of it was new to Javon. He had a harder time.

Javon: We tried our best to not let Mr. Jackson see our frustration, but he would catch it at times. Some days, he'd call us and ask us to do something last minute. He'd call us at six-thirty in the morning and say, "I need you guys to get some things from the store." We'd have to get up out of bed, put on our suits, our equilibrium all messed up, driving over there with an attitude. He could tell. He'd say, "Hey Javon, what's the matter? I don't see a smile."

He was so sweet and disarming and gentle all the time. That made it really hard to stay mad.

Bill: I wasn't getting any petty cash and I'd damn near maxed out my credit cards, but the way he was still shopping, you'd think there was no problem. During the day, we would go to these antique stores on Park and Lexington Avenue in the city, the ones with those big antique globes. He would pick out a bunch of things that he wanted and have me make arrangements to get it.

There's a mall in New Jersey off Route 4, The Mall at Short Hills. We went there a few times. Near one of the entrances where we'd go in, there was this huge Ferris wheel, an indoor amusement park type of thing. He checked it out as we walked past, and then on the way back to the car, he said, "Bill, I want you to find out who makes that Ferris wheel. See what it costs. I want that."

You can only imagine what was going through my head. Where the hell was he going to put a Ferris wheel? Dude didn't even have a house; he was crashing in someone's basement. I went back to the mall later that evening and took a picture of the manufacturer's tag and did some follow-up, and the thing cost about $300,000. I gave him the information. Thankfully there wasn't any further discussion about it.

What was really difficult was knowing that he had the cash to pay us. He carried enough cash on his person that he could have made us whole at any time. We didn't ask, and he didn't offer. We knew how he felt about that money. That was separate. It was for him and his kids. He didn't think of that money as part of the money for his business. It was frustrating. He'd give you a thousand dollars because he wanted something. Something ridiculous, unnecessary. He'd call and say, "Bill, I left some money at the back door. I need a flat screen TV and some new iPhone attachments." We'd go pick up whatever it was. Then, when we dropped it off, sometimes we'd try and keep the change. You know, so we could eat something? He would ask for the change.

Javon: The anger, the animosity, the frustration—me and Bill started taking it out on each other. We'd go on details and not say a word to each other unless we had to. I remember one night we almost went at it. I'd been hand-washing my shirts and my suits and hanging them up in the shower and using a hair dryer to dry them. Stranded in this cheap hotel, living on soup and crackers. I went to tell Bill I couldn't take it anymore. He didn't even want to see me. I banged on his door for an hour, yelling at him, before he even let me in. When he finally opened the door, I could tell he was really pissed off. I told him, "I need to send my suit to the cleaners, so I'm gonna need some money for that. You're gonna have to call Ms. Raymone and let her know."

Bill lit up. "What the *fuck*?! We both need our suits cleaned. Why is this about you?!"

"Well, what the fuck you want me to do? You're the one communicatin' with Ms. Raymone!"

We got into it for a good twenty minutes, going back and forth.

"I maxed out all my credit cards!"

"I maxed out mine too!"

We kept throwing all these complaints at each other, but everything one of us was going through we were both going through. I had a newborn back at home. Bill was a single father, away from his daughter. We had to catch ourselves. Like, wait a minute. Why are we fighting with each other? We were tired of it. We both could have used a drink, but we couldn't afford one.

There were days we were so frustrated we were begging for someone to take it out on. There were days we *wished* somebody would try to hurt the boss. We *wished* somebody would come at us, because that person was going to get fucked up. I had a brass-knuckle stun gun that puts out 950,000 volts per second. I kept telling Bill that I was itching to use it. I said, "Please let somebody say something crazy to Mr. Jackson or walk up to him in the wrong way. Please let somebody get out of line."

Bill: We wanted to whip somebody's ass in front of Michael Jackson. Just to show him our frustrations. We wanted him to be right there to see it. That's how we felt.

We'd let him get a few kicks in too, 'cause we knew he had some frustrations of his own to work out. "Hey, Mr. Jackson, come kick this motherfucker. Get a few good hits in."

Javon: The question we get all the time is "Why did you stay? Why didn't you quit?" It sounds strange, but we felt like staying was not just our professional obligation, but it was the most practical thing to do. We knew exactly how much money he owed to other people. If we left, we'd be at the back of that line with everybody else. We'd never see a dime.

Bill: We decided that no matter how hard it got, Mr. Jackson wasn't leaving our sight, because as long as he was standing there next to us, they'd have to pay us eventually. So that was the practical side of it. But on the other side, the personal side, I can tell you exactly why we stayed. We stayed for the kids, for Paris, Prince, and Blanket. You couldn't turn your back on them. You knew what they were up against. Isolated. Alone. What were they going to do if something happened to him? It was like what he told me on the phone in Virginia: as much as he loved them, there were certain things he couldn't do for them on his own. We sacrificed time with our own kids to be able to give them that, and we were afraid of new people coming in and not caring as much.

Javon: We kind of broke security protocol. You're not supposed to become that attached to your clients. But we were around them sixteen hours a day and we couldn't help it. Any time we might have thought about leaving, we'd bring the kids something from the store and they'd light up, saying, "Thank you, Javon! Thank you!" and we'd just melt.

We always felt needed. We felt like we were doing something important, more than you'd get from just a regular job. We'd be driving on a detail and Mr. Jackson would say, "You guys, I'm really proud of you, and the kids really like you. You're doing a really good job. I don't want you to think I'm not appreciative." Times like that made us feel good. This was *Michael Jackson* telling us this. I don't care what nobody says, when Michael Jackson is telling you that you did a good job, you just take it differently than working a regular nine to five. And when we finally did get paid? He got so excited about it. He wanted so much for us to feel good about working for him.

It was after we'd been in New Jersey for a couple weeks, when we went and did the photo shoot for Italian *Vogue*. The magazine put us up at The Carlyle in Manhattan on the Upper East Side. The shoot was at a studio off the West Side Highway on 53rd or 54th Street, this huge loft in an old warehouse building. It had an elevator big enough for our SUVs, so we drove the trucks right into the building and rode up and parked on the floor where they were doing the shoot. They had racks of clothes and all this expensive jewelry for him to wear.

Mr. Jackson was in the makeup chair getting ready when Ms. Raymone showed up. She came in with a stack of mail and packages to give him. In that stack were two envelopes for me and Bill. When she handed him that? He *stopped* the photo shoot. He just stopped everything. He jumped out of his chair—makeup half done, with the smock still on, curlers in his hair—and he ran across the room waving these envelopes, going, "Bill! Javon! I've got a surprise for you!"

He had this huge smile on his face as he handed them to us. "See? Here you go! I *told* you guys. I promised. I'm sorry it took so long. Thank you so much for sticking by me. Anybody else would have left." We said thank you, and he said, "Now we can go back to work, right? I need your morale back. Now you can give me some smiles again, okay?"

It was so heartfelt. He was so proud of himself that he got us paid. We were excited, too. Then we opened the envelopes.

Bill: It was half. Raymone paid us half of what we were owed. She came over after Mr. Jackson left, and she said, "Are you guys satisfied now?" Like she was doing us a favor. That made us real hot. I told her we'd discuss it with her later.

When the shoot was over, we got in the car and Mr. Jackson said, "Everybody's happy? Are you guys happy?"

I forced a smile. I said, "Yes, sir. We're good."

I wasn't good. I was pissed. I was pissed off that I didn't get all of my paycheck. But I'd seen the excitement on his face, the joy that he had done this for us. *He* was happy, and it was so rare to see him happy. How was I going to take that away from him?

Javon: Later that night, we were back at The Carlyle. I ran into Raymone and two of her colleagues in the restaurant and she was flagging me down. "Javon, come here! Come here! How are you doin'? What's goin' on?"

Raymone was always more cordial to me in person than to Bill. I wasn't on the phone getting in between her and Mr. Jackson, so in her eyes I was just the errand boy. So I walked over with a little fake smile, and she could tell it was fake. She said, "Where you going?"

I said, "Going to get something to eat."

"Oh, sit down with us and have a drink!"

I didn't want to be difficult and make more tension than there already was, so I sat down with them for a while. When the check came, I caught a glimpse of it. The bill came to $2,300 for the five of us. They must have been drinking the good stuff. I just sat there looking at the check like, Damn, that's most of what I'm short right there.

Raymone said, "Javon, what's the problem?"

I didn't think it was appropriate to say anything with other people there, so I said, "Nothing. I'm just not in a good mood right now. I'm going to go back up to my room."

"Okay, you have a good night."

Bill: I think she thought we were stupid. Like we couldn't see right through what she was trying to do with Mike LaPerruque. Like how she'd rented that condo in Vegas under Mr. Jackson's name and then had us drop her off there routinely without thinking maybe we'd put two and two together about it. Mr. Jackson clearly didn't trust her. Why was she still in the picture? We didn't know.

Fortunately, we didn't have to worry about Mike LaPerruque for very long. He fell out of favor with Mr. Jackson right after he showed up. Couple days after the *Vogue* shoot, we were in Jersey driving home from the mall. It was me, Mr. Jackson, and Mike, and it came over the radio that O. J. Simpson had been arrested in Las Vegas. This was the time he got busted for armed robbery, trying to steal some of his own sports memorabilia from some people at a hotel. This news came over the radio, and Mike LaPerruque said, "They finally got him! They finally got O. J.!"

Mr. Jackson was in the backseat. He said, "What? What's that about O. J.?"

Mike said, "They finally got him."

"What do you mean they finally got him?"

"He was arrested, in Vegas."

Mr. Jackson didn't really react. He just said, "Oh." We stopped a few minutes later, and Mike had to run inside a store to get something, and Mr. Jackson said, "Bill, I didn't like that."

I said, "What's that, sir?"

"I didn't like that comment about O. J. O. J. and I were friends. No one knows this, but he stayed with me at Neverland after he was acquitted."

I sat there thinking, *Whaaat?* I'd never heard that before.

I didn't get a clear sense on whether he thought O. J. was guilty or not, but I think his sympathies were with O. J. on the way he was hounded, how even after he was acquitted, people never left him alone. Mr. Jackson said he knew exactly what

O. J. was going through. He said, "O. J. should have just left the country. He should have left and never come back."

So after Mike made that O. J. comment? Mr. Jackson wasn't feeling him so much. It was also obvious early on that Mike was feeding Raymone information, and Mr. Jackson didn't like that, either. He said, "That's not the same guy that used to work with me." Mr. Jackson didn't fire him. He stuck around, but we started to go on details without him.

About a week after the *Vogue* shoot, we did the second one for *Ebony*. That was a big deal. They put us up at the Four Seasons. The shoot itself took place at the Brooklyn Museum. The whole place was shut down for the day. *Ebony* took it over. We brought Mr. Jackson in around eight in the morning. He had a dressing room, racks of designer clothes. There was all this activity swirling around him. The magazine people were there, a lot of executives.

It was one thing to see fans screaming and trying to get at him. When you have fans, you're trying to be a buffer; you're in a protective mode. Here, I wasn't trying to push anyone away, so I could see just how all these people approached him and interacted with him, how deferential everyone was. These were all successful, important people in the industry, but they all bowed to him. Everything moved around him. Everywhere he stepped his presence would shift the whole energy of the room.

When it came time to do the shoot, he was excited. He was doing all these poses, just crazy poses, grabbing his crotch and dancing while the photographers snapped away. At one point, he spun around and his pants ripped in the back, and he just turned around and ripped it again and damn near ripped his pants off, and everybody was cheering him on. He went into full performance mode. For me, a kid who grew up on the Jackson 5 and *Ebony*? That was amazing to see. A real live *Ebony* magazine shoot. Michael Jackson. *Thriller*. It was goose-bump time.

That day, I saw a side of him that I hadn't really seen before.

When he got up in front of the cameras, it was like a bright light turned on inside him. His whole demeanor changed. This was my first time meeting the King of Pop. Up to that point, I'd only ever worked for Michael Jackson. Those were two different people, I realized. The King of Pop had designers and stylists hanging all over him. Michael Jackson did his own laundry. Javon and I, all we'd seen was him hanging out in pajamas with his kids and going to the movies; that was the guy we knew. But this other guy, this King of Pop, he was unfamiliar to us.

Javon: After the *Ebony* shoot, we were expecting we'd go home. There wasn't really anything important left to do. But Mr. Jackson wanted to hang out. Every morning, we'd drive the teacher over to the Cascios' for school. We'd stay close to the house, just in case Mr. Jackson needed us. We'd circle the block and see if there were any paparazzi. But there were never any problems because it was such a quiet neighborhood. The majority of the time, he just stayed at the house and sent us on errands. Sometimes we wouldn't hear from him for three or four days.

You could tell that he and the Cascios had a long history together. He was so relaxed and happy there. That was one of the best times I remember as far as him being in a good place, just relaxing around other people. We'd never seen him like that before. I knew he was happy, because one day, I went to pick him up and he got in the car and I said, "Mr. Jackson, looks like you've gained weight a little bit. You look good."

He said, "Yeah, Javon. I'm eating good. Angel's mom is making me fat. They're feeding me all kinds of Italian food. The kids can't get enough."

Bill: Mr. Jackson was also using that time to work on his music. Angel Cascio had that studio in the basement, and the two of them would spend hours down there. There were also a few meetings about *Thriller 25*. Peter Lopez arranged for Mr. Jackson to meet with the R & B artist Ne-Yo. There was also a meeting with Kanye West; they discussed working together on the remix of "Billie Jean" for the anniversary album.

Javon: When Kanye West met Mr. Jackson? He was totally starstruck. They met at Lyor Cohen's house, the president of Def Jam Recordings. Me and Bill were outside with the truck, and we saw this little guy and a tall guy walking down the street, and as they got close, we saw that the little guy was Kanye. We were like, *Wow, that's Kanye West.* We walked Kanye in, and once Kanye saw Mr. Jackson, *he* was the one who was starstruck. He started gushing. "Oh my God, Mr. Jackson, it's such a pleasure and an honor to meet you. You just don't know. I'm your biggest fan. I love you so much."

Mr. Jackson said, "God bless you. Thank you. I'm a fan of your work too."

The whole time, Kanye was like a kid in a candy store. I've never seen somebody be so humble. To see him that way was surreal. Everybody knows that Kanye can be very arrogant, and here he was, just amazed to be in the same room as Mr. Jackson. When Ne-Yo was introduced to Mr. Jackson, he was just as starstruck as Kanye. Ne-Yo was so nervous, he couldn't stop shaking. Experiences like that made you remember just how special Mr. Jackson was to people.

Bill: One day Mr. Jackson called and asked me to come to the house. When I arrived, he said, "I need you to do me a favor. I need you to bring a package to a friend of mine in the city."

"Yes, sir."

"Now, Bill," he said, "I want you to be prepared for when you meet him. He's been through a terrible tragedy. When he was a baby, his father set him on fire. His name is David; you may have heard of him. They made a movie about his life."

"Yes, sir."

"Bill, when you see him, you'll be startled. So you have to prepare yourself so that he doesn't see that you look shocked."

"Yes, sir."

Then he handed me a package. It was wrapped in newspaper and bound up with a few layers of masking tape. It was at least an inch thick. Just from the size and the feel I could tell it was money, a lot of it. Along with the package, he gave me David's number; he'd be expecting my call when I got into the city.

As I drove over the George Washington Bridge into Manhattan, I couldn't help but wonder what David was going to look like. Was he handicapped in some way? In a wheelchair? I didn't know. When I hit the Henry Hudson Parkway, I called him and we arranged to meet across from Madison Square Garden. I got to the arena, pulled over, got out of the car, and called him to let him know I was there. He said he was a block away. Couple minutes later, I noticed this guy coming toward me, a slim, Caucasian dude with a green hat that was pulled down, covering his face. As he got closer, he looked up and said, "Bill?"

I tried not to stare. His entire face was scarred from being burned. His ears, nose, and hands were all deformed. I could only imagine what it was like for him, being out in public. I said, "Hey, Dave. How you doing?"

"I'm good, thanks. How's Michael?"

"He's doing great."

I gave him the package. He said, "Thank you, and tell Michael I love him."

"I sure will." I gave him a hug and said, "Take care of yourself."

He pulled his hat back down and walked toward the subway station. I got in the truck and headed back to New Jersey.

Beyond that, there wasn't a whole lot going on. We just kicked it around the Cascios for almost two months, running errands, going to the mall. Part of it, I think, was that Mr. Jackson was just comfortable there. He didn't want to leave. The stability he got from their family life was something he didn't get very often. But it was also becoming obvious that we weren't leaving because he couldn't afford to. By the end of October, it wasn't just payroll that was messed up. There was no more money, period.

Javon got up one morning and went down to the hotel gym to work out. When he came back, he couldn't get in his room. He went to the front desk to see what was going on, and they said there were some problems with the card on file. Checkout was at some automatic time. When the payment didn't go through, he'd been locked out. He called me and I went downstairs and talked to the manager. They told me there was an outstanding balance that needed to be paid. They couldn't let us back in the rooms until it was taken care of.

Raymone's office was dealing with that bill; it went directly to her. Hotel management told me they had been talking to her about it. I called her and of course she wasn't answering my calls. And she knew it was important why I was calling, because she'd been talking to these people at the hotel. I ended up talking to someone else in her office, and I just got the usual excuse: "Mr. Jackson's money is tied up right now."

We hung out in the lobby for a couple of hours, and finally we were told we could get back into our rooms. I checked with the hotel to see whose credit card had been put up, and it belonged to this woman who worked for Raymone. Some junior person in Raymone's office was putting up her personal credit card to cover Michael Jackson's bills.

Javon: At first, I thought Ms. Raymone was just procrastinating in paying the people, that it was just a temporary thing. Then the reality started setting in. It was very disturbing. What's going on here? Are we just kicked out for a couple hours, or should I be packing my stuff to go home? Why am I getting kicked out of hotels when I work for Michael Jackson?

We had a company card that we used to put gas in the trucks. That got cut off too, right around the same time. Bill started using his own money to buy gas. We were already so deep in the hole, and he started going and putting fifty dollars into each truck every couple days just to keep us to where we could function. I told him he was crazy. I said, "Bill, this ain't your responsibility. We should make an example out of this. The next time there's an important detail, we'll just tell Mr. Jackson, 'We don't have any gas and we can't come get you.' Then they'll have to do something."

Bill said he wasn't going to do that because it would make us look bad. Bill took it like he was a soldier on a mission; that was his mentality. Just because other people aren't doing their job doesn't mean you stop doing your job. He kept saying, "Nah, I'll put the gas in the vehicle." I don't know where he got the money from, who he borrowed it from. All he'd tell me was, "I took care of it."

Bill: It had come to the point where we were just barely holding things together. Last week of October, Mike LaPerruque and I took Mr. Jackson into the city for a dinner with Peter Lopez at Mr. K's, this Chinese joint on Lexington Avenue. I didn't sit in on the dinner or anything, but I have to assume it was related to the phone call they'd had back in Virginia: "Can you help me find my money?"

Javon: On the night of the *Ebony* photo shoot, we were driving Mr. Jackson through Midtown on our way back to the hotel. We were near the Apple Store, around 57th street, and we saw a billboard for Tyler Perry's *Why Did I Get Married?*, this movie that Janet Jackson was starring in. She was front and center on this big poster up on the side of a building. We were sitting at a red light and Mr. Jackson looked up at the billboard and said, "Is that my sister? What is that? Is that a play she's in?"

I said, "No, that's her movie, sir. She's in a movie."

"When does it come out?"

This movie had been out for a few months. The billboard for it was all torn and faded around the edges—that's how long it had been in the theater. But I didn't want to tell him that. I said, "It just came out, sir."

Then real soft, almost in a whisper, he said, "Oh. I wonder why no one told me."

Me and Bill looked at each other. We were shocked. Like, how does he not know that his own sister is in this big movie? We knew he was isolated. We knew he didn't have many friends. But how had he not even had a casual conversation with someone in all these months to say, "Hey, Janet was really great in that movie"? How was he that cut off from the people in his own life?

As we drove off, he said, "I wonder if it's a good movie."

I said, "Yes, sir. I've seen it. It's an excellent movie."

And that was all he ever said on it. He never mentioned it again.

Bill: At the time, seeing how much his affairs were out of order, I thought, This is just how it is. Now, looking back, I honestly believe that if his relationship with his family had been better, if he'd had the same relationship with his own family that he had with the Cascios, his life would not have been like this. That's where the problem was.

There were a few conversations that I had with Grace about the early days, when his life was more organized. I remember one time she said that when Mr. Jackson was married to Lisa Marie Presley, that was a really good time for him. Grace felt that she really loved him and that he really loved her too. Things were more in order because of that trust they had. Lisa Marie made sure the wrong people weren't getting in his ear, that people weren't using him. Or she tried to, anyway. And if you're in a position like

Michael Jackson was, you have to have that person who's in your corner, someone who's not there to get a paycheck, someone who doesn't have an agenda.

When we first got there, and Mr. Jackson wouldn't let his family past the gate without an appointment, I thought that was messed up. But with all the nasty stuff we'd been told about them, it sort of made sense. We'd heard that the family was rotten, that they were trying to feed off him, that they wanted to control him. We heard that they were going to try and kidnap him. Whenever nasty stories turned up in the tabloids, we'd hear that someone in the family had leaked it.

But honestly, after being around for a while, with most of the family I never got any kind of rotten vibe. With Randy? Yes. Randy was just Randy. He and Michael had that falling-out over some business deal. And Jermaine, he was friendly enough, but whenever he called or came around, he always seemed to have an angle, some deal he was working that he was going to get himself in on. Jermaine was the one that left the group first; he was supposed to have the solo career that blew up, but that never really happened for him. There might have been some jealousy there. Jermaine also tried to sell a book during the trial, and I don't think Mr. Jackson ever forgave him for that. Jermaine wasn't as tight with Michael as some people may think, at least not from what we could see.

But everyone else? Jackie and Rebbie and Tito and the rest? I never got a bad vibe. They were always cordial, always respectful. The only vibe I ever got from them was concern. They were concerned about their brother. Even Joe Jackson. As nasty as he was to me the times I met him, as terrible as the stories are about him in the press—people want to make him the bad guy but it was more complicated than that. That was another thing Grace said that stuck with me. She said the only person who never stole from Michael Jackson was his father.

For me, I'm the youngest of six. My relationship with my father wasn't the best. He was a former military man who played by very strict rules. He was the disciplinarian. I was on the other end of that coming up. That was true for a lot of black families from that time. The world wasn't always a safe place for young black people, and the odds against making it felt so overwhelming. Gangs. Crime. Trouble at school. So if you got out of line, the belt came out. That's how it was. Mr. Jackson even made that comment to me once, when we were talking about our families. He said he didn't know why the media had made such a huge deal over the way his father used to discipline them. It was not uncommon back then. And to take a family from where they were? From Gary, Indiana, to as far as they made it? I think it's hard to judge Joe Jackson if you didn't live Joe Jackson's life. If he hadn't been who he was, who knows if the world would have ever heard of Michael Jackson.

I understood why he wasn't close with some of his siblings. But all of them? The whole family? It didn't make sense. Out of eight siblings, with all those nieces, nephews, and cousins, they couldn't all be bad people. That's just not possible. But we were given direct instructions that no one in the family was allowed to reach him except his mother. She was the only one who had his number, but the siblings would always convince her to divulge it. After I set up that iPhone for him, I must have changed his number four times in the first six months. Each time, it was to get away from his own family.

Even his mother—she had an open invitation to visit or call, but sometimes she'd call me and wouldn't ask to speak to him. Maybe she didn't want to bother him, didn't want him to think she was intruding. She'd call me and I'd ask if she was trying to reach her son and she'd say no. She'd just say, "Is he okay? Is he eating?"

"Yes, ma'am. He's good. He's watching a movie with the kids."

"Oh, good. Thank you so much."

And that was it. She was just checking on him, like mothers do.

And that was the vibe I got from most of his family too. They were just checking in on him. Which is why I had the feeling that his relationship with his family had suffered under all these handlers over the years. And without anyone from his family there, too many different people were able to reach in and put their hands in the basket and pull some money out, or manipulate him in the fragile state he was in. He really didn't have anyone protecting him on that angle. He had security to protect his physical being. He had the best lawyers in the country taking care of his record deals and his publishing catalog. He had all that. What was missing from the organization was people who really gave a fuck about Michael Jackson.

14

After two months in New Jersey, Michael Jackson suffered two serious blows in rapid succession. That October, Sheikh Abdullah of
Bahrain, weary of trying to extract a settlement from Jackson's lawyers, filed a lawsuit against the singer in London, seeking to recoup
the $7 million he'd paid for the never-delivered album and stage
musical promised under the deal for Two Seas Records. Unlike the
frivolous claims that ate up so much of Jackson's time, this suit was
potentially crippling. The all-encompassing language of the contract
Jackson and Abdullah had signed gave the sheikh rights to any new
recording or live-performance projects the singer might undertake.
Jackson insisted that he'd been misled into signing a contract whose
terms weren't fully explained. Abdullah claimed he'd been used and
deserted. Either way, Jackson's ability to work was all but paralyzed
until the issue could be resolved.

Just days after Abdullah's claim was made, Fortress Investment
Group made a move to foreclose on Neverland. On October 22, the
group filed a Notice of Default and Election to Sell with the state of
California. Jackson owed the full principal of his $23 million mort-
gage on the estate, plus $212,963 in interest. He had just ninety
days to settle the account, or Neverland would be sold to the highest bidder.

In the autumn of 2007, Michael Jackson found himself marooned
in the New Jersey basement of Connie and Dominic Cascio, his

resources tapped. As he had done so many times before, when beset by trouble, Jackson turned to a wealthy, powerful figure for help.

Bill: One evening, after we'd been in New Jersey for a while, Mr. Jackson had us pick him up at the Cascios' house and take him to meet with Londell McMillan, another one of these high-powered entertainment attorneys. Londell handled business for Prince, Stevie Wonder, Lil' Kim, and he'd done some cases for Mr. Jackson in the past. I knew of Londell from other clients I used to work for, but I hadn't heard his name come up with Mr. Jackson until that night.

They met at a mall off Route 4, the Westfield Garden State Plaza. We pulled our car into the parking lot, and Londell pulled up in his vehicle alongside ours. It was about nine o'clock and it was dark, starting to get cold out. Londell climbed in the back with Mr. Jackson, and Javon and I got out and stood outside to let them discuss what they had to discuss. They signed some documents. Whole thing lasted less than half an hour.

After that, I started hearing Londell's name in a lot of places where I used to hear Raymone's. Before that, it was always "Call Raymone." Now it was "Call Londell." I got the feeling that was the beginning of Raymone being on the way out.

Javon: While we were in Virginia, Reverend Jesse Jackson had come down for a visit. He was a longtime friend of the family, and while he was there, he'd invited Mr. Jackson to attend his birthday party, which was going to be in Los Angeles the first week of November. We didn't hear about it again until New Jersey. We were about two, maybe three, weeks out from the party, and Mr. Jackson said he wanted to go, that he promised Jesse Jackson that he would be there.

Bill: Getting to L.A. was a story in itself. First, Mr. Jackson wanted to drive back. He wanted to rent a luxury bus and spend a few days on the road. He had me looking into that. He also asked me to start looking at houses to rent in Vegas, and he gave me specific instructions not to tell Raymone I was looking at houses. So I started making calls to realtors, got some listings and printed them out for Mr. Jackson. Then everything with the trip came to a complete stop. I called Raymone to discuss the travel itinerary, and she said, "That's not happening. I don't know how you guys are going to get back to the West Coast."

I said, "Do you mean that you don't know how we're going to get to Jesse Jackson's birthday party, or you don't know how we're getting out of New Jersey, period?"

She just said that he couldn't afford it, that he didn't have the money to send everyone back. She said they could maybe afford to fly out just Mr. Jackson and the kids, without security or the schoolteacher or anybody else. I told Mr. Jackson that she'd proposed that, and he said, "That's such an idiot statement. She's such an idiot. What about you guys? Who's going to protect my kids? No."

He told me to call Londell. Londell was the fixer now. I called him, told him the whole story. Londell called Jesse Jackson, who agreed to put up the money for us to travel and stay in L.A. So arrangements were made for us, Mike LaPerruque, Mr. Jackson, his hairstylist, the kids, and the schoolteacher to be flown into L.A. three days before the party.

We flew out commercial. We drove in to JFK from New Jersey, and I made arrangements with some people I knew to meet us at the airport and take the trucks back to the Cascios' house; the plan was to have them shipped back to Las Vegas for us to use once we returned there. Prince's dog had to be shipped too. We could take the cat on the plane in a carrier, but the dog was going to have to stay with the Cascios and be shipped later. Prince, he cried his eyes out when he had to leave that dog behind. He was in that backseat, sobbing the whole way to the airport. I asked Mr. Jackson, "Is he okay?"

He said, "Yeah, he'll be fine. He's just upset, but I told him you'll make sure Kenya's okay. You'll take care of it, right?"

"Yes, sir."

At JFK, we were met by airport security and a few management officials. They knew we were coming in, and Mr. Jackson and the kids were cleared to go straight to the plane. Javon and Mike LaPerruque escorted them to the gate. I stayed with the bags. Mr. Jackson told me, "Bill, make sure you count the bags, because a lot of my stuff has gone missing at airports."

"Yes, sir."

There were about thirty bags. I was keeping a special eye on the case with the Oscars. He also had a Louis Vuitton briefcase and another leather case with all his jewelry and makeup. These two TSA guys were scanning each bag. I was watching and keeping track. The Louis Vuitton case was the last to go through. As that was being scanned, they said to me, "Sir, we can't see inside this bag through our scanner. We need to open it."

I said, "I don't have the key, and I don't know the combination."

They said, "We have keys to open it. May we?"

"Sure."

They opened it. I couldn't see what they were looking at; they were on the other side of the scanner. But they opened up this briefcase, and one guy looked at the other guy, and that guy looked up at me and gave me this stunned, wide-eyed look. Yo, you talk about nervous? I didn't know what was in that bag. I was getting ready to say, "That shit ain't mine," when they said, "Sir, could you step over here?"

I was still in the middle of taking things out of my pockets; I hadn't even gone through the metal detector yet. They said, "Don't worry about your pockets, sir. Just come on through."

I went to the other side and they turned the briefcase around. There was at least $300,000 in there. Ten-thousand-dollar stacks.

Nothing but the Benjamins. And these two guys didn't know who I was with. Mr. Jackson had gone through separately. They thought this belonged to me. My first instinct was to run. My mind snapped into ghetto mode, you know? I'm a black man at the airport with a suitcase full of cash. I didn't know what to do.

They said, "You have to claim this."

Just as they were telling me what I needed to do and who I needed to call, the manager who'd escorted Mr. Jackson to the plane happened to be walking back. I flagged her down and said, "Ma'am, can you please tell them who I'm with?"

The manager looked down and saw the briefcase and said, "Oh, you're with the . . . " She gestured back toward the gate. "Right. You're fine." She turned to the two agents. "He's fine. Let him through."

They let me through, and I got the carry-ons and headed to the gate. You talk about relief? I thought I was going to be detained. I didn't know what.

We flew into LAX and we were met by a car service and a couple other security guys who worked for Jesse Jackson. The schoolteacher, the hairstylist, and I were going to stay at a hotel by the airport. Mr. Jackson and the kids were staying as the guest of some friend of Jesse Jackson's in Beverly Hills. Mike LaPerruque was from L.A., so he stayed at his own house, and he didn't live too far. Javon had his people in L.A. too; he stayed with his grandmother. I took Mr. Jackson and the kids to the house and then crashed at the hotel.

The party was at the Beverly Hilton two days later. I got in touch with Jesse Jackson's people to go over the arrangements, which way we'd be coming in, what time, where. That night when we arrived, Jesse Jackson was outside waiting for us. Lots of big names. Larry King. Don Cornelius from *Soul Train*. We got out of the car, and the flashes from the cameras started going off—boom, boom, boom! They were all around us. Everywhere. We did the whole red carpet thing and then went inside.

As I was walking Mr. Jackson to his table, I saw Berry Gordy. I knew he'd been instrumental in Mr. Jackson's career coming up at Motown, but I'd never heard Mr. Jackson mention his name before, so I wasn't sure if there was some animosity between them. I whispered to Mr. Jackson, "Sir, there's Berry Gordy." When Mr. Jackson saw him? He damn near knocked a woman down rushing over to see him. He ran straight over to Berry Gordy and grabbed him and gave him the biggest hug.

It was a real friendship hug that they gave each other. When I saw that, I felt good about it. After the event, we went upstairs to a suite for the after-party, and Mr. Jackson and Berry Gordy were talking again. I couldn't hear what they were talking about, but just from the looks on their faces, I could tell the conversation was deep. At one point, I did hear Mr. Jackson say, "Thank you. I miss you. I could use your help." Maybe he was really opening up about the state he was in, the problems he was having. I couldn't tell for sure, but it was good that he could talk to someone who went back that far, someone he knew. Once the party was over, we got the cars ready. Jesse Jackson walked him to the door and thanked him for being there, and we bounced.

The next morning, I got a call from the hotel desk around eleven. They said, "Will you be checking out today?"

I said, "I don't think so."

"Well, we only had a prepayment for three days, and we're going to need another credit card to put on the account by noon."

I called Mr. Jackson and made him aware of the situation. He told me to call Londell. I called Londell. Londell said, "Why are you guys still there?"

I said, "I don't know. Nobody told me any different."

He said, "Only three days were paid for at the hotel. He's supposed to be out of the house he's staying at too."

"Really?"

"Yeah. That guy has other guests coming in. We told him that Mr. Jackson only needed the house for three days."

Londell told me the rest was up to us. "Figure it out," he said. Those were his exact words. I called Mr. Jackson and told him that Londell said there was nothing he could do and that we were going to have to leave the hotel. Mr. Jackson said, "Okay. I'll call you right back."

That was at noon. One o'clock came and I was still sitting in my room, waiting. I stayed there until three, when they finally came and kicked my ass out. The schoolteacher and the hairstylist were there with me; they got kicked out too.

I had just enough room on my card to pay for one room for one more night, so I got a room for the schoolteacher. She needed a place to stay and we had a bunch of luggage that had to go somewhere. The stylist, she left and stayed with friends. I figured I'd wait and find out what to do with myself. I called Mr. Jackson a couple of times. Didn't hear from him. I was pissed. I decided to give it until seven o'clock. I said, "If he doesn't hit me back by seven, I'm out of here." I sat in the hotel lounge with my bags all afternoon. I called Mr. Jackson one last time at 7:30, and his phone went straight to voicemail. I didn't know what was going on. All I knew was that I had to get home. I've been away from my daughter. I'm broke. I'm ready to go home.

I had no credit card, just a little bit of cash, so I called a friend of mine and had him book a car for me to drive back to Vegas. I called Javon and let him know what was going on.

Javon: Bill was like, "I'm not going to stay here if nobody's on the same page. I'm gone."

I said I'd stay in L.A. a little while longer, but eventually I had to get back to my family too. I asked Bill, "Is there anything I need to do? Do I need to check on him?"

He said, "He has your number. If he hasn't called, then I guess he's fine."

I totally lied to my family about the whole situation. I told them that Mr. Jackson just gave me a little time off because we had been on the road for so long. I didn't want to tell my grandmother, "I'm here because I don't have money for a hotel." I didn't want to create a panic about how deep in the hole I was.

Bill: I knew that Vegas was the next stop, and since we didn't know where Mr. Jackson was going to be staying, I needed to go back and start looking into that anyway. My mind was running through all kinds of options. I just knew I had to figure something out. I got back to Vegas late that night. Early the next morning, around eight o'clock, I was sitting at my kitchen table looking at houses online when the phone rang. It was Mr. Jackson. He said, "Bill, I need one of you guys to run out and get me a radio. I don't have any music in this house."

No mention of anything that happened the day before. The schoolteacher. Getting kicked out of the hotel. Like it never happened. I said, "Mr. Jackson, I'm in Vegas."

"Vegas? What are you doing in Vegas?"

"Mr. Jackson, I called you last night, remember? I told you they were kicking me out of my hotel, so I came back to find you a place to stay for when you come home."

"Well, who's here with me and my kids?"

"Javon's there, and Mike is there too."

"When am I coming back to Vegas?"

"That's what I'm working on right now."

"Okay. Find out where we're going to stay and call me back."

Then he hung up. I felt like Alice in Wonderland. I had no idea what was going on.

Javon: Mr. Jackson didn't call the whole time I was in L.A. I stayed about four or five days and finally decided to head back myself. I had my sister book me a flight.

I was happy to be home, especially when I saw my baby. But it was also kind of like a letdown. I didn't want to tell my girlfriend what was really going on. She could tell I came back kind of distraught. I'd been gone all this time, and I didn't have a lot to show for it. I should have come back bearing gifts, and I had nothing but the clothes on my back and a piece of luggage.

It was bittersweet. It was sweet because I got to see my family, and it was bitter because with work, it was here we go again. I was looking at a stack of bills that had piled up. In my head I was thinking, Should I hold on or look for another job? Do I walk away now and call my old company, see if maybe I can get back on there? Here I was at Christmastime and I couldn't even buy presents. That's when the reality of it set in: I wasn't going to be able to do Christmas for my kids this year. Bill kept saying, "Hold on." But I was thinking, I don't know how much more of this I can take. I was really in a bad place.

Bill: Thanksgiving came and went. Pretty soon, Christmas was approaching, and Mr. Jackson was still at the house in Beverly Hills, the one he was only supposed to be at for three days. He'd talked his way into staying for three weeks. I was going around Vegas, looking at houses, hotels, trying to come up with a plan. I called Raymone, tried to work something out through her. She was no help. She said, "Bill, I don't know." Okay. Next call: Peter Lopez. I couldn't reach him. He was out of the country. Next call: Londell. Londell said he'd help out and he put me in touch with his assistant. I told her about the Green Valley Ranch, the place we'd stayed before when we had to evacuate the Monte Cristo house.

She said, "Okay, we'll just have him go back there. We'll put it on Londell's credit card and he can be reimbursed."

We hired a bus to drive Mr. Jackson and the kids from L.A. to Vegas. I called him and told him that he was coming back to the Green Valley Ranch. When he stayed there before, he was in the Presidential Suite. It had an indoor pool. The kids liked it. He told me he wanted the same room. I called Londell and told him. Londell said, "How much is it?"

I said, "Twenty-five hundred a night."

"What the *fuck*!?"

"Yo, man, I'm just tellin' you what he wants."

Londell damn near lost it. He started off about Mr. Jackson needing to get his finances under control. He said, "I'm not putting him in a $2,500-a-night room. Put him in a regular room. He needs to know how fucked up his finances are." We talked about the spending for a bit. He finally agreed to pay for a suite for two weeks, but it wasn't the Presidential Suite. I just called Mr. Jackson and told him it wasn't available. While we were on the phone, he asked me about Mike LaPerruque. He said, "Is Mike coming with us to Vegas?"

I said, "Yeah, as far as I know."

He said, "Well, we can just . . . hold off on that. We'll send for him later."

I knew what he meant. That was the last we saw of Mike LaPerruque.

Javon: We stayed at Green Valley Ranch for a couple of weeks. Bill and I both had rooms directly across from Mr. Jackson's, but a majority of the time, I was in Bill's room because that's where we had CCTV monitors set up for the cameras outside Mr. Jackson's suite. We would take shifts watching the monitors, doing patrols. He wasn't really leaving his room much. Grace wasn't around, and the kids were on winter break from school, so the teacher wasn't around much, either. After a few days, Prince's dog arrived. The kids got real excited about that.

The whole time, Mr. Jackson made it seem like he was just chilling for a bit until he moved into that house off Durango, that $55 million estate. He kept talking about it like it was his house. He kept saying, "That's going to be my house." And when he said it, he was completely convinced of it. He'd say, "I've got some deals that are about to go through. I'm going to buy this house, and you guys are going to be fine. Don't worry." While we were out shopping, he even told us, "You guys look for some golf carts. We're going to need golf carts for you to patrol the property once we move in."

We kept thinking, How is he going to afford this? How? But who were we to say that Michael Jackson *didn't* have some big deal about to happen? He's Michael Jackson. And we'd put in so much time, sweat, and tears, we wanted to believe it was true. We wanted a reason to stick with him and see things turn around.

Bill: The schoolteacher had a place to stay. She had a small apartment that was still available because it had been paid for in advance for a year, so it was available for her when we got back. Grace was traveling. She'd been in Jersey for about three days and then she'd bounced. I hadn't seen her since. That got me thinking about her apartment at the Turnberry, where Raymone had her place too. I didn't know if Grace was coming back, but I knew Raymone's had to be empty. So I said to Mr. Jackson, "Why don't you stay at Raymone's apartment?"

He said, "Raymone has a place in Vegas?"

"Yeah."

"Where?"

"At the Turnberry Towers."

He didn't know what that was. I had to explain it to him. High-end, gated community, luxury condos. He said, "Bill, I need you to find out who's paying for that."

I called the property manager that was renting them out and he said, "I can't give that information to you."

I said, "Well, if the apartment is in Michael Jackson's name then surely you can give the information to him."

He said he could, so I put Mr. Jackson on the phone and that's when he learned that the apartment was being paid for out of an account Raymone controlled on his behalf. He was livid. He told me he wanted both apartments, Grace's and Raymone's. He said, "I want my mom to have one of those apartments and I'll stay in the other one."

I said I'd get right on it. I called Raymone and told her, "Mr. Jackson wants the apartments."

She said, "What apartments?"

"The ones over at the Turnberry."

She seemed caught off guard. She said that we didn't have those anymore. A friend was letting her use them.

I didn't say anything. I knew this was one of those times I should just play dumb and stay out of it.

A few days later, she came out to Vegas because that situation got ugly. The first thing she said on the way home from the airport was, "Bill, we don't have those apartments anymore. I don't know why he thinks that we have those apartments and that we were paying for them out of his money." I didn't argue with her. She didn't need to justify herself to me; she needed to justify herself to Mr. Jackson.

I took her to meet with him. Whatever went down between them in that conversation, I have no idea. The apartments never came up again. They were gone. They were unavailable. Maybe the rent was already late on them? Maybe Mr. Jackson had known about them at one point but then forgot? That wouldn't have surprised me. It was never explained. But that was the last I ever saw or heard from Raymone Bain.

After two weeks at the Green Valley Ranch, the manager called me and said, "Mr. Whitfield, we're going to need another credit card. The card that was on this account has been withdrawn."

I got in touch with Londell. He confirmed that he'd withdrawn his card. He said two weeks was all he'd agreed to do and he couldn't run an endless tab for the hotel. It was like, You're on your own.

I went to Mr. Jackson and told him, "Sir, the credit card on file is being declined. We're going to need another card to put on the account."

He said, "Okay. So give them another card."

He said it like I could just reach into my pocket and pull out a Platinum American Express. I said, "Sir, I don't have another card to give them."

He didn't really have an answer to that. He just expected me to call someone and handle it. I went back to the hotel manager and tried to negotiate for more time. He wouldn't budge. He wanted us gone by the end of the day or the hotel would have us removed. If word of something like that got out to the tabloids? I couldn't let that happen. I was scrambling. Javon was already packing up our security gear and putting it in my car so that it wouldn't get locked inside the room.

I couldn't call Raymone. Couldn't call Londell. Finally, I got a hold of Peter Lopez. He said he'd work on something and call me back. He called me back a couple hours later and said, "You guys are going to go to the Palms." Peter was friends with George Maloof, the owner of the hotel, and he'd agreed to put up Mr. Jackson and the kids for a couple of days.

We had to be out of the Green Valley Ranch in a matter of hours. Packing his things was an ordeal in and of itself. Michael Jackson didn't pack his own luggage. When he was ready to move, he would just pull all his stuff into the middle of the hotel suite and leave it for us to pack up. That was the usual routine. When I was packing up his room, I went into his bathroom to check for stuff in there. I opened the door, and the whole bathroom was covered with posters of Bruce Lee. There were stacks of books about Bruce Lee, framed pictures of Bruce Lee next to the sink. There was a shirt with a Chinese dragon on it hanging on the wall. It was like he'd decorated the bathroom to look like a Chinese restaurant. I didn't even know where all this stuff had come from. The Bruce Lee pictures really caught my attention. The kung fu poses reminded me of some of the dance moves that Mr. Jackson did in his videos. Was he in here practicing his dance routine? Was he meditating? I could only wonder.

Late that night, we headed to the Palms. I was in direct contact with George Maloof about where and what time we were coming in; he was handling it personally. We came through the loading dock and took the service elevator up. They were putting Mr. Jackson in the Hugh Hefner suite. That place is huge, almost four thousand square feet. Two stories, penthouse level, amazing floor-to-ceiling views of the city. There's an elevator inside the suite. It even has its own bowling lane. This room typically went for twenty thousand dollars a night. George Maloof gave it to Mr. Jackson for free.

Once we got there, Peter Lopez was supposed to meet us. I was exhausted. I'd been working since dawn. Normally, any time we hit a new hotel, I'd be out on point. I'd do a full advance of what's going on, find out if the rooms next to us were occupied, who the residents were, etc. But to be honest, I couldn't motivate myself to do it. I was just walking around the suite and checking out the view. At that point in time, I was on my own. Javon had a family situation. He'd taken a few days off.

George Maloof came upstairs to talk to Mr. Jackson and show him where everything was. Peter Lopez called and said that he was coming over with Akon; Mr. Jackson wanted to do some studio time with him. This was after midnight, and they were talking about a studio session. I didn't know what I was supposed to be doing. I told Mr. Jackson that I'd be outside. I grabbed a chair, went into the hallway and set up outside his door, killed some time on my iPhone. About forty-five minutes later, Peter Lopez and Akon came up. I greeted them both and called Mr. Jackson to let him know they were here. Mr. Jackson opened the door, and they all went inside.

I sat there for another two hours. The battery on my phone died, and I was stuck there with nothing to do and no way to communicate. Now it was close to three in the morning. I was dead tired, wondering what was going on. Were they ever going down to the studio? I knocked on the door. No answer. And I knew they were all right inside the suite. I just sat there, falling asleep, nobody telling me what was going on. Finally I said, "Fuck this. I'm out. I'm going home."

I got up, went to the elevator, and pressed the button for the lobby. I was gone. I went down to the parking lot, got in my car, and plugged the phone into the charger. I sat there for a minute, wondering if I should really just leave. Then the phone rang. It was him, all frantic. "Bill! Where are you?"

"I'm downstairs, Mr. Jackson."

"Downstairs? Downstairs where?"

"I just came down to uh . . . " *Shit.* "Sir, I just came down to check something at the front desk."

"Bill, you can't just leave me. You just can't leave me and my kids."

"Yes, sir. I'm on my way back upstairs."

"Okay. We're going to the studio. Do you know where the studio is?"

"Yes, I know where the studio is."

"Okay, we'll be at the studio, but I need you to watch the kids."

"Yes, Mr. Jackson."

By the time I got back upstairs, they were at the studio already. I sat back down in that chair, tired, hungry, and pissed off.

They didn't come back upstairs until about eight-thirty that morning. I needed to go home. I needed rest. I called Javon. He was tied up. I called Mr. Jackson and told him I needed to run home and get something to eat. He said, "Who's going to stay here with the kids?"

"I'll get someone from hotel security."

"Can you trust them?"

"Yes, sir."

There was a dude I knew who worked security for the hotel; he had done a few details for me in the past. I found him and told him I needed a favor, explained what it was. He said he had to clear it with his supervisor. I told him I'd do him one better and call George Maloof right then and clear it with him. I called Maloof and told him what I was going to do, and he said it was fine. So this guy went up and sat in front of Mr. Jackson's door, and I went home and crashed. I slept until late that afternoon. When I woke up and looked at my phone, I had all of these missed calls from Mr. Jackson. He'd been blowing me up all day. Little stuff, errands, packages to pick up.

As I was going through all these messages, I seriously felt like I was done. My daughter was upset with me, crying that I was never home. I couldn't afford to get any Christmas presents for her or the rest of my family. Things were not cool at this time. But I also didn't know what to do except go back to the Palms and see it through, see what was going to happen. So I showered up and went back later on that evening.

Akon was still in town. They were doing more studio work. There was actually a lot going on, all of a sudden, a lot of faxes going back and forth, things for him to sign, more so than usual. Something was in the works. It seemed like some kind of deal was maybe about to go off. But whatever was supposed to happen didn't happen fast enough. We were getting closer to Christmas.

Mr. Jackson was insisting that he did not want to have Christmas with his kids in a hotel, but it was obvious that there wasn't going to be any alternative.

Once Mr. Jackson knew he'd be staying, he came to me and said he wanted the place to look "Christmassy." He asked me to go get a tree and decorations and lights. I said, "Mr. Jackson, there isn't any money to—"

"Oh, how much do you need?"

"I don't know. Two, three hundred bucks?"

He went over to a table where he had a stack of hundreds and he gave me a thousand. I went out and bought him a tree, some lights, a bunch of little reindeer figurines. I brought all that back, and he and the kids decked it out.

Two days before Christmas, he came to me and said he wanted to set up a shopping trip to get the kids presents. I called FAO Schwarz and made arrangements to shop there after the store closed that night. Javon was back on board by this time. We drove down to the store, met the manager by the loading dock and took an elevator up to the back entrance. We went through, aisle by aisle. Mr. Jackson was picking things out, train sets and stuffed animals and dolls. An associate was following him with this empty stockroom cart, this big cage. It was huge, and Mr. Jackson was just filling this thing up. I was standing there watching him and looking at Javon, and we were not thrilled with the situation. Javon was in my ear on the radio, telling me how he couldn't even buy diapers. At one point, Mr. Jackson was looking at these girls' dolls and he picked one up and looked at me and said, "Bill, aren't you getting anything for your daughter?"

I said, "No, sir. We haven't been paid yet."

"Oh."

That was all he said. Then he turned around and went right on shopping. At that moment, I wanted to slap the shit out of him. I saw myself doing it, too, in my mind. I envisioned it. I saw myself slapping the shit out of him, him falling back over this big pile of action figures. I saw the headlines coming out the next day: Michael Jackson's Security Slaps the Shit Out of Him.

But of course I didn't say or do anything. I just let it go.

Javon: I was standing a couple feet away, and I could see the look on Bill's face. After Mr. Jackson walked away, Bill radioed me and said, "Can you believe he just asked me that?!"

I said, "Bill, why don't you let *me* ask him if he's going to buy your daughter something. Let me. I'll do it."

Because I'd had it. I was tired of tiptoeing around the facts. I wanted to talk to Mr. Jackson and tell him, "Look, Christmas is important to us too. We're fathers too. We want to do the exact same thing for our kids that you're doing for your kids right now, but we can't. So let's get this straight. How are we going to make that happen?"

That's all I was really thinking about. I didn't care about all our back pay. I just wanted enough money in my hands that I could do Christmas. I didn't even have to take my kids to FAO Schwarz. That's all overpriced toys, anyway. I could take them to KB Toys and get them a little something. That's all I needed. And I was ready to get in Mr. Jackson's face and tell him that. I was tired of not saying anything. But Bill kept saying, "Let me handle it. I'll figure something out. I'll talk to Londell."

Bill: When Michael Jackson saw kids in Africa living in poverty, or when he saw kids with cancer living in hospitals, his heart would immediately go out to them. He could read a fan letter about a family going through financial hardship, and he'd literally start to cry. He could be the most sensitive and caring person you'd ever met. In his lifetime, he gave hundreds of millions of dollars to charity. And I'm not just talking about handing the big check over to the United Way in front of the cameras. I'm talking about him personally reaching out and helping people in need. Like with Dave, the guy in New York who'd been burned. There were dozens of people like Dave over the years. In some cases, Michael Jackson literally saved their lives.

That compassion was totally genuine, and it came through in his music, too. Which is why so many of his fans saw him as a saint, this incredibly generous and loving person. And he was. On that level. But when it came to the pain caused by his own actions to the people right in front of him? He couldn't see it. He didn't want to see it. Given the life he'd lived, being isolated from such a very young age, I don't think he ever really developed the skills you need to cope with personal relationships. So he shut those feelings out, refused to deal with them. If you had people that worked for you and they hadn't been paid for months, you'd understand how that would mess them up. You'd know it. You'd see it. He didn't. He couldn't. And that's why I kept saying to myself, "It's not his fault. It's not his fault."

Once we finished all the shopping, we went up to the register. Mr. Jackson was standing behind me while I watched the clerk ring everything up. The bill was close to ten thousand dollars. When the guy gave me the total, I turned around to Mr. Jackson, expecting him to give me cash as usual. Instead, he pulled out a credit card. I didn't know where that credit card came from. I didn't even know he had one. It was new. It still had that white activation sticker across it, like it had never been used. I gave the credit card to the guy. He swiped it. It wasn't declined, but it came up as "Not Authorized."

I said, "Mr. Jackson, did you authorize the card?"

He said, "Yes, I authorize you to use it."

He said it totally straight-faced. Like, "Sure, Bill. You can use it." He thought that's what it meant to authorize a credit card, like his words were some kind of "abracadabra" that would magically make the thing work. I tried talking to him, seeing if he'd called the number to activate it. He honestly didn't know what I was talking about. He'd never had to handle that for himself. He just kept saying, "Oh, there's plenty of money on there. Do it again. Do it again."

Guy swiped it again. Nothing. Couple more times. Nothing. I was whispering back and forth with Mr. Jackson, seeing what he wanted to do. He said, "Just tell them we'll come back and pay for it."

I was like, Does he really think they're just going to let him walk out of here with ten thousand dollars worth of toys and come back and pay for it later? *And* he wants everything gift-wrapped? I knew that wasn't going to happen, but I asked the manager anyway. I said, "Is it possible that we can come back and pay for this?"

He just gave me this look, like, Really? Do you really think I'm going to do that?

I was trying to negotiate something with this guy and meanwhile I had Mr. Jackson in my ear, going, "I shop here all the time. Just tell them it's okay." So finally I was like, Okay, call Londell. It was almost four in the morning New York time, but I didn't care. I called him, told him the situation we were in. Londell said, "Put the manager on. I'll see if he'll take my card over the phone." Londell gave them his card number, paid for everything, and that was that. We got it all wrapped, took it back to the Palms, and put it under the tree.

After that, I was pretty much on hiatus. I made arrangements with hotel security to have people do shifts in front of his door, so that Javon and I could get a little time off. Those guys showed up, and I went home. I was spent. I felt like I needed to vent to somebody. Since Londell had got us out of a few different jams, I thought it would be okay to vent to him. I called him to talk about a few things and I filled him in on my and Javon's situation. He was stunned. He said, "You guys haven't been paid since *when*? Do you need something? What do you need?" Fortunately, he got it without me really having to beg for help or embarrass myself like that. He wired us $2,500 so that we'd have some breathing room for the holidays. That was a huge relief.

Christmas came without much happening. I called Mr. Jackson that afternoon to wish him and the kids merry Christmas. He asked me, "Did your daughter get everything that she wants?"

I said, "Yes, sir. She's good."

He said, "Does she have an iPhone?"

"No, sir."

"Get her an iPhone and tell her it's from me. I'll pay you back."

It felt good that he did that, like maybe he recognized a little bit of what we were going through. So I bought my daughter an iPhone and wrapped it up for her like it was from him, and he did reimburse me for it. A couple days later, I was speaking to Mr. Jackson on the phone and I said, "Sir, my daughter would like to thank you for the iPhone."

He said, "Yeah, sure."

I gave her the phone and they talked for a minute. She said thank you, and he said, "You're welcome." I could just see the joy on my daughter's face while she was talking to him. She couldn't believe she was on the phone with Michael Jackson. That was one of the few bright spots in that time.

Right after Christmas, we were asked to change rooms. Some high roller was coming in for New Year's, and they wanted a paying guest in that room. Peter Lopez called me and said, "Bill, we have to get Mr. Jackson into another suite." We moved to a smaller room on the opposite side of the hallway.

While all this was going on, one morning UPS delivered these three packages to my house. There were three big boxes wrapped in Bubble Wrap. The eBay account Mr. Jackson used was set up in my name, and whenever he ordered something, it was shipped to my house. I called him and let him know that his package arrived. He was real excited and asked me to bring it right over.

I drove the boxes over to the Palms and got a luggage cart to bring them from the car to the room. I brought them in, and Mr. Jackson was like, "Great, great!" We got a knife and started opening these boxes. We opened up the first one and the only thing in it was these legs, like a set of life-sized mannequin legs. Kind of a porcelain color with red shoes on. That was odd. Then we opened up the second box. Inside that one was a torso. It had these wings on it, coming out of the back. I pulled this thing out and I was thinking, Huh, this looks like Tinker Bell. But this can't be Tinker Bell. Tinker Bell's tiny, and this thing is enormous. Then we opened up the third box.

Yep. This is Tinker Bell, dude.

We put this thing together, and I was standing there looking at a damn near seven-foot-tall Tinker Bell. He loved it. He wanted it in a certain area of the room. He was going, "This is great! This is great!"

That was a difficult moment. Here I was, really bending over backwards to try and help him in whatever little ways I could, but he was still doing the same things that got him in this mess. He can't even pay for the roof he's living under, and he's off buying crap on eBay? In some ways I blamed him, and in some ways I didn't. There were times I felt this situation was his responsibility and I was furious with him. Other times, I felt this was all because of what other people had done to him and it wasn't fair and I was angry at them. There were days when I felt I really understood him and what he was going through, and there were days I didn't understand him at all.

Javon: That day we were at FAO Schwarz, that's the angriest I ever was with him. But even then I couldn't stay mad at him for more than ten minutes. I'm sure he said something on the way home that made me forget all about it. There was just something about him, his demeanor. He was so sweet and soft-spoken. You could be in a bad mood, and his good spirit and his energy would instantly soften you and cheer you up. That's just the way his inner being rubbed off on people. He knew how to make people love him. Just the way he spoke to you made you think that everything that came out of his mouth was genuine.

I saw how this man brought smiles to everyone that came around him. Everyone that came in contact with him, from celebrities to average Joes, he brightened up their lives. We couldn't see why, in business, he couldn't put people in place that he could trust. We couldn't believe that as brilliant as he was, he could be taken advantage of the way he was being taken advantage of. It made you feel sorry for him and for the kids. They were living out of suitcases. There was no structure about where they were going to stay. It made you want to protect them and make sure nothing happened to them. That's why it stopped being just a job for us. It was more like you felt you were on a mission.

You'd see him in his naive stage and you'd think, This guy can't even authorize his own credit card. He's so used to people taking care of him, maybe it's really not his fault that we're not getting paid. But at the same time, he could set up a sting with the paparazzi to test me to see if I'm trustworthy or not. To me, that's a guy who's very clued in and very aware of what's going on. So which was it?

I had a harder time with it than Bill. I would get more upset, and Bill would always talk me down, saying, "It's not Mr. Jackson's fault." And I'd say, "But Bill, at some point it *has* to be his fault." Yeah, he had all these people taking advantage of him, but he's the one who hired those people. And even if other people did this to him, whatever problems you have in your life, they become your fault eventually if you haven't done anything to fix them. That's why you always wanted to grab him and tell him, "Mr. Jackson, man up! It's time to take a hold of what you built. All it takes is for you to put your foot down." But he couldn't. He was afraid to give orders. He'd walk on eggshells around his own employees. I couldn't fathom it.

Bill: Whenever I hear that whole thing about how Michael Jackson missed out on his childhood or how he never got to be a kid, I hear it different than most people. He wants to play with toys and ride roller coasters and have sleepovers and this and that. Okay, that's some of what he missed out on. That's part of what childhood is, but it's also a lot more than that. "Clean your room." That's childhood. "Take out the garbage." "Apologize to your sister." That's childhood. It's not just about playing games and having fun. Childhood isn't just about being a child. It's about becoming an adult. Because eventually you will be an adult, whether you want to or not.

He loved all those stories about Peter Pan and all that. But I sometimes wondered if he really got what that story's about. I think he just took from it what he wanted to take. Because what happens in that book is that the children leave Neverland and go back to their parents and grow up. That's the point. That's reality. You do have to grow up. But if the people around you never pushed you to do that? If nobody taught you the things that you needed to learn? Then you're not going to have the skills that you need to be able to deal with the world. Did Michael Jackson miss out on his childhood? He missed out on a lot.

New Year's Eve came around and we were still at the Palms, still waiting for something to happen. That night, Javon took off to be with his family. I went down to the hotel by myself. There were guys posted at his door, but I wanted to be nearby, just in case he called. I figured something might come up. New Year's Eve at the Palms is crazy. There's two or three different nightclubs in there, so it's packed.

I settled in at one of the restaurants downstairs and had dinner. I sat there most of the evening, wondering if things were going to get better. Because if it kept getting worse, I was going to have to do what I had to do to take care of my family. You talk about soul searching. That's exactly what it was. Midnight came, and I was walking through the lobby and this huge crowd was all around me, counting down and ringing in the new year. I stood there in the middle of all of those people laughing and drinking and having a good time, and I just wasn't happy. I was not happy, because I didn't see the light at the end of this tunnel.

PART THREE

THIS IS IT

15

January 2008 found Michael Jackson still at the Palms, working around the clock in the hotel's studio in an effort to deliver his long-overdue tracks for *Thriller 25*—tracks he had to deliver even though Sony had informed him that he wouldn't actually be seeing any income from the album's release. The label would be keeping any royalties it generated to cover Jackson's half of the administrative costs from the Sony/ATV catalog, which the singer had fallen behind on.

In addition to the work for the album, Jackson and Londell McMillan had indeed been finalizing a deal to avert the singer's short-term cash crisis. Barclays bank had purchased and refinanced the $300 million loan Jackson had taken out against the Sony/ATV catalog. HSBC and Plainfield Asset Management, a hedge fund, had lent the singer an additional $70 million against Mijac, the catalog that held the rights to Jackson's own music. And Sony had guaranteed Jackson's new debt load in exchange for the first right of refusal to buy him out of the Beatles catalog if he defaulted. However, Fortress Investment Group did hold on to the $23 million note on Neverland; if Jackson failed to save it from foreclosure by March 19, the investment group stood to make millions from dumping the estate at auction.

Most of this new $370 million influx Jackson would never see. It went to settle old lawsuits and claims and to cover outstanding expenses, like the $300,000 in back pay owed to the staff at Neverland.

Jackson received an $11 million living allowance, and the balance of what remained was set aside for the sole purpose of covering the interest payments on the new loans.

Amazingly, on paper, Michael Jackson was still not broke. The cash value of his assets—the publishing catalogs, his property holdings, his vast collection of cars and antiques—was still greater than his debts. But he remained cash poor. Short of liquidating everything he owned and walking away from the business of being the King of Pop, his only real option, as he had known for some time, was to go back onstage.

After several years in financial free-fall, Michael Jackson was once again standing on his feet, at least temporarily. But this new state of affairs created as many problems as it solved. When the world believed that the singer was broke and broken, most people were content to just leave him be. Now, word was beginning to circulate that the King of Pop might be coming back to life. Over the Christmas and New Year's holidays, as Bill and Javon had suspected, their employer had dismissed Raymone Bain; in one of the many settlements to come out of the new loan package, she was paid a considerable amount of money to go away. There was now a power vacuum at the center of his organization, and all sorts of people were rushing in to fill it.

Bill: After a couple weeks at the Palms, I heard that Michael Amir was in Vegas. He was going to be around, helping out. He'd first been introduced to Mr. Jackson by Feldman, back when we were staying at the Monte Cristo house. That's when his name first came up. Then he was around while we were in Virginia. He started out like an intern. He was cataloging all of Mr. Jackson's books with a computer program, helping Mr. Jackson with his film projects, doing stuff like that. Whenever he came to town, I had to make arrangements to get him from the airport, so we'd spoken a number of times. We were cordial. We were cool.

When Michael Amir hit Vegas, he called me and asked if he could use one of the trucks because the boss wanted him to go on a couple of errands. Before, whenever Mr. Jackson sent him to get film equipment at Best Buy or wherever, either me or Javon would drive him. I didn't give him the keys to the truck. I didn't know him that well. I wasn't okay with that. Then at the Palms, he was suddenly asking for the truck and telling me that the boss said it was okay. I checked with Mr. Jackson and he said it was fine, so I didn't question it too much.

Pretty soon, though, Michael Amir was communicating with Mr. Jackson every day. Since Grace wasn't around, he started taking over some of the things that Grace used to do. I started to notice that, when he came up to the Palms, he wouldn't even have to ask us if Mr. Jackson was in his room or the studio; he already knew, and he'd go straight to wherever Mr. Jackson was. They seemed to be getting closer and closer. On the one hand, I was cool with it because I wouldn't have to do so much running around. On the other hand, I also wondered what his agenda was.

At the same time, we were still under a lot of pressure to find a house. We needed to get the hell out of the Palms. The Maloof brothers weren't putting Mr. Jackson up out of charity. When Peter Lopez made that deal and told George Maloof, "Michael Jackson's going to come and stay at your hotel," I'm pretty sure Maloof said yes under the impression that Michael Jackson would be eating in his restaurants, making appearances in his nightclubs—generating press. But Mr. Jackson didn't do any of that. He just worked in the studio and took the service elevator back upstairs. And once it was clear that he wasn't leaving his room? That free ride was over. Time to go.

Around mid-January, Mr. Jackson called me and said he'd found a house and that he was going to be moving. That was news to me, because he'd had me working on all those arrangements during Christmas and New Year's. Then Mr. Jackson said, "Call Michael Amir. He'll give you all of the details."

Michael Amir?

There it was. He'd stepped up. It had happened almost over-night. Suddenly he wasn't just a gofer. He was coming to me and Javon and saying, "Mr. Jackson needs you to do this or do that." He was in Mr. Jackson's ear now. He'd taken over the house search without me even knowing about it. That made me nervous. Not because I didn't like the guy; he and I never had problems. But it was always suspect when people were maneuvering and being secretive around Mr. Jackson. I'd seen how that played out with Grace and Raymone and Feldman before. But I wasn't there to question what Mr. Jackson wanted. I just called Michael Amir to find out what was going on with the house.

As soon as he told me about the place, I knew which one he was talking about. I had passed it a few times and seen it was avail-able, but I'd never even considered it because I knew Mr. Jackson wouldn't have picked it. The house was this Spanish hacienda-type estate on Palomino, right off Rancho, north of where the Monte Cristo place was. I knew the area. It's not a great neighborhood. The neighbors' houses were right up on top of it, and Rancho is a real busy street, which meant a lot of traffic, a lot of eyeballs to worry about.

It was also near a school; there was an elementary school right across the street. I saw that and I was like, Are you kidding me? The flak he's going to get over that? I know Michael Jackson wasn't a child molester, but there are still people out there who think otherwise. Parents started complaining almost from the day he moved in, saying that it was dangerous to have Michael Jackson living near a school. It was all over Vegas. It made the local news. Knowing how much he wants his privacy, why would you put him through that by renting that house? Plus, you're teasing Prince and Paris and Blanket every day. All the other kids playing across the street and they've got to hear it? Terrible idea. But nobody asked me.

Javon and I didn't even help with the move. Michael Amir made the arrangements. He had six or seven guys from the Nation of Islam come out, and they packed everything up at the Palms and brought it over. Once Mr. Jackson was at the house, word came down that these guys from the Nation were going to be handling security at the house, and Javon and I would be working alongside them, handling the logistics of taking Mr. Jackson on details. That surprised me because he got a lot of flak for using Nation of Islam people during his trial. That was the whole reason I'd been brought on in the first place.

Javon: As far as the Nation moving him into the Palomino house, I didn't see it as us being pushed aside. I was relieved. I needed the break after being on the road with him all that time. And there was still plenty of things me and Bill were doing. We had the relationships with all the restaurants and theaters he liked to go to, so we still handled the details when he left the house. That didn't change. Plus, I knew that the Nation was very protective of Mr. Jackson. Those guys are dedicated. They're soldiers. Nothing was going to happen to him on their watch. And with them watching the house, working for Mr. Jackson became more like a regular nine-to-five type gig again. Show up for work, provide your service, and go home. Which was fine with me.

Bill: They never set up the security trailer at the new house. The word was always, "He's not going to be here that long." Now, was I being told that because he really wasn't going to be there that long or because they didn't want us around? Were people trying to push us away? I would call Peter Lopez and ask, "What's going on? What's my job now? Do I still have a job?"

Peter would say, "Don't worry, Bill. He loves you guys. Everything's fine. There's a lot going on right now, a lot of changes happening, but you guys are fine."

I took a wait-and-see kind of attitude, but things were definitely different. All the faxes and emails I'd been getting? More and more, those documents weren't coming at me anymore. A lot of that was now going to Michael Amir. Mr. Jackson and I never had a conversation about it. It was just that one day I was doing all that stuff, then it started to taper off, then all of a sudden I wasn't doing it at all.

Michael Amir had become the new Feldman, and I was fine with that. I preferred it that way—I really did. I was cool with not being that dude. We've all had bosses that get on our nerves. Michael Jackson was my boss, and some days he got on my nerves. It was all the little things, the tedious stuff. The phone calls. "I want this." "I need this." "Find me a Ferris wheel." I didn't want to deal with his lawyers and managers anymore, either, all the politics and the backstabbing. If somebody else wanted to step up and do all that? Cool. Take it. Call me when you need me for security. If I got a call from Greg Cross or someone saying they needed to send or fax something, I'd just say, "Hold on. Let me get you Michael Amir's number." I wasn't dealing with any of that anymore.

The mood wasn't the same. The fans didn't come back at this new house, and they'd been such a big part of what kept his spirits up. There were a few that came by from time to time, but not in the same numbers, not the way they did at the Monte Cristo house. This new area, this location, it wasn't private. There was no strip of property outside the gate for them to camp out on. You also couldn't have fans hanging out all day in front of an elementary school.

A lot of the fans didn't even know where he'd moved. Since Raymone was gone, she wasn't sending along any of the fan mail. And her address was the only one that a lot of the fans had. I didn't know where the fan mail was going. There was no office. It was just getting lost, I guess. Some of the fans who knew me would reach out to me. They were hearing things about him doing a show. I didn't have much information to give them. They'd send me cards and ask me to pass them along. They'd say, "Tell him we miss him. Tell him we love him."

I was also getting a lot of questions about the *Thriller 25* album. The anniversary of the actual release date had come and gone back at the end of November. All sorts of stuff had been planned, TV specials, appearances. None of it had happened because he wasn't cool with it. As far as he was concerned, that album was perfect. You don't go back and add hip-hop beats to *Thriller*. It's a classic, and you don't touch it. But they told him he had to.

Javon: Sony had told him to get in the studio with some of these younger artists and do these remixes to make himself new and hip again. But he didn't do it with enthusiasm. You could tell that. That's why it was so down to the last minute with those sessions at the Palms. He kept putting it off and putting it off, and the remixes kept taking longer and longer to finish. The whole month we were at the Palms, Mr. Jackson basically never left the hotel because he was working with will.i.am in the studio the entire time. Me and Bill spent most of our time in the lobby of the studio with will.i.am's security, keeping an eye on them while they were in there working.

Bill: It wasn't until after the album came out that Javon and I learned that Mr. Jackson had thanked us in the liner notes. He didn't tell us he was going to do that; we learned about it from friends who bought the album and saw our names. When I got a copy of the disc and saw it, I was like, Wow! That got me excited. It felt good, after everything we'd been through, to be acknowledged like that. It felt like our small contribution was appreciated.

Javon: When I saw my name in the liner notes? That was one of the most joyful moments of my life. Nobody can take that away from me. That album will never be duplicated. It will outlive my kids' kids' kids' kids. The way the Internet is, no one will ever sell over 100 million copies ever again, and that makes it the number one album in human history. So to have my name be a part of that? It was all worth it.

Bill: When the album hit, it was a huge success. Went straight to No. 1 in the U.S. and in a lot of other countries. Outside, in the media and in the music press, there was all this hype about the twenty-fifth anniversary of this album, but inside the camp it barely registered. You'd think it might have gotten him excited, been a jolt in the arm or something. But honestly, he didn't talk about it like it was a big deal. I heard more excitement in his voice talking about going to see *Spider-Man 3* than I ever heard when he was talking about *Thriller 25*.

It was not a happy time, those months after the Palms. On the surface, it was business as usual, but the mood in the house was kind of gloomy. The Monte Cristo house, as many problems as it had, there was at least an effort to make it a home, building the library and the dance studio, the classroom for the kids. At Palomino? There was no studio built in there, no classroom, no library. It wasn't a home.

When the kids' birthdays came around, there was no more going all out like before. No more clowns and jumpers. The people around him now, they just didn't have the same vibe. I feel like Javon and I, being dads, we just brought more of a fatherly touch to doing that job. We knew all the things you need to know to raise kids in this town. If he wanted a clown, we went out of our way to find one. Trampolines and decorations and cakes, we did all that. The team that was with him now, most of them didn't live in Vegas. They were from L.A. If Mr. Jackson said, "We need to find a clown," they probably wouldn't have known where to start.

Javon: The new team hadn't been around the family enough to know their likes and dislikes, their dos and don'ts. We knew what kind of cereal each of the kids liked, that sort of thing. But we weren't around the house to help out and go that extra mile for them anymore. We were just handling transportation and protection whenever he left the house. And there weren't nearly as many outings at that time, either. The nights we used to drive down the Strip and go people-watching? There were no more of those. He stayed in. Taking the kids to Krispy Kreme and Circus Circus? We maybe did that once or twice.

Bill: His demeanor had changed. He was more quiet, more withdrawn. Three days would go by and I wouldn't hear from him, and I used to hear from him four or five times a day, every day. So I'd call him and say, "Hi, Mr. Jackson. It's Bill."

"Hey, Bill."

"Is everything okay?"

"I'm fine. Is there a problem?"

"No, sir. No problem. Just haven't heard any communication in a while. Wanted to make sure everything's okay."

"Sure. Thanks for checking in."

And that'd be it. I didn't know what was wrong; I just knew something wasn't right. You could tell by what was going on with the kids. Whenever he moved to an unfamiliar place or was surrounded by strange faces, he kept the kids closer to him. The freedom he allowed them at Monte Cristo or in Virginia, letting us take them out, going to playgrounds and such, those days were over. The kids were always under his wing now. That meant his guard was up.

I started to get an uneasy feeling about the direction everything was going. For a year, he didn't make a move that I didn't know about. Then one day, around late February, maybe early March, I got a call from Peter Lopez. He said, "Bill, Michael is wondering where you guys are."

I said, "What do you mean 'wondering where we are'?"

"Why aren't you guys in L.A.?"

"He's in L.A.?"

"Yeah."

"Mr. Lopez, we didn't even know he was in L.A."

The other team had taken him to California without telling us. Peter seemed just as confused as I was. He said, "Bill, what's going on here?"

I said, "I don't know. Talk to Michael Amir."

Couple days later, Mr. Jackson called me himself and said, "Bill, where are you guys? Why aren't you in L.A.?"

It made me feel incompetent, but I didn't know what to tell him besides the truth. I said, "Sir, I didn't know you were in L.A. Nobody told me."

"Oh. I thought they told you. Just speak to Michael Amir—and see if you can find out when I'm coming back to Vegas."

Huh? Find out when you're coming back? I wanted to say, "Why don't *you* tell *me* when you're coming back? How do you not know? How are you not the person who decides that?" But he wasn't. He had no control over what was going on around him.

There were a couple more times that he disappeared to L.A. without me knowing. I found out later via Peter Lopez that whenever Mr. Jackson was asking for me and Javon, people were telling him that he couldn't reach us. But I wasn't getting any missed calls. Michael Amir had my number. He knew exactly where I was. He just didn't call. Pretty soon, it reached the point where I didn't have Mr. Jackson's direct number anymore. The iPhones that I'd set up for him and his mother in my name? The bill on those was never paid. The charges had run up close to two thousand dollars, and they got disconnected. Mrs. Jackson called me because she couldn't get in touch with him anymore. I had to give her Michael Amir's number because that was the only way I had of reaching him.

Sometimes I would call Michael Amir myself and say, "Listen, I need to talk to the boss."

He'd say, "Sure, I can give him a message for you." And there'd be that tone in his voice, that tone you use when you're just trying to get somebody off the phone.

I'd just say, "Fine. Have him call me." But I'm sure he wasn't putting any of my messages through.

It was weird. Michael Amir had taken on that same possessive attitude that Feldman had. Much as I was happy to let go of that gatekeeper role, I felt uneasy about not knowing everything that was happening. Things started to get fishy to me. I wanted to know what was going on. Maybe I was feeling a little jealous myself, but I knew that Mr. Jackson was easily influenced. I knew that somebody had his ear.

This had all started back at the Palms, because that's when the money showed up. Right after Christmas, he'd made this deal. It was one of the last things I handled back when all the communication was still going through me. This huge transfer of cash came in. At the time, I thought it was maybe an advance on doing a concert or part of the *Thriller 25* deal. I found out later it was a loan. That big loan consolidation that Raymone and Greg Cross had been fighting about? That deal had finally gone through. That was the money that got him moved into the Palomino house. That's what allowed me and Javon to finally get paid a little something. Not all of our money, but about three months' worth. Enough for us to have some faith.

But even with this new loan, regular paychecks never came back. Two months would go by, and you'd get some of your money. Another month, a little more. There was still no organized management. I pushed it as far as I could with Londell and Michael Amir. It was like listening to Raymone all over again. They'd say, "Man, things are just so messed up. We're trying to work on some things. We're trying to get everyone paid."

Whatever. I didn't press it because I'd learned not to expect any different. But I don't think they knew that I knew just how much money was going through the mill. One of the last documents I handled for Mr. Jackson as we were leaving the Palms was a fax he needed to sign, authorizing some wire transfers after this loan came through. This document was five pages long, just page after page of names—attorneys, managers, creditors, banks. Seemed like everybody that Mr. Jackson owed money to was on that form, and they were all lining up to get paid.

The biggest chunks went to make back payments on his loans. There was a $5 million wire transfer for Transitional Investors, $1.3 million for Signal Hill Capital. A lot of it was for lawyer fees. There was $1.35 million for Greg Cross's firm. Londell's firm, Dewey & LeBoeuf, they got $1.5 million, plus there was a transfer of $276,000 for Londell himself. Raymone's consulting firm took $413,700, and Raymone personally got a lump payment of $487,570; that was the money she got to walk away. There was even a $775,000 payment to cover his back taxes from 2006—whoever was handling his money hadn't been paying his taxes.

Over $56 million went out the door with one signature. And that was just one document on one night, so it had to be one little piece of what was going on. And it wasn't like he was doing this with new income. This was coming from another loan. This was taking from Peter to pay Paul. It was all part of cleaning house. When Raymone got cut out, all these new handlers came in, and this was their plan: settle all the old business so we can get down to new business.

You started hearing a lot more talk about doing a show, how much a concert could generate, where's the best place to do it. Those conversations had always been going on, but they were usually in the background. Now the talk was getting louder, more specific. Word started going around: Michael Jackson is going back to work. You started to see a lot more activity going on. This machine was opening up. And as it opened up, more people were coming through. More faces. More phone calls. Kenny Ortega, the choreographer, suddenly he's in the mix. This guy, Frank DiLeo, who'd managed Mr. Jackson back in the 1980s. I'd never even heard his name before, but now he's back in the picture. There were new people coming on payroll. This guy needs a thirty-thousand-dollar advance to start working. That guy needs a fifteen-thousand-dollar retainer to come on board. The money is getting ready to be made now, and everybody wants a piece.

I could see the stress getting to him. There was this weight just coming down on his shoulders. I remember a conversation we had at the Palms. I'd just driven him back to the hotel, and we were in the elevator headed up to his room. We were coming from a meeting where he'd finalized some deal. Probably it was those loan papers, something big. And as we rode up in the elevator, he had this look on his face. It was like he was getting himself ready for something he knew was about to happen, something he was dreading. He said, "You weren't here before, Bill, so you haven't seen it yet. But you're going to."

"Haven't seen what, sir?"

"The vultures," he said. "They're going to start coming now. Everybody is going to want something, and nobody is going to trust anybody else. You're about to see the ugliness in people. Just wait."

16

While talk of a possible Michael Jackson comeback began to circulate, the March 19 deadline to save Neverland from foreclosure still loomed on the horizon. Just days before the cutoff, Jackson's attorney Londell McMillan made a statement to the Associated Press, claiming that "a secret deal" had been made to keep the estate from going to auction. In reality, that "deal" was simply another extension, giving Jackson an additional two months to locate an investor willing to bail him out.

Then, in April, through his brother Jermaine, Michael met a man named Tohme Tohme, a heavily accented Lebanese businessman of somewhat mysterious origin. Tohme referred to himself as "Dr. Tohme Tohme," even though, as near as anyone could tell, he was not a doctor of any kind. Tohme was a middleman, a facilitator, someone adept at leveraging his network of relationships to broker deals in the real estate and entertainment worlds. After meeting with Michael and learning of Neverland's impending fate, Tohme tapped into that network to connect the singer with billionaire Tom Barrack, owner and CEO of the private equity firm Colony Capital.

Barrack met with Jackson in Las Vegas and subsequently agreed to buy out Jackson's $23 million loan in exchange for a 50 percent stake in the property. Properly restored, Barrack believed, Neverland could easily be worth $60 million or more. Colony would cover the cost of rehabilitating the estate, and then together they would sell it, each pocketing a share of the proceeds. Tohme Tohme was in for a finder's fee, and soon would be in for a lot more.

The speed with which the Neverland deal came together convinced Jackson that Barrack and Tohme were the kind of people he ought to be in business with. That summer, he hired Tohme to succeed Raymone Bain as his manager. After seeing the state of Jackson's financial affairs, Tohme began aggressively pushing his new client to go back onstage. Tom Barrack, too, saw the potential in a Michael Jackson comeback; he knew what restoring the singer's public image would do for the resale value of Neverland. Colony Capital, among its many interests, was owner of the Las Vegas Hilton, where Elvis Presley had made his historic comeback in 1969. Barrack broached the idea of Jackson performing there, but Jackson still balked at the idea of a Vegas show.

Barrack then put in a call to his friend and fellow billionaire Philip Anschutz, owner of the Anschutz Entertainment Group, with the notion to put Jackson and AEG together for a show at AEG's O2 Arena in London, not knowing that AEG was already thinking along identical lines. The promoter was very keen to get in the Michael Jackson business and had been ever since Raymone Bain set up the first meeting between Jackson and AEG Live CEO Randy Phillips the year before. During their first sit-down, Jackson had been deeply ambivalent about the deal AEG was proposing. Since then, circumstances had changed.

Bill: Once I handed things over to Michael Amir, I started to be less aware about what was going on with the business side. I didn't want to know. Who his new manager was? Didn't care. Who his new lawyer was? Didn't care. It had nothing to do with me.

I had a few dealings with this new person Tohme Tohme. His office tried to get me and Javon to sign non-disclosure agreements. Because of the way we'd come on, when there was a gap in security, there was no one around to make us sign them. Then pretty quickly we were the ones in the position of getting other people to sign them. So now this Tohme Tohme guy was trying to get us to agree to one retroactively, saying we couldn't get all of our back pay until we did. Our paychecks were being used as leverage again. I wouldn't do it. I took it as a sign of disrespect. I knew it wasn't coming from Mr. Jackson; he'd never asked that of me. I felt I'd earned his trust by the way I did my job. So now that I was being asked to do it, I saw it as a sign of what was going on in the organization: all these new people maneuvering for control, inserting themselves between me and Mr. Jackson.

After that, I didn't deal directly with Tohme Tohme's people. I let all that go through Michael Amir. But I'd still pick up bits and pieces of what was going on. In June, we took Mr. Jackson to a meeting at the Las Vegas Hilton with the owner, Tom Barrack. They had dinner at the Japanese restaurant there, Benihana. Barrack was there to talk to him about their plans for fixing and saving Neverland, about him possibly being a headliner at the Hilton. All those Vegas headliner discussions had been going on for over a year, but that summer, I started hearing not just about the Vegas gig but maybe a tour, a concert overseas. London, maybe. But by that point, I'd heard about so many different things—concerts, appearances, whatever—and none of it ever panned out, so I didn't put much stock into it.

Javon: I didn't feel like he wanted it. I didn't feel like he ever wanted to go back onstage. When he was with us, it didn't seem like he missed it at all. He was more excited about starting a new chapter of his life, being around his kids every day. He didn't jump into perform- ing at the Wynn, and they made some really good offers to per- form there. If he talked about music or dancing, it was purely from the creative side. Any time the conversation turned toward the business or commercial side, there was no joy, no enthusiasm.

Bill: Every now and then, though, you'd get a glimpse of this other part of him, like when we were at the *Ebony* photo shoot in Brooklyn. I always called it the King of Pop mode. There were two sides of him. There was Michael Jackson, the family man, the father, and there was the King of Pop. Michael Jackson wanted his privacy. He was desperate for a normal life, but at the same time, if you've been the greatest in the world at something, I think it's hard to let that go. He would say, "I want everyone to leave me alone." But then when we took him out on details and got caught out by the fans and he was getting that love? Oh, yeah. He liked that. He'd light up. When the stylist used to come and get his hair and makeup looking good and he had his new Roberto Cavalli outfit on? When we had dinner at the Wynn and we'd walk through those casinos and people were shouting his name and saying, "We love you"? All that King of Pop stuff? He'd eat that up.

Javon: There was one night when we were at the Palms. He wanted to go to the club downstairs. He didn't want to make an appearance or be seen; he just wanted to slip in and hang out for a little while, do some people watching. This club had a private upstairs balcony that overlooked the crowd, so we set it up for him to go down there.

We were in the club for maybe two to three minutes when all of a sudden the DJ started playing one of his songs. They were mixing it with a lot of samples from other artists. Mr. Jackson was bopping his head along to it, and he said, "Wow, I didn't know that they still played my music."

We were like, *What*?! We told him, "Sir, they still play your music all the time. In bars, clubs. You still hear it everywhere."

He said, "Really?"

He seemed surprised. I think he felt like a lot of people had forgotten him or he wasn't as popular anymore. It really made him happy to hear his songs in the club like that.

Bill: People often reached out to get permission to sample his music. Peter Lopez handled a lot of that. He would call me and say, "Bill, tell Michael that Kanye West wants to sample such-and-such tune. What does he want to charge?"

I'd relay the message to Mr. Jackson, and he'd say, "Nothing. Tell them it's fine if they just use it. The more they use my music, that means my music stays alive."

He could have charged a fortune, but he didn't. He just wanted his music to be out there in the world. It was important for him to keep that King of Pop title, to be remembered.

One time I was driving with him, and I had on this morning radio talk show and they started doing one of those call-ins. They were asking listeners, "Who do you think was better, Michael Jackson or Elvis Presley? Call in and let us know how you feel."

I turned it up. I wanted to hear what his reaction would be. People were calling in and giving their opinions, saying they liked one or the other. For a while, Mr. Jackson was just being quiet in the back. He wasn't making any comments, but I could tell he was listening. Then he just burst out, "Elvis couldn't *touch* me! I sold more records than him *and* the Beatles! They can't touch what I'm capable of doing." He still had that performer's ego. It would come out of him from time to time.

Javon: Being the entertainer he was, it was like Dr. Jekyll and Mr. Hyde. He didn't want the bad side of fame. He wanted to be left alone when negative stuff came up, but he didn't want to be left alone on a good day. Any time he did talk about performing again, he'd say it was because he felt he owed it to his fans. What do you do as an artist if you leave your audience behind? If he didn't tour or do any records or anything, he'd be turning his back on his fans, and he was *huge* on his fans. They were his biggest supporters. So that weighed on his decision. "I need to do it for them," he'd say.

Bill: He'd also talk about doing it for his kids. He'd say that now that they were old enough to appreciate who their father was and what he did, he wanted them to see it themselves. He'd say that he would have loved for his kids to see him and his brothers perform together, to see how it all started. But then that's all he'd do. He'd just say it. Any time a deal or an opportunity to do it came up, like with the Vegas thing, he'd drag his feet, back away, make some excuse.

So there was some desire on his part to perform but, in our opinion, not that much. That's not why he went back to work when he did. This concert everybody was talking about, it was being put together because of his financial obligations. It wasn't "Hey, we should do a show." No. It was "Hey, you *gotta* do a show. You have to do a show to get out of this hole." Who wants that? He was a perfectionist. He wanted to do things on his own time with his own personal stamp on them, and who can do that under that kind of pressure?

I had my doubts about why he was being steered in this particular direction. He had other options. He still owned half the Sony catalog. Why not sell that and settle your debts and go somewhere and start over? If he really wanted to be left alone, why not do that? Part of the reason he wouldn't sell it was that he hated Sony. Letting them take the catalog would have felt like they'd beaten him. But from the things I was hearing, I also got the sense that people didn't want him to sell the Sony catalog. If Michael Jackson sells his half of the Sony catalog, nobody gets paid except Michael Jackson. If Michael Jackson endorses something, nobody gets paid except Michael Jackson. But if Michael Jackson does a show? *Everybody* gets paid.

That's where the pressure was coming from. They were starting to put dollar figures in his face, saying, "This will wipe out your debts. This will pay off every lawsuit." And that was always how he wanted to handle things. "Take care of it." "Get rid of it." "Make it go away." He became convinced he could put everything behind him if he had enough money to pay everyone to get lost. That's not how it works. If you're at the top, people come after you. More money, more problems. That's the game. You know that, and I know that, but I don't think he saw it that way. He was inside the bubble, thinking about the glory days.

When *Thriller* first came out, he was *the man* in everybody's eyes. What issues did he have? What drama did he have other than making badass music? You didn't hear all the negative crap. Back then, he really did have enough money to buy his way out of just about anything. He could buy a place like Neverland and escape. That's why he wanted to be able to buy the house on Durango. That place was like Neverland. It was so huge, you couldn't see him and he couldn't see you. That's the time he wanted to get back to. He thought he could buy his way back there. In his experience, that was the answer: get enough money to get out.

So I think that's why he agreed to do a concert. And knowing him? The way he handled money? The suitcases full of cash? That's why he agreed to something overseas. He came to Vegas to be a headliner, but if he'd been a headliner here, everybody suing him could have put liens on that show. Do the same show in London, and it's a lot harder to go after that money. My guess is a lot of it was going to stay overseas. Numbered accounts. Cash in safety deposit boxes. Keep it hidden from everyone, including his own lawyers and managers. That's how his mind worked. That's why he decided to do this concert. He thought if he could make enough money over there, he could get out with his kids, and this nightmare of all the vultures and the lawsuits and the drama would finally end. But it wasn't really going to end. As long as he was Michael Jackson, it was never going to end.

17

By late September 2008, Tohme Tohme and Tom Barrack's preliminary talks with AEG had borne fruit, leading to a handshake agreement to stage a series of concerts at the O2 Arena in London the following year. Shortly after the deal was struck, Jackson left Las Vegas for an open-ended stay at the Hotel Bel-Air in Los Angeles, where he began taking meetings with the various choreographers and musicians he hoped would join him for the new show.

In addition to landing the AEG deal, Tohme Tohme continued to make things happen for his new client. He even strong-armed Sony into forking over the $12 million in royalties it had withheld from the sales of *Thriller 25*; since Sony Music and Sony/ATV Music Publishing are two separate entities, the company had no right to hold revenues from one to cover administrative costs from the other. Jackson instructed Tohme to take the *Thriller 25* windfall and save every penny of it for one thing and one thing only: to use as a down payment on the massive estate on Durango that he had been eyeing since the year before. That house, his soon-to-be Wonderland, was the reward Jackson promised himself for going through with the concerts in London.

The music industry was now buzzing with the news that Michael Jackson was going back to work, and everyone began elbowing their way in to get a piece of the action. Second in line, behind AEG, was the Jackson family. While making a public appearance in Australia that October, Jermaine Jackson announced to local reporters that the Jacksons, including "Michael, Randy, and the whole family" were "in the studio and planning on being out there next year." This was news to Michael, who was not in the studio with his brothers, wasn't speaking to Jermaine, Randy, or anyone else, and had no intention of joining them in any kind of tour. The day after Jermaine's comments to the Australian press, on Halloween, Michael released a statement saying that he loved his family dearly but had "no plans to record or tour with them."

From that point, the jockeying around Jackson's comeback started to get strange. Joe Jackson began meeting with a concert promoter, Patrick Allocco of AllGood Entertainment, promising a Jackson reunion that included Michael. In spite of Michael's public denials, Patrick Allocco decided to believe what Joe Jackson was telling him—the lure of being in the Michael Jackson business was just that powerful. Joe Jackson instructed Allocco to reach out to Frank DiLeo, whom Joe described as "Michael's manager." But Frank DiLeo had no business relationship with Michael Jackson and hadn't since he was fired in 1989. Still, DiLeo met with Allocco and claimed to be in a position to bring a deal to Michael for a family reunion. On November 26, DiLeo signed an agreement with AllGood Entertainment to produce a Jackson family reunion concert.

Even if Michael Jackson had been interested in the idea of a reunion, there was little chance that AllGood or any other promoter would be able to match what AEG was willing to put on the table. Tohme Tohme had started negotiations for the London concerts, and he was making steep demands—a large cash advance, a house in Los Angeles for Jackson and his family to live in until the show. AEG agreed to all of it.

On November 17, Sheikh Abdullah's case against the singer went to trial in London. Grace Rwaramba was called to testify, and Jackson was subpoenaed to testify as well. To avoid the public spectacle of the singer going back on the witness stand—and because no deal for the O2 shows could be finalized until Abdullah's claim was resolved—AEG stepped in and paid the sheikh a $5 million settlement, releasing Jackson from the contract he'd entered into three years earlier. But just as Sony did not keep refinancing Jackson's debt out of simple charity, AEG wasn't helping the singer out of the kindness of its heart, either. Jackson's obligations didn't go away. They merely shifted from his wealthy Middle Eastern benefactor to his corporate American one. AEG expected a return on its investment.

Philip Anschutz, Tohme Tohme, Tom Barrack, Randy Phillips, Joe Jackson, Jermaine Jackson, Patrick Allocco, Frank DiLeo, Londell McMillan, Peter Lopez, Michael Amir Williams—the list of players jockeying to be a part of Michael Jackson's billion-dollar comeback was growing longer with each day. Before it was over, Jackson's former adviser and longtime attorney John Branca would rejoin the pack as well. Some of these people had only the best of intentions, a true desire to see the singer free of debt and back on top. Others were driven by different motives. But all of them shared one thing in common: they now had a vested interest in seeing Michael Jackson back onstage in the summer of 2009, whether he was ready for it or not.

Bill: Once the plan for the concert started to take shape, that took precedence over everything else. Now it was King of Pop mode, full-time. We'd take him on a detail once a week, maybe every two weeks, but he was going to L.A. for a lot of meetings, spending more time there.

I would still get phone calls because I was the keeper of a lot of information. Anything anybody needed from the past year—a phone number, a document—I'd get a call to help locate that. All that stuff we put in storage in Vegas and in Virginia, we were still handling that. From the minute Mr. Jackson got back to the Palms, he was asking about all the film equipment that we'd left in Virginia, so we were making arrangements to have a lot of that shipped back.

It was like he was trying to create two different worlds. There was his personal life, and then there was this whole show-business machine that was gearing up, and he was trying to keep them separate. There were things on a personal level, things that he didn't want the concert people to become a part of. The school-teacher, her working visa was up, so she was going to have to go back to Bahrain. Mr. Jackson was trying to get her citizenship. So he had me taking her back and forth to meet with an immigration attorney, working on her papers. I was dealing more with personal matters like that.

We were trying to maintain a connection to him, handling those sorts of things. But that private, personal realm was getting pushed more and more to the side, and we were getting pushed out with it. We didn't feel that it was being done through him; it felt like we were being shut out by others. I had the impression Mr. Jackson didn't really know how much we'd been pushed aside, either. Even though I wasn't right there with him all the time, he acted as if I was still handling some of the things that I had been handling before, that I was just one layer removed. He was still telling people, "Call Bill." I would still get calls from lawyers, production people, business people, some of them I'd never heard of before. They'd call me and say, "Hey Bill, I just spoke to Michael. He said to send you these documents to have signed." But I wasn't handling those things anymore. That was all Michael Amir now.

I certainly didn't expect that Javon and I would be the top thing on Mr. Jackson's mind now that there was so much going on. But I felt like his not knowing about our situation was a symptom of his not being fully aware of what was going on underneath him. When he spoke to me about Michael Amir, he spoke as if the two of us had a good working relationship, like we were partners and everything was cool. "Oh, just call Michael Amir." He didn't know what was really going on.

Javon: Michael Jackson had an effect on people. It's hard to describe. Once he let people in, they started feeling possessive of him. Like, *He's mine!* People didn't do it on purpose; he brought it out of them because he was bigger than life. He's calling them personally, giving them leeway to dictate certain stuff, and they start to feel like, Okay, he trusts me. They see how vulnerable and hurt he is. They see all these other people trying to use him and take advantage of him. So they start to think, If *I'm* the one in control, *I'll* make sure he's okay.

So once he lets someone in, pretty soon they're starting to speak on his behalf, as opposed to letting him make his own decisions. They know if they do it, they won't get that much flak, because they know Mr. Jackson doesn't question things. They start to feel like they're in control, but to keep that control, they've got to manipulate everybody else that's trying to get at Mr. Jackson. So they're spreading lies about this person or telling Mr. Jackson not to trust that person.

Then they start lying to Mr. Jackson too. They're telling him, "Yes, sir. No problem, sir," and at the same time, they're going behind his back and doing something else because they feel that they know best. They convince themselves that they're lying to him for his own benefit. That's what everyone around him did, in front of my eyes. That's what Feldman did. That's what Raymone did. Greg Cross. Michael Amir. Everyone. If Michael Jackson let you in his circle, it's inevitable that you'd do it too.

Bill: He had that effect on people, making them feel special, and we certainly felt it too, the way he made us feel that working for him was more than just a job. We felt protective of him in that way, but we didn't succumb to the petty fights like everyone else. Javon and I, we saw all that going on and we made a conscious decision to stay out of it.

It wasn't necessarily that those other people were bad people. There was just a force that dictated a lot of this madness. Bad energy. It surrounded Mr. Jackson. Raymone and Michael Amir? I was cool with both of them when we met. Under different circumstances, I don't know that I ever would have had a problem with either one. But the way it was around Mr. Jackson, nobody trusting anybody, so much money and power in play, it just sucked you into all this drama. People look at what happened to Mr. Jackson and they want to blame somebody. "It was Dr. Murray." "It was Tohme Tohme." "It was his family." Nah. That wasn't it. It wasn't any one person. It was everything.

The fact that someone like me wound up in that gatekeeper position, that was an accident. I fell into it because there was nobody else there. Most of the people in his orbit were there because they were trying to get something by being associated with him. I wasn't. I wasn't trying to be a player in the music industry. I wasn't trying to use Mr. Jackson's celebrity to make myself a film producer. My ambition is to do what I'm doing. I like doing personal protection, I'm good at it, and it's where I want to be. So my only concern was to take care of this person's well-being. When it came to all that business with the loans, people playing games and whispering in his ear, "Don't trust this one," or "Don't trust that one," I wanted no part of it. And when people realized I wasn't getting sucked into that? That's what made me the bad guy. You're the bad guy because you won't be one of the bad guys. Mr. Jackson trusts you, so therefore we can't trust you. That's how corrupt his world had become.

Javon: It's not that we're better than the people who came after us. We're not. It had more to do with the time we were with him. It was more personal on our watch. When we came in, there were no shows in progress. It was such a small circle, a skeleton crew. That's what I always try and explain to people. At the Monte Cristo house, during those months in Virginia: *it was just us.* We were it. Grace would be gone for long stretches, other people might pass through here and there, but for days and weeks at a time, there were no other people around. We'd be out in a field in Middleburg popping firecrackers, alone with Michael Jackson and his kids. It was surreal. We didn't believe we were living it half the time.

The only people there were me and Bill, and we weren't going to compete against each other. But let's call a spade a spade. If there'd been ten, fifteen other people around? Bill would have had so much hatin' on him. Somebody would have tried to cut-throat him the minute Mr. Jackson put him in that gatekeeper position. Bill would have *had* to play those games, or he wouldn't have lasted three weeks in that spot.

Bill: Around late October, Mr. Jackson took another trip to L.A. He was staying at the Hotel Bel-Air, which was where a lot of meetings were taking place. This time he didn't come back. There was no "We're out of here." It just happened.

Javon and I were still in Vegas. We didn't know what our standing was at that point. I only got one call to go out to California. His *Gone with the Wind* Oscars, he wanted those again for what-ever reason. I drove all the way to L.A., passed the briefcase off to Michael Amir in the lobby of the hotel, and was told that was all they needed me for. I got in my car and came back home. Couple weeks later, word came down that he was moving out of the hotel and renting a house, this mansion in Holmby Hills. I got a call that he wanted everything from the storage facility in Vegas, all five of those huge units. Arrangements were made for everything to be picked up and shipped to L.A.

I was worried. Going back to California was something Mr. Jackson had to do for the show. I didn't think he would have ever moved back there by his own choice. The past few months, I'd started to see a side of him I'd never seen before. This was not the same guy that we worked for in Virginia. He was falling into a mode, I felt, of doing what others wanted him to do. You talk to people who worked with him and they tell you how, onstage or in the studio, he was in total control. That wasn't him when he was sitting down and dealing with people for business.

It was like when he was on that three-way call with Raymone and Greg Cross and he threw the phone and screamed, "I should have my father kick their asses." Your father? Really? You're fifty years old. But his whole life, whether it was Joe Jackson, Berry Gordy, Quincy Jones, he always had these powerful figures around him, moving him in this direction or that direction. That's what he knew.

I'll never forget this one time we were driving in the car. Normally we'd listen to classical music when we were driving, but this time I had the radio on an R & B station and Bobby Brown's "My Prerogative" came on. When the song ended, Mr. Jackson said, "Bill, can you play that again?"

I said, "I'm sorry, sir. That wasn't a CD. That was the radio."

So he asked me to go out and get a copy of the album for him. I went to Best Buy, picked it up, and for the next few days, he had me play that song again and again, all day long. Bobby Brown's "My Prerogative" was the only thing Michael Jackson ever asked to listen to in the car besides classical music. He said he wanted to record it, make it part of his comeback. He played it over and over and over, singing along until he'd memorized every last word: "I don't need permission. Make my own decision. That's my prerogative." He'd be in the backseat singing those words, and he sang that shit with conviction. It's *my* prerogative. Do what the fuck *I* want to do.

I keep that song on my iPhone today. I listen to it every now and then. But I don't hear it the way Bobby Brown sings it. I hear it the way Michael Jackson used to sing it. *Just leave me alone. I made this money, you didn't.* But he didn't know how to get there.

By January, once we'd shipped most of his stuff out to L.A., things in Vegas were basically dormant. We'd get a call once a week or so from Peter Lopez or Michael Amir, some errand Mr. Jackson needed us to do, but that was about it. Javon and I both started picking up some part-time clients to fill in the gaps. I was in a difficult position. Part of me felt like I should be in L.A., watching his back. I'd gone from running errands and watching the front gate to receiving documents and handling sensitive information, and he had faith that I wouldn't sell him out to the tabloids. I felt like he trusted me, and it's nice to feel trusted. He had so little faith in other people, I liked that I was able to give him that feeling of being able to count on someone. I missed that part of it. I knew some of the guys on the L.A. security team. I could have reached out to them, talked to Peter Lopez, inquired about getting out there. I didn't.

The truth is I chose to back up. I took pride in working for Michael Jackson, for *Mr.* Jackson. But that was in Virginia. This was a different time. He was no longer Mr. Jackson. This was King of Pop mode now. I didn't know this dude. I didn't know this era. It was a world that I didn't want any part of. You saw what was happening. You saw these people coming at him from all angles, everybody with their hands out. You saw him becoming this character, putting on this persona, in order to deal with them. I didn't like those people and I didn't trust them and I didn't want to work with them.

We kept hearing that this was just a lull, that we'd be going back to work soon, that something was coming up in London that would involve an overseas trip. I didn't believe any of it at the time. That was one thing you learned quickly in Mr. Jackson's world. You didn't believe anything until you saw it happening with your own eyes. I didn't feed into what I heard from people inside his camp, and I definitely didn't feed into anything I was hearing on the news. When it came to Michael Jackson, the media knew very little of what was actually going on; they just circulated a lot of rumors and gossip. So even as all these reports started leaking out about a comeback tour, something big on the horizon, I paid that no mind. In my experience, nearly everything the media said about him was wrong pretty much all the time.

I was actually with him when I heard that he died. The first time I heard that he died. We were in Virginia, driving. We'd just left Walmart and we were heading back to Chuck E. Cheese's to pick up the kids. Mr. Jackson was sitting in the seat behind me when the radio announcer came on and interrupted the broadcast and said, "Hold on, we have an announcement . . . Hold on just a minute, folks . . . Yes, we've just received breaking news that Michael Jackson, the King of Pop, has passed away."

I turned around and said, "Mr. Jackson, did you hear that?"

"No, what?"

"On the radio. They're saying that you died."

He just laughed. He said, "Yeah, I get that all the time."

18

On March 5, 2009, Michael Jackson stepped onstage at the O2 Arena in London. Dressed in black and standing at a podium before a striking red backdrop, he waved to the four hundred journalists and seven thousand screaming fans assembled to hear him, and announced the multimedia stage show spectacular he called *This Is It*.

"And *This Is It*," Jackson said, "really means this is it. This will be the final curtain call. I love you. I love you all."

To the casual observer, Jackson looked to be mounting the comeback of all comebacks. Three months before, in early December, AEG had agreed to move him out of the Hotel Bel-Air and into a new home at 100 North Carolwood Drive in the exclusive neighborhood of Holmby Hills. The seventeen-thousand-square-foot mansion cost $100,000 a month, an expense the promoter was holding against Jackson's earnings from the O2 concerts. Shortly after New Year's, Tom Barrack and Colony Capital had deployed a small army of contractors to rehabilitate Neverland, spending millions on the landscaping and repairs needed to return the estate to its former glory.

By the end of January, Jackson and AEG had agreed on the terms for *This Is It*. Jackson was given an advance of $6.2 million, which he guaranteed with a commitment to perform ten shows in London that summer. What Jackson didn't know at the time was that AEG was already forecasting that the demand for tickets would far outstrip the seating capacity of just ten shows. And Tohme Tohme, having seen Jackson's finances up close, knew that ten performances alone would never be sufficient to wipe out the singer's debt. Tohme and AEG had already explored raising the number of performances if consumer demand called for it.

Immediately following Jackson's March 5 announcement, fans were told they could register online for a pre-sale drawing of tickets. Over a million people registered in just the first twenty-four hours. Tohme and AEG immediately began to talk about increasing the number of shows, first to twenty, then to thirty-one, and finally to a total of fifty live shows. Jackson reluctantly agreed to the increase on certain conditions. AEG had to rent him an estate outside London for the extended residency. And, to ensure that he remained in proper health, AEG had to hire a personal trainer, a personal chef, and a personal physician. For this last position, Jackson insisted they hire Dr. Conrad Murray, his private physician from Las Vegas. When tickets for *This Is It* went on sale the following week, all fifty shows sold out in a matter of hours, and seats were soon being auctioned off on eBay for as much as fifteen thousand dollars apiece.

Back in Los Angeles, preparations for the concert's July 8 launch date were already underway. Kenny Ortega, who had served as Jackson's choreographer for the *Dangerous* and *HIStory* tours, was hired to helm the massive production. Hundreds of dancers were flown to L.A. from all over the world for auditions. The final show would include more than twenty production numbers, each one set against its own individually designed set piece, all at a cost that was rapidly approaching $30 million.

As the production geared up for launch, the maneuvering that had been going on behind the scenes ramped up as well, reaching new heights of absurdity. When Frank DiLeo failed to secure a deal for AllGood Entertainment to stage a family reunion show with Michael Jackson, Joe Jackson partnered instead with a longtime acquaintance named Leonard Rowe. Rowe, a concert promoter, was an ex-convict who'd been imprisoned for wire fraud in the early 1990s.

At Joe's behest, Rowe went to Patrick Allocco of AllGood Entertainment, claiming that he, not Frank DiLeo and not Tohme Tohme, was Michael Jackson's manager. Allocco paid Rowe a fifteen-thousand-dollar retainer on the promise that he could set up a meeting with Katherine Jackson—the only person in the family whom Michael actually spoke to—in the hopes that she could convince her son that joining the family for a reunion would be the better deal. Leonard Rowe prevailed upon Katherine to intervene. Fearing that fifty shows in London would jeopardize his health, she agreed that the reunion was best and started lobbying her son. Meanwhile, Frank DiLeo was busy forging an alliance with Jackson's personal assistant, Michael Amir Williams, who by this point controlled virtually all access to the singer. Williams, who had never liked or trusted Tohme Tohme, saw DiLeo as a better ally to have inside the camp. And so the personal assistant opened the door for the former manager to get back in Michael Jackson's ear.

By the end of March, Tohme Tohme, Frank DiLeo, and Leonard Rowe were all moving independently about Los Angeles, each claiming to be Michael Jackson's manager. Underlining the confusion, on April 2, an industry news site published an article entitled, "Will Michael Jackson's Real Manager Please Stand Up?" By that point, many in Jackson's camp were actively working to counter the influence of Tohme Tohme, telling Michael that Tohme had served him poorly by backing him into the fifty shows in London.

On April 14, Jackson agreed to meet with his father and Leonard Rowe to hear out their proposal for the reunion concert. By the end of the meeting, Jackson had signed two letters, one naming Leonard Rowe as his manager and another stripping Tohme Tohme of any and all authority to represent him. Around the same time, Frank DiLeo started to take meetings while brandishing a letter, allegedly written and signed by Michael Jackson, naming DiLeo as his manager and representative. With Tohme Tohme out of the picture, and Michael's world in complete disarray, DiLeo convinced AEG that he could control the family and their access to Michael and keep everything running smoothly until London. By mid-May, DiLeo was working out of an office at AEG. The promoter also kept up cordial relations with Tohme Tohme, who was intimately involved with the London deal whether Jackson wanted him to be or not. AEG was covering all its bases.

On May 25, Jackson sent a letter to Leonard Rowe renouncing any business relationship the two had ever had, finally closing the door on the idea of a Jackson family reunion, a deal that had never actually existed but had somehow consumed a great deal of attention for close to six months. Two weeks later, its efforts stymied, AllGood Entertainment sued Jackson for $40 million, claiming that the singer and his manager Frank DiLeo—who, after being hired by AEG, appeared to be Jackson's manager—had agreed to perform at a Jackson family reunion. Therefore the deal to perform at the O2 Arena was a breach of the "contract" with AllGood. As a compromise, AllGood said it would settle for a percentage of the profits from the London shows.

The "vultures" Michael Jackson had worried about were arriving right on cue, and the stress began taking its toll. Jackson was regularly missing rehearsals, showing up late, and exhibiting erratic behavior. He was losing weight, plummeting to a dangerously low 130 pounds, and his insomnia was worsening. On June 19, Kenny Ortega would later recount, Jackson showed up for rehearsal in an alarming state, too weak to run through the show. The director sent Jackson home and then, later that night, sat down and emailed AEG's Randy Phillips, expressing his concerns. "He appeared quite weak and fatigued this evening," Ortega wrote of his star performer. "He had a terrible case of the chills, was trembling, rambling, and obsessing. Everything in me says he should be psychologically evaluated. If we have any chance at all to get him back in the light, it's going to take a strong therapist to help him through this as well as immediate physical nurturing."

"I believe that he really wants this," the email concluded. "It would shatter him, break his heart if we pulled the plug. He's terribly frightened it's all going to go away. He asked me repeatedly tonight if I was going to leave him. He was practically begging for my confidence. It broke my heart. He was like a lost boy. There may still be a chance he can rise to the occasion if we get him the help he needs."

Bill: I watched the London press conference on TV. When I saw him at the podium, announcing the concerts, that was the first time I thought, Wow, this is really happening. Up until that point, I'd really paid no attention to it.

What struck me about the press conference was when he said, "This is it. This is the final curtain call." I don't think people knew exactly what he meant when he said that. He meant this is *it*. Over. Done. I'm not doing this no more. It wasn't going to be like the Eagles or Frank Sinatra, these people who retire, come back, retire again, then go back on tour one more time. No. Michael Jackson was out.

As reluctant as he was to perform again, I believe he'd genuinely worked himself up to be excited about doing those initial ten shows. The King of Pop had taken over. He was excited because what was being asked of him was doable. When they upped it to fifty shows, he was livid. I remember there was talk of fifty shows back at the Palms. It was fifty before it was ten. Fifty was the original number, because that was how many shows he really needed to do to make this big money they were waving in his face.

Back when all these concert discussions were in the beginning stages, he'd talk to us about it in the car. He'd say, "They want me to do fifty shows. I *can't* do fifty shows." He didn't say it like he was refusing to do it. He said it like it was ridiculous they were even asking him to do it, like they were asking him to jump off a fifteen-story building and survive. Like, Can you believe they really expect this? He'd talk about his age, all the wear and tear of doing those world tours, how he'd messed up his back, his knee. It was the same way he spoke about not committing to five nights a week in Vegas. "I can't do that many shows. I just can't."

It seemed like a bait and switch. It was originally fifty shows, then it was lowered to ten to entice him to do it, then they raised it back to fifty again. I heard they got Mr. Jackson to commit to it by saying he'd break the record for the number of shows sold out by Prince, because Mr. Jackson was always competitive about being compared to Prince. That was one story that was going around. But the reality was that Mr. Jackson was already in debt to AEG for so much money. He'd taken this multimillion-dollar advance on the shows, plus AEG was paying for that mansion in L.A. So when they told him it was fifty shows, it wasn't like he could pay back what he'd already taken. He was boxed in. He didn't have a whole lot of options.

Javon: I never believed he was going to do fifty shows. After spending all that time with him? No way. Never. He was always so frail, so skinny. He could have gained ten pounds and he'd still be too skinny.

And it wasn't just the physical aspect. It was his demeanor. Some days he was upbeat, other days he was down. Like with Elizabeth Taylor's birthday. He could be up, totally in a good mood, ready to go, but if one little thing threw off his day, that was it. He'd shut down. There's no way he was going to be able to get through months and months of performances without some drama in his world shutting him down.

I wanted to believe it would happen. I wanted to root for this big comeback. But he was so unpredictable. Even with that press conference, I still didn't believe that this concert was actually going to happen. I wasn't going to believe it until he was onstage with a mic in his hand, singing.

Bill: Shortly after the press conference, things on our end started to move again. I was getting calls from Peter Lopez. Mr. Jackson was going to be renting an estate outside London. He wanted us to handle security. Javon and I were in touch with a company over there, telling them what equipment we would need. We were getting pictures of the house, floor plans, that sort of thing. Once the shows started, we were going to handle security at the estate and escort Mr. Jackson to and from the arena, where AEG's people would handle everything. Again, I had the feeling that Mr. Jackson was trying to keep that barrier between his personal life and his professional life. So we were going to London. That was definite.

Pretty much everything with the house was set up through Peter Lopez. I'd been looking to reestablish that personal connection with Mr. Jackson we felt we'd lost, and for me, Peter Lopez was the anchor. He made us continue to feel like part of the team. He'd say, "Listen guys, Michael trusts you. All this other stuff is going on, but don't worry about it. I spoke to Michael. He wants you guys in London." I felt good about that. I also had several conversations with Brad Buxer, Mr. Jackson's musician friend who spent all those nights with him in the studio on Monte Cristo. Brad would say, "Bill, you *gotta* go. You have to be part of this. Just sit back, and it'll be cool when we get to London."

Talking to Peter and Brad, hearing their enthusiasm, that made me feel a lot better. They were the guys who were there for Mr. Jackson even when there was no money to be made, so they were the only people I felt I could really trust. Once it was confirmed we were going to London, I drew up a proposal, a new contract to include provisions for our traveling and working overseas, and I sent it to Peter Lopez. That was passed on to the new management, but I never heard back from them.

There was a big management shuffle going on. Once the London announcement was made, and once the fifty shows were sold out, it was like blood in the water to all these sharks. You thought it was bad before? Now everybody was coming out, trying to grab onto this thing. Since the Palomino days, everything had been going through Tohme Tohme. Then, in April, right in the middle of the run-up to London, all of a sudden he was out. Mr. Jackson fired him. Whoever wanted Tohme out, they'd gotten in Mr. Jackson's ear and convinced him that this guy couldn't be trusted.

Joe Jackson had been trying to put together a Jackson reunion show at the Superdome. He was always trying to pull that one, trying to get the brothers back together. We knew Mr. Jackson didn't want to do it. Whenever the subject came up, the boss would just shrug and roll his eyes and say, "That's all Joseph." Mr. Jackson did make the statement once that he would love for his kids to see him perform with his brothers. But he also didn't want anything to do with his father's business plans, and doing anything with his brothers would involve his father. But Joe was leaning on Katherine to get Mr. Jackson to do it. The family didn't trust Tohme Tohme, so they were taking sides with whoever was trying to push him out.

Even after Tohme Tohme was fired, he was still going around, claiming to be Michael Jackson's manager. Somehow this Frank DiLeo character had leveraged his way in and gotten himself hired by AEG in some capacity, and now he was claiming to represent Mr. Jackson too. It was chaos. Total confusion. These people were all out signing deals, saying they were Michael Jackson's manager. And because Mr. Jackson would sign whatever was put in front of him, there were all these conflicting contracts and letters of agreement going around, and everybody was threatening to sue everybody else for violating this deal or that deal.

I was a step removed from all that, but I saw everything that was going on in the industry around the show. There weren't many people who had Michael Amir's direct number, and not everyone knew that he was the new gatekeeper. My number was the last point of contact a lot of people in the business had for Mr. Jackson, and I was getting calls all the time. It was insane. All these producers and other types who'd worked on his older albums, they were calling me up and saying, "If Michael plays such-and-such song in the show, he's going to owe royalties to so-and-so. He needs to call my attorney." I was getting calls like that every day. Did anybody call just to say, "Hey, tell Mike 'Good luck'?" No. There was nothing like that. It was a feeding frenzy. Everybody was calling to say why they should be involved and what they should get out of it. I just passed all the messages up the chain to Michael Amir.

Javon: Even Ms. Raymone came back around, trying to get another cut. Back when we were living on Monte Cristo, she'd set up a dinner with Mr. Jackson and someone from AEG. It didn't go anywhere at the time. She couldn't put the deal together, but now that AEG had come back to Mr. Jackson to try again, she said she was owed something on that. Even though Mr. Jackson had paid her hundreds of thousands of dollars to cut her loose, she came back after the London announcement and sued him for $44 million. When we first heard that, we were like, *What?* After all that damn money you got paid? You clown. You snake. You've been eating off this guy forever, and now you want $44 million off a deal you couldn't make happen? What a joke.

We could tell he wasn't being looked after properly, because all of a sudden, he was all over the news. The paparazzi had him everywhere. Seemed like pictures of him were popping up on TMZ.com practically every day. When I saw all those pictures of him in L.A., all I could think was, "What the hell is going on?" The paparazzi had him staked out, and the people handling his security were taking him in and out the front doors of places in broad daylight. We couldn't believe he was out like that. We never took Michael Jackson through the front door of anywhere if we could help it. Here they had him parading around in front of the cameras nonstop.

Part of it was just him being in L.A. and having all this new excitement around the show, but even in L.A., if you want to avoid the paparazzi, you can do it. It's more difficult. It requires more planning and more effort, but celebrities do it all the time. Famous people who don't want to be seen are not seen. But the people handling Mr. Jackson didn't seem to care about his privacy. They cared more about putting him out there to generate buzz for this tour. Shame on anybody and everybody who allowed him to go out like that.

Bill: Meantime, this whole massive production was gearing up, like a huge jet engine getting ready for takeoff. But the stories I was hearing about Mr. Jackson were pretty much what I expected. I knew some of the people working on the show just from being around the music business, and we knew a couple guys on the security team. I'd hear from them. They'd say, "He wasn't himself today." This wasn't that new to us. I heard there were a few rehearsals that he missed because he was tired. I'd had a few calls now and then from Grace. She'd say, "The boss is tired working on them shows."

Those rehearsals were seven, eight hours straight of intense, physical work. To do that every day, day in, day out, for weeks? You need rest. I knew he didn't sleep much. But when he was on our watch, without the show, if he didn't sleep, he could always take it easy the next day. Send the kids to a playground with us while he took some downtime. But if he was expected to grind out those rehearsals every day, he was going to have to get his sleep eventually.

That film they made of the rehearsals? *Michael Jackson's This Is It*, the documentary? I've never seen it. I can't watch it, because I know what was going on behind the scenes. I know everything that was happening. It'd be like watching a magic show after you've already seen how the tricks are done—you know it's fake. All those people talking about how great this show was going to be and how excited Mr. Jackson was. It all sounds fake to me.

Michael Jackson was a perfectionist, so if he was going to do this show, he was going to commit himself to doing his absolute best for his fans. He was committed in that sense. But did he really want to be there? I don't think so. I think he wanted to be in Virginia, out in a field setting off firecrackers with his kids. I think he wanted to be in that bar in Georgetown, knowing what it's like to just kick it having a beer with some friends. I think he wanted to be free.

At the end of May, after all this buildup, all this hype, they announced that the first London shows were being postponed by a week. Around that same time, Peter Lopez started asking about me and Javon going to L.A., that maybe we should be in L.A. for this last leg before going overseas. Peter and I would be on the phone talking about the house in London, and then eventually he'd ask, "So, when are you guys coming to L.A.?"

That kept coming up, and I just wasn't—I don't want to say I wasn't excited, but there was still business that was not taken care of. The contract proposal I'd submitted to the management company, it'd been three months and I'd still heard nothing back. I trusted Peter and believed in what he was telling me, but he wasn't in charge of making any of this happen. Management was. But Michael Amir never returned my calls, and with this changing cast of characters over there, I actually had no idea who was in charge. It was worse than the days with Raymone. At least with her, I knew who the point of contact was for day-to-day business. AEG was in charge of running the concert, but on Mr. Jackson's side, in his organization, it was total confusion. I was even still carrying that outstanding iPhone bill, the one Mr. Jackson and his mom ran up. I had AT&T on me about paying this two-thousand-dollar bill, and I couldn't even get anyone in Mr. Jackson's camp to talk to me about that.

It didn't exactly make you feel comfortable about working with them. I was cautious about it. I couldn't leave my daughter again, and I knew Javon wasn't leaving his family again, without certain reassurances. Travel schedules. Payment schedules. Accommodations. None of that was in place. So whenever Peter Lopez would bring up the subject of L.A., I would kind of drag my feet, waiting to see what kind of answer I was going to get on these arrangements.

Finally, around the middle of June, Peter called and he didn't say, "Maybe you should be in L.A." He said, "Michael wants you guys in L.A." He told me to hit up Michael Amir to make the arrangements to fly over. I knew calling him was pointless. I tried anyway. No response. He wasn't returning Peter Lopez's calls on the matter, either. I didn't really press it that much. Whatever Mr. Jackson wanted us there for, it didn't really seem that urgent. And at that point, we were only a couple weeks out from leaving for London. What sense would it make for us to go to L.A.? I just sort of assumed nothing was going to happen until we left for overseas.

About a week later, I got another call. This one came in at around eight-thirty at night, that much I remember precisely. It was Mr. Jackson calling this time. I hadn't heard from him in a while. His specific question was, "What happened to you guys? Where are you? Why aren't you in L.A.?" I told him I'd been trying to make the arrangements but wasn't getting anywhere. He told me to try Michael Amir again. I told him I would, and that was all we said. He didn't give me a reason for wanting us there, nothing.

I felt like, What is going on? He was surrounded by people over there. What did he need us for? Did he want us in L.A. just because? There were only a couple reasons I could think of. I knew he didn't like having the kids surrounded by strangers, and Grace was already in London. Maybe he just wanted a familiar face at the house. He also used me a lot when he needed someone to say no for him, to pull him out of meetings, to step in and say, "Mr. Jackson needs to leave now." Maybe people were getting to him and he needed that buffer. I honestly didn't know. The last time he had me go to L.A., I'd driven all the way there and sat in a hotel lobby just to hand over those Oscars and turn around and come home. Was this just going to be that again?

It was the exact same situation I'd been in two years before, almost to the day. I was here in Vegas and he was in Virginia, saying, "Where are you guys? When are you going to get here?" I couldn't get Raymone to make the arrangements, but it didn't matter. He needed us; we went. Now, we hesitated. That's what had changed. For Mr. Jackson, we'd drive cross-country without thinking twice about it. And if it was still just Mr. Jackson calling and saying he needed us, the kids needed us, I think we would have got in the car and gone, no questions. But were we willing to do the same, leaving our own kids, to get in the middle of all this King of Pop business? It just didn't feel the same. So much had happened since then.

I did that thing I used to do sometimes when Mr. Jackson made strange or unusual requests, like when he asked me to find him a helicopter simulator or a Ferris wheel. I'd wait a few days before doing it to see if he'd drop it or if he'd bring it up again. That way I'd know if he was being serious or if it was just a whim. And that's how I felt about him calling me to go to L.A. It didn't seem urgent. So that's what I told myself. I thought, If it's important, he'll call back. He didn't call back.

19

On June 25, 2009, at 12:26 p.m., paramedics burst into Michael Jackson's bedroom at 100 North Carolwood Drive, responding to a 911 call placed just minutes before. They found Jackson unconscious and not breathing. After numerous attempts at resuscitation failed, at 1:07 they put him in an ambulance and rushed him to the UCLA Medical Center, just three miles away. A little over an hour later, at 2:26 p.m., Michael Joseph Jackson was pronounced dead of cardiac arrest. A full autopsy was ordered to determine the exact cause.

Three hours later, Michael's brother Jermaine emerged from the hospital and issued a statement confirming what the world had already known for some time. The tabloid website *TMZ* broke the news of Jackson's death just minutes after the coroner's pronouncement was made, triggering an unprecedented surge of media coverage. In the hours after Jackson's death, Internet traffic spiked by 15 percent worldwide, crashing Wikipedia, Twitter, and the website of the *Los Angeles Times*. The rate of status updates on Facebook tripled.

As the wider world Googled and tweeted and streamed the news of Jackson's death, a crowd of fans and onlookers started to gather outside UCLA Medical Center to stand vigil. Other gatherings sprang up outside the Carolwood mansion and at the gates of Neverland. By the evening, huge crowds had assembled outside the original Motown headquarters in Detroit and the Apollo Theater in

Harlem. By the next morning, spontaneous gatherings had spread to the streets of London, Paris, Mexico City, Nairobi, and Moscow.

A televised public memorial was held for Jackson on July 7 at the Staples Center in Los Angeles. Jackson's brothers, each wearing a single white glove, acted as pallbearers, bringing the singer's casket out onto the stage. Eulogies were given by a range of luminaries, from Brooke Shields to the Reverend Al Sharpton to Motown's Berry Gordy. In between the speeches, musical performances of Jackson's greatest hits were performed by Mariah Carey, Stevie Wonder, and Jennifer Hudson. Over 31 million viewers watched the broadcast in the United States. More than 6.5 million watched in England, 18 million in Brazil, and millions more in other countries. In addition to the television audience, 33 million streamed the video online, making Michael Jackson's farewell the most-watched memorial of a public figure in world history.

The global outpouring that followed Jackson's passing demonstrated just how popular the singer remained. In just the week that he died, Jackson sold 2.6 million digital downloads and over 800,000 albums. In the last six months of 2009, he sold 9 million albums in the United States and 35 million albums worldwide. *Michael Jackson's This Is It*, a documentary film compiled from the concert's rehearsal footage, was later released for a two-week limited theatrical run. It earned over $261 million, making it the highest-grossing music film of all time. *Billboard* magazine estimated that in the year after Jackson's passing, his fans generated over $1 billion in revenue for the parties that inherited control of his interests.

On September 3, 2009, Michael Jackson was interred in a private ceremony at Forest Lawn Memorial Park in Los Angeles. In the weeks that had passed since his death, the events surrounding it had started to become clear. The most jarring news had come on August 27, when the Los Angeles coroner's office ruled Jackson's death a homicide, citing its cause as "acute propofol intoxication with benzodiazepine effect."

Propofol, a powerful anesthetic, was a drug that most people had never heard of, as it is used only in hospital settings to render patients unconscious for major surgery; if used without the proper instruments to measure oxygen levels, heart rate, and blood pressure, it can be extremely dangerous. Under the intense physical and emotional stress of putting the London shows together, Jackson's insomnia had become crippling. Desperate for sleep, he'd increasingly turned to his personal physician, Dr. Conrad Murray, to help him by administering nightly doses of the drug.

On the evening of June 24, Jackson had arrived at the Staples Center for full-dress rehearsals. After weeks of seeming weak and fatigued, the singer appeared full of renewed energy and ran through the entire program, giving a show-stopping performance that director Kenny Ortega described as "bioluminescent." Jackson left the arena at twelve-thirty, returning home for yet another sleepless night. Trying to bring him down from the evening's performance, Dr. Murray first administered heavy doses of the sedatives lorazepam and midazolam. But by the time the sun came up, Jackson still hadn't slept, and at 10:40 a.m., Murray gave him a final push of twenty-five milligrams of propofol.

An hour later, by the doctor's own account, he discovered that Jackson wasn't breathing. After several panicked minutes trying to administer CPR on his own, Murray ran downstairs screaming for help. Jackson's L.A. security team, joined by Prince and Paris Jackson, followed Murray back into Jackson's bedroom and witnessed the doctor frantically trying to bring their father back to life. Nearly half an hour passed between the time Jackson was found not breathing and when 911 was called.

Eight months after Jackson's death, in February 2010, Dr. Conrad Murray was charged with involuntary manslaughter for administering the fatal dose of propofol. When the doctor's trial finally got underway in the fall of 2011, Dr. Christopher Rogers, chief of forensic medicine for the Los Angeles County coroner, testified that while Michael

Jackson was underweight and fatigued from the rehearsals, his health was otherwise normal for a fifty-year-old man. But for the events that transpired on June 25, 2009, the singer could have conceivably lived well into old age. On November 7, 2011, Murray was found guilty of manslaughter and sentenced to four years in prison.

During the trial, Bill Whitfield, the head of Michael Jackson's Las Vegas security, was called to testify in the hope that what he and his team had learned during their time on the job might offer a clearer picture, and a better understanding, of what happened on the day that Michael Jackson died.

Bill: That morning, I was out running errands, still debating whether or not I should go to L.A. By the time I got home, I'd pretty much decided that I should. I should just get in my car and go. Find out what's going on. But the second I walked into the house, my phone started blowing up. *Blowing. Up.* Emails. Text messages. Voice mails. I answered one call and it was a buddy of mine, and he said, "Yo, what's up with your boy?!"

"What are you talkin' about?"

"Your boy's dead, man!"

"Who?!"

"Michael Jackson!"

"Get the fuck outta here."

I didn't believe him. I'd heard that before. Had to be a rumor. But my phone just kept ringing. I was seeing names of people I knew back in New York, people I hadn't spoken to in a long time. I got scared. I got up and turned on the TV, and it was breaking news on every channel.

Javon: I was at Best Buy doing some shopping, and all of a sudden, my phone started ringing like crazy. At the same moment that started, one of the sales girls in the CD section shouted out, "Oh, no!

Michael Jackson dead!" I reached for my phone to answer it and it was my cousin Jeff. He said, "Mr. Jackson's gone."

"Are you for real?!"

"That's what they're saying. Let me find out more and call you back."

I took a pause. All I could think was, Where are the kids? Did they see their father when he died? Who has them right now? I rushed home so I could see the news for myself.

Bill: On the TV, camera crews were camped outside the hospital. Now it was all real. The newscaster was saying, "We're waiting for an announcement from one of the family members." That's when I saw Jermaine step up to the podium, and I was thinking, Is he really getting ready to say what I think he's getting ready to say? Jermaine was pausing and taking deep breaths, and finally he said, "My brother, the legendary King of Pop, Michael Jackson, has passed away . . . " I just fell back on the couch in shock.

Javon: Once I heard it confirmed by the coroner's office, I went in the bathroom by myself and I just broke down and started crying. I was looking in the mirror, and my heart dropped and my chest was really hurting. I just kept thinking about the kids. Where are they? How are they taking it? They didn't really know the rest of his family that well. He kept them away from everybody. The only other person they'd ever really known was Ms. Grace. With their daddy gone, who were they going to go to now? Who was going to take care of them?

Bill: When they showed the footage of the ambulance leaving his house, my first thought was, They waited for an ambulance? Why didn't they take him to the hospital? Why didn't they just grab him and rush him to the hospital at the first sign of something wrong?

In the days after, all I could think was, What if I had been there? Could I have done something? Would it have been different if I'd just gone to L.A. when he called? Later on, when I heard the actual 911 call, I heard them on the phone telling the operator, "We have a gentleman here. He's not breathing." Fuck that. I would have thrown him in the car and rushed him to the hospital myself. It was only a couple miles away. I would have got him out of there. He's not breathing? Let's go! We gotta go! Maybe it would have been different if I'd actually been there. Maybe I'm just imagining how I would have reacted, but I really don't think I would have just sat around waiting for the paramedics.

That scenario kept running through my mind: What if? I kept playing it back and forth in my head. But I can tell you what did *not* cross my mind when I heard that he died. I didn't even think about Dr. Conrad Murray. Didn't imagine for a second that he might have been involved. Propofol? I'd never heard of it. He wasn't using anything like that to sleep when he was around us, and we knew he wasn't because he was never asleep.

All I ever really knew about Michael Jackson and prescription drugs was what everyone else knew, what you heard in the media. There aren't too many negative things I haven't heard about Michael Jackson, and it's all just rumors, so I always tried to go by what I saw with my own eyes, and I didn't see much. There was the time he wanted to go to the hospital in Virginia in the middle of the night. That was unusual. The camera he tore up at the Four Seasons? There was something going on there. But that was really it. In all that time of being in really close, personal contact with him, that was all I saw. The Michael Jackson I knew, most of the time he'd be reading a book or helping the kids with their homework. That was the guy I worked for.

Dr. Murray visited Mr. Jackson maybe three or four times in the months I was with him. And the few times he came, it was because the kids were sick. Paris had the flu, Blanket had an upset stomach, something like that. If Dr. Murray was treating Mr. Jackson, bringing him prescriptions on the side, I wouldn't know, of course. But he was never at the house more than an hour, hour and a half, tops. Never overnight. If Dr. Murray was helping him to sleep, he wasn't doing it on my watch. And why not? Why wasn't Dr. Murray in Virginia? Why wasn't he in New Jersey? He wasn't there because Michael Jackson didn't need all that. The King of Pop brought that on, because he had all these vultures after him, trying to do all these shows, all that pressure. The King of Pop brings all the drama.

Javon: For weeks after, I was kicking myself. I kept thinking, What if I'd been there? I can't say for sure how I would have handled it, but if I'd been there when they pronounced him dead, I know I'd have blamed myself. I would have said, "Was there something I didn't do right? Did I wait too long to call the ambulance?" Something. That would have destroyed me, having him die on my watch, his kids thinking that we didn't do what it took to keep their daddy alive. Not being there, at least I had some closure.

Bill: I started to feel that we weren't supposed to be there. We were not supposed to be a part of that, the scenery of him passing away. Everybody that was part of that has to carry it for the rest of their lives. Someone actually said that to me, too. One of his fans said that to me. She said, "He was going to die in L.A. This show, this pressure, it was going to happen, and maybe your relationship went the way it went because he wasn't supposed to die on your watch. You weren't supposed to carry that burden on you." I think about that still. "I wasn't supposed to be there." Was I not? Maybe that's some crazy thinking, but I wonder about it. I hold onto that.

Looking back on it now, in some ways I'm more relieved than sad. I've accepted it. Part of me honestly believes that he didn't die. He left. I'm leaving this place. I'm leaving this shit, this life. I'm out. Because it was never going to be right for him. Never. Not in this world. He was never going to have the life that you and I have, to just get up and go, be free. Michael Jackson was going to have vultures swarming him; he was going to need security following him, watching his every move, for the rest of his life. Who wants to live like that? There was no peace for him here. That's what I say to myself. Now, he'll rest.

That's how I started to feel in the months after it happened, but it took me a while to get there. Right after he died, there was about a week before the memorial at the Staples Center. I was in touch with a woman from AEG, because they were handling the arrangements. I told her that I needed tickets for me and Javon. Then, maybe two days before the ceremony, we were getting ready to head out and I got a call. I answered, and there was this woman crying on the other end of the phone. She said, "Bill, it's Joanna."

Joanna? I didn't know any Joanna. I said, "Who?"

She said, "Bill, it's me. Joanna. It's Friend."

Oh. Friend. From Virginia. I said, "Hey, how you doing?"

She just kept crying. She said, "Bill, I must see Michael. I must say good-bye to him. Can you please help me, Bill?"

She started begging me to help get her into the memorial. She didn't call it that, though. She had that thick Eastern European accent, and her English was just okay. She didn't know the word for memorial. She kept calling it a "show." She said, "Bill, I must go to show." But there was no way for her to get in. Mr. Jackson had kept her a secret from everyone. There was no one else for her to contact. Nobody knew who she was. She just kept saying, "Bill, *please!* You must get me in!" I didn't know what I could do. I told her I'd call her back. Then I called Javon and told him what was up.

Javon: I didn't want to go. By that point, I was so frustrated. I'd been seeing all of these articles in the newspapers and all the shows on TV. Everything was Michael Jackson, Michael Jackson, Michael Jackson. It was to the point where *Dancing with the Stars* would be on and they'd ask the contestants, "How do you feel about Michael Jackson passing?"

I was fine with the people who just said, "Well, he was a great entertainer and we'll never forget his music." That didn't bother me. But I couldn't stand all the celebrities coming out of the woodwork, trying to act like they were his best friends, like they were talking to him on a daily basis. People would say stuff like, "Yeah, I was chilling with Michael about a year ago . . . " And I'd just stare at the TV like, No, you weren't. I was with him the whole time, and you weren't there.

I knew this funeral was going to be fake. I didn't want to be around the fakeness. I knew I wouldn't be able to keep my composure. I told Bill, "If I go, I'll hurt somebody. For real." I wanted to pay my respects and have my one-on-one time with Mr. Jackson, but I knew it wasn't going to be like that. I was already apprehensive about it when Bill called about Friend. So I said, "Bill, you go and represent us and give my ticket to her. She should be there."

Bill said, "Are you sure?"

I said, "Yeah, I'm sure."

Bill: Part of me didn't want to go, either, for the same reasons, but I was more torn about it than Javon. I felt like it was important to attend. I called Friend back and kept in touch with her and arranged to meet her in L.A. She wasn't even in the States when she called; she made it over from Europe in less than a day.

The morning of the memorial, I headed over to the SLS Hotel in Beverly Hills, where they were distributing the tickets. I went and stood in line, got the tickets and went back out front to wait for Friend. I saw a bunch of people who'd won tickets on the radio— they were doing radio giveaways. You could win a spot at Michael Jackson's memorial. That really bothered me. Eventually I heard this voice yell "Bill!" from behind me. I turned around, and it was Friend. She was still crying, looked like she hadn't stopped crying for the past ten days. She came over to me. I gave her a big hug, gave her the ticket. Then I didn't see her again until we were both inside.

Outside the Staples Center, it was crazy. Police everywhere. Blocks and blocks cordoned off. I parked in a garage, must have been about ten blocks away, and I walked. His fans were lining the streets behind the police barricades, holding up signs and flowers. People were dressed like him, with the mirrored sunglasses and the fedora. Just thousands of people.

Once I got inside and got to my seat, I could tell right away that this thing was going to be exactly what we thought it was going to be. This wasn't going to be a real, genuine thing. It was going to be Hollywood, a place to be seen, a who's who. I looked around and saw all of these celebrities. People were talking, laughing, socializing. Even the Kardashians were there. Really? Javon would have lost his mind if he'd seen that.

There were about 1,500 people in the section I was in, and I only saw about forty, fifty people who were actually, genuinely, in mourning. I saw the girl with the red car who used to always park outside the Monte Cristo house. She was there. When I saw her, I said to myself, that's who should be in here. They should take all these fake-ass people and put them out in the streets, open up the doors, and let his fans in. They're the ones who deserve to be here for this. His fans were the only ones who never deserted him. Whenever the fans said, "We love you, Michael," he'd always say, "I love you more." And he meant it. They meant more to him than he did to them. He cared for them so deeply that in some ways they constituted the only sustained, committed relationship in his life—his only real love affair.

Once the program started, I really didn't pay too much attention to what was going on onstage. I was more lost in my own thoughts. I felt like the people up there were all saying good-bye to a different person than I was. All the artists that were performing— Usher, Mariah Carey, John Mayer—I didn't pay them no mind.

I really didn't. Friend was right. This wasn't a memorial. It was a show. That's exactly what it was.

At the end, they brought the Jackson family onstage. Some of the brothers said a few words, and then someone said, "Paris wants to say something." When I heard that? I went straight for my coat pocket and pulled out my sunglasses and put them on. I knew I was going to water up the minute she started to speak. She stepped up and they brought the microphone down for her. She started talking and when she said, "Daddy was the best father you could ever imagine," I just lost it. I completely lost it. I didn't even hear the rest of what she was saying. It was too painful. It was words I didn't want to hear.

Then she started to cry, and the moment she did that, I realized I'd never seen her cry before. I'd only ever seen that little girl cheerful and smiling and laughing. Prince and Blanket too. Prince cried when he had to leave his dog in New Jersey, but that was the only time. Other than that, I'd never seen those children crying or hurt or upset. They were just the happiest kids. They loved their daddy and loved each other. They were the happiest family, always.

After Paris spoke, Marlon Jackson came up to thank everyone for coming. He and the other brothers went over to the coffin to carry it offstage. "Man in the Mirror" started playing, and people were shouting, "We love you, Michael!" Looking at all that going on, there was one memory that kept running through my mind, a conversation I'd had with Grace back at the Monte Cristo house when I first started working there. She and I were in the garage. I was putting together some of the security equipment, and Grace was at the little workstation she'd set up. Mr. Jackson had told her to try and get in touch with somebody. She was getting frustrated and she said, "The boss wants me to get in touch with this person, and I keep leaving messages, but nobody's calling me back. It's like he forgets sometimes that some people don't want anything to do with him after all this mess."

I said, "What mess? What are you talking about?"

"The trial," she said. "Since the trial, a lot of people just don't call back anymore."

She was giving me the heads up, filling me in on how things worked, like she often did. She started telling me about the days right after the trial was over. "After he was acquitted," she said, "we had a party at Neverland for him to celebrate, and nobody came."

"Nobody?"

"A few people," she said, "but not many."

She said they'd put together a guest list of all these friends and people Mr. Jackson had worked with over the years. They invited close to three hundred people. Maybe fifty showed up. And a lot of the people who did come were people that worked for him. People that worked the grounds at Neverland. People from his lawyer's office. People who were paid to be there. Everyone else called and said they couldn't make it or they had other things planned. "And he knew," Grace said. "He knew why they didn't come. People called him and told him that they loved him and that they were praying for him, but very few people would go public and say that they believed him. A lot of people act like his friends but they're not really his friends. If he's not making them money, they're not really around."

When that trial was over, Mr. Jackson really wanted to believe that his life would be like it was before. He thought the world would see he was innocent, that he'd been wrongly accused, and then everyone would come back to him and love him again. But that didn't happen. It broke his heart. We keep having all these trials and depositions, people going around and pointing fingers and asking questions, everybody suing everybody, all this bickering over who or what killed Michael Jackson. To me it's perfectly obvious what killed Michael Jackson.

As I sat there in that arena, looking at all the people packed into the seats around me, I couldn't get that conversation with

Grace out of my head. I just wanted to be alone with my thoughts, to have my own moment to grieve. But I couldn't. Because all I felt was anger. That overtook everything else. I sat there with all these people getting up onstage and talking about what a great friend Michael was and how much he meant to them, and the only thing I could think was: Where were they? Where were they when days went by and the phone didn't ring? When he couldn't sleep at night and had no one in the world to talk to? Or when it was Paris's birthday and no one showed up to watch her open presents, except the nanny and a couple of security guards? Where were they when he was getting turned out of hotels and his kids were living out of suitcases and we didn't even have money to put gas in the vehicles? Where were these people then?

Where were all these people when he needed them?

ACKNOWLEDGMENTS

Bill: No one walks alone on the journey of life. Many people joined me, walked beside me, and helped me along the way by continuously urging me to write this book. Apart from the efforts of Javon and myself, the success of this project depended largely on the encouragement and support of many others. I would like to take this opportunity to express my gratitude to the people who helped me see it through.

First and foremost, I want to praise and thank God for gracing me with the blessing of protecting one of his angels, Michael Joseph Jackson.

I want to thank my family for their support and encouragement: my mom, Mary; my brothers, Calvin and Richard; my sisters, Carol, Lisa, and Stephanie; and my daughter, Aleiya, whom I love more than life itself, especially for all her understanding in spite of the hours my journey with Michael Jackson took me away from her.

I want to thank the abundance of friends that have supported me during this journey, all those who talked things over, read, wrote, offered comments, and gave me their honest opinions. Though there are too many to mention everyone by name, I want to especially thank Angela Jimenez for her friendship, support, and being a true fan.

I want to thank Craig Pyette and Amanda Murray and their teams at Random House Canada and Weinstein Books, respectively, for believing in our story and making it possible for us to share it with the world.

I want to thank Peter McGuigan and his staff at Foundry Media for believing in this project and Tanner Colby for taking the time to research, write, and piece our story together.

I want to thank the true and dedicated fans of Michael Jackson. Without them this book would not have been necessary. It's for them that we wrote this book, to share a side of Michael Jackson that they deserve to know. I hope it will give closure to those that need it and bring belief to those who lacked it.

Last but not least: I thank Mr. Michael Jackson for trusting and believing in me. As I protected him in life, I will continue to protect his honor in death.

Javon: Thank you, Lord, for never giving up on me, for never turning me away from receiving your mercy. You know me better than I know myself and knew that I was destined for greatness. I hope that your light will always shine through me.

Mom, thanks for being the rock and a great example of what a woman should be. Without you, there is no me.

Dad, thanks for always teaching me "Family First."

To Taneka, Tiffany, and Tasha, I'm blessed for having such strong sisters that lead by example and are never afraid to tell me what I need to hear instead of what I want to hear.

To my little brother Josh, I'm proud of the man you've become, never a follower, always a leader.

To my oldest baby, Patrice, I am honored to be your dad. You are such a beautiful queen. The sky is the limit for you. Continue to keep God as your rock. Dad is always here for you.

To my son, "Lil Javon," from the day you were born, I knew you are destined to be someone great. I hope I make you as proud as you make me. I couldn't ask for a better Junior.

ACKNOWLEDGMENTS

To my little princess daughter Honesty, You are my corazón. Thanks for always keeping a smile on daddy's face.

To Gran-mommy, I love you much. I'm so blessed for you to witness the book come out. I strive to always make you proud.

To Granny, thanks for always giving me tough love. I needed it. I love you.

To Uncle Kev, you have always been a second dad. You showed me that nothing is handed to you in this world, you have to go get it yourself.

To Kiera, I am blessed to have you as my friend and mother of my son. I wouldn't have it any other way. I love you.

To Mayra, you're such a great example to our daughter of what a lady should be. Keep up the good work. I love you.

To Cousin Jeff, this book would not have been possible without you having faith in me. Much respect, King!

To Cousin Tay, I'm proud of the dad and man you have become. Thanks for having your big cuzzo's back through the good and bad.

To Peter McGuigan and the staff at Foundry Media, thanks for shopping our project around and believing in us and not forcing us to compromise our integrity.

To Tanner Colby, thanks for listening to us and bringing our vision to life.

Thanks to all my family and friends for your love and support: Auntie Carol, Uncle Ed, Aunt Gwen, JJ, Desi, Krystal, Darren, Cousin Trina, Dimawi, Lil E, Virgil, Cousin Jason, Sonic, Tafari, Susie, Angela, Marlon, Buck, Sed, Ron, Pastor Carey, Trineka, Calvin, Jamori, Delaney, Seabraum, Jason. Rest in peace Sonny, Auntie Paula, the Gibson Family, Melody, Danthony. I wish I could list you all. . . .

And last but not least, Aisha, my best friend in the world. You stood by me at my lowest point and never treated me different. You have a friend for life. I love you always.

INDEX

BILL WHITFIELD, a New York native, and JAVON BEARD, who grew up in South Central Los Angeles, served for two and a half years as the personal security team for Michael Jackson. They have appeared on *Nightline* and *Good Morning America*, and have worked with numerous other high-profile clients, including Sean "P. Diddy" Combs, Andre Harrell, and Shaquille O'Neal.

TANNER COLBY is the co-author of the *New York Times* bestseller *The Chris Farley Show: A Biography in Three Acts* and *Belushi: A Biography*, and author of *Some of My Best Friends Are Black: The Strange Story of Integration in America*, which was nominated for the Andrew Carnegie Medal for Excellence in Non-Fiction by the American Library Association. He is also a frequent contributor to *Slate* magazine.

The body of *Remember the Time* has been set in Adobe Garamond. Designed for the Adobe Corporation by Robert Slimbach, the fonts are based on types first cut by Claude Garamond (c.1480–1561). Garamond was a pupil of Geoffrey Tory and is believed to have followed classic Venetian type models, although he did introduce a number of important differences, and it is to him that we owe the letterforms we now know as "old style." Garamond gave his characters a sense of movement and elegance that ultimately won him an international reputation and the patronage of Frances I of France.